*MacBride's Brigade*

To

William Forgrave
of
Glarryford, Molepolole
and
Ballinamallard

# MacBride's Brigade

## Irish commandos in the Anglo-Boer war

DONAL P. McCRACKEN

FOUR COURTS PRESS

This book was set in 10 on 13.5 pt Janson
by Carrigboy Typesetting Services, County Cork for
FOUR COURTS PRESS LTD
Fumbally Lane, Dublin 8, Ireland
Email: info@four-courts-press.ie
*and in the United States for*
FOUR COURTS PRESS
c/o ISBS, 5804 N.E. Hassalo Street, Portland, OR 97213.

A catalogue record for this title is available from the British Library.

ISBN 1-85182-499-5

Printed in Great Britain by
MPG Books Ltd, Bodmin, Cornwall.

# Contents

# List of illustrations

## TABLES

## CREDITS

The following persons, institutions and books are gratefully acknowledged as the sources of illustrations:

The Board of Trinity College, Dublin (photograph formerly owned by Michael Davitt), no. 2; Davitt, *The Boer fight for freedom* (1902), nos 9, 11, 12, 13, 14 & pp 107, 127; Fitzgibbon, *Arts under arms* (1901), no. 16; *The Graphic* (18 October 1899), no. 3; Hillegas, *With the Boer forces* (1900) no. 15; KwaZulu-Natal Archives, no. 17; KwaZulu-Natal Museum, no. 7; *Le Petit Journal* (1899), no. 8; D. McCracken, p. 39; Brian Mooney, no. 1; National Library of Ireland, p. 73 National Museum of Ireland, no. 21; Preller, *Kaptein Hindon* (1916) cover & no. 5; Priem, *De oorlog in Zuid Afrika* (1900), no. 10; *Report on military operations in South Africa and China*, (1901), no. 20 & p. 109; Rosslyn, *Twice captured* (1900), no. 4; Unger, *With 'Bobs' and Kruger* (1901), nos 18, 19; Wilson, *With the flag to Pretoria* (1900), no. 6.

# Preface

This is the story of a band of Irishmen who went to war in Africa. In the tradition of the Wild Geese, they joined a foreign army to fight the hereditary enemy. They fought well, but it would be naive to imagine they affected the fortunes of war. None the less, MacBride's brigade was consistently to be found in the van and earned for itself the respect of the Boers, perhaps more so than any of the half dozen foreign units in the Boer army. But it was more than respect. There was affection too. As one Boer commander observed of the Irish corps:

> This party adapted themselves to our conditions sooner and more easily than any of the foreigners with us. Where the German and the Hollander, nearer to us in blood perhaps, felt and looked out of place, you could not pick Patrick out of a herd of the wildest Boers. There were fieldcornets bearing the names of Kelly and O'Brien. This little band of men could curse like heretics, and their profanity was at times quite picturesque. (Schikkering)

Ten thousand kilometres away in Ireland the impact of MacBride's brigade was stunning. It galvanized nationalist Ireland out of its lethargy created by the Parnellite split and set the nationalist movement on the road which would lead to independence. The Boers recognized this and illicitly siphoned cash to the Irish Republican Brotherhood to undermine recruitment to Irish regiments in the British army. They had only limited success, and as at Fontenoy Irish fought and killed Irish on a distant battle field. There was talk of foreign government intervention on the Boer side, but nothing substantial materialized. Ultimately, the Boers came to realize that as far as aid in the form of foreign armies was concerned, they were alone. Even the nature of the European pro-Boer movements was not all that it might seem. One day on the veld Arthur Lynch maliciously showed Louis Botha a newspaper which reported the defeat of John MacBride at the South Mayo parliamentary by-election. The Boer general read the piece, put down the paper, stared across the rolling veld and said nothing.

MacBride's brigade was formally called the Irish Transvaal Brigade or the Irish corps, though in fact MacBride was its commander for only a couple of months. A more accurate title might be Blake's brigade but Colonel John Blake was Irish-American and back home in Ireland they wanted a home-grown hero. Whatever we call them, the commando was an undisciplined crowd, more so than the average Boer commando. They were easy going, they could be boisterous and they could be downright stubborn. On one occasion in April 1900 it was reported that they were refusing to fight because the Boer authorities had ordered the strong-willed Church of Ireland cleric, the Revd Dr John Darragh, over the border to Lourenço Marques.

Irish fighting units had operated in South Africa for nearly a hundred years and on 25 June 1900 the Irish Transvaal Brigade was vividly reminded of this. As they passed through the small settlement of Bronkhorstspruit, they found the welcome shade of peach trees which had grown up over the previous twenty years. In the first Anglo-Boer war the Connaught Rangers had been ambushed here. Many of the men had had their pockets filled with ripe peaches picked from a nearby orchard. They were buried in their uniforms and the peach grove which soon grew up marked the spot.

Ten years ago the *Irish pro-Boers, 1877–1902* appeared. It told the story of the impact of developments in South Africa had on Irish politics. Here the other side of the coin is now told – the tale of the men who fought on the hot and dusty veld. It is not a conventional military history, but an adventure story, long forgotten in Ireland.

The Boer army had only one permanent unit. the Transvaal State Artillery. The remainder of the army of the Transvaal Republic and the Orange Free State Republic was made up of commandos. These units varied in size from several hundred to several thousand men and were allied to the different districts and towns in which they were raised. They were democratic in structure, electing their officers and held together by belief in their cause and by loyalty to their officers rather than by a strict military code. Every burgher (white citizen) in the commando had a horse and a rifle. Uniforms generally were not worn, though the widespread wearing of slouch hats and bandoliers gave the impression of a uniform. African men were an important component of many of the commandos, acting in the capacity of auxiliaries.

The Irish commandos did not differ materially from many of the Boer units save that they were meant to represent the Irish sympathizers in the republics. They also gave their officers British titles such as colonel, major and captain rather than commandant and fieldcornet as used by the Boer commandoes. Only the state artillery used British titles. Like the Boer commandos the Irish fighters were not paid.

# Acknowledgements

I first began work on the Irish-South African link in 1976. Much information contained in this volume has thus been gathered over two decades and in two hemispheres. Some of those who encouraged me in this quest are now no longer with us. In particular I would single out T.K. Daniel, who for a number of years summered in Africa bringing with him welcome news of the Irish history world and providing encouragement for the launch of the Ireland and Southern Africa Project. For this particular book I am grateful to the following individuals:

In Ireland: Hilda Allan, Desmond Byrne, William Forgrave, Donal Guilfoyle, Anthony J. Jordan, Maire Kennedy, Sean McCracken, the late Emeritus Professor T.W. Moody, Brian Mooney, Pádraig O Cuanacháin, Dr and Mrs Maurice O'Connor, Ulick O'Connor, Art and Sheila O'Leary, Dr Tony O'Reilly and Commandant Peter Young.

In South Africa: Dr Peter Brain, George Chadwick, Mark Coghlan, Liezel Hannemann, Emeritus Professor J.L. McCracken, Patricia A. McCracken, Ambassador Eamon Ó Tuathail, Brian Spencer, Shelagh O'Byrne Spencer, Kribashnie Perumal, Dr G.D. Stephenson, and M.W. Wessels.

In Britain: Dr Donal Lowry and Muriel Berry Walsh; in France; Pierre Joannon; in Uganda, Robert Law; and in America, Mark Antolowitz.

I should also like to thank the staff of the following archives, institutions and libraries: Archives Diplomatiques du Ministère des Affaires Etrangères, Paris; British Library; Cory Library for Historical Research, Rhodes University, Grahamstown; Don Africana Library, Durban; Irish Military Archives, Dublin; Johannesburg Public Library; KwaZulu-Natal Museum; Killie Campbell Collections, University of Natal, Durban; Ministry of Defence Library, London; National Archives of Ireland; National Army Museum, London; National Library of Ireland; the Newberry Library, Chicago; Public Record Office, London; Public Record Office of Northern Ireland, Belfast; South African Archives, Pretoria; South African Library, Cape Town; South African National Museum of Military History; Trinity College, Dublin, Library; Military Academy Archives, West Point; University of Durban-Westville; University of Melbourne; University of Stellenbosch Library; University of the Witwatersrand Library; and the War Museum of the Republics, Bloemfontein.

# Introduction

We are afraid we could not induce the Irish labouring classes to come to this colony in anything like sufficient numbers. They know nothing of it beyond having a dim idea that it is associated with Kaffir wars; but they know all about America and Australia, or think they do, having heard them talked about from their infancy by those who had friends there – and away they pour across the Atlantic, sometimes to a glutted labour market, where they find themselves worse off than at home. There is much in a name.[1]

*Cape Town Daily News*, 2 February 1876

The waves of nineteenth-century Irish emigration did not break on the South African shoreline. The huddled masses, yearning to breathe free, went elsewhere. To Africa came only the Irish soldiers of the queen, the Irish missionaries of God, the Irish servants of the colonial domains – and the adventurous, intrepid and foolhardy.[2]

It is true that a few Irish emigration schemes to the Cape colony had taken place – the 300 Irish 1820 settlers were dumped at the edge of the Namaqua desert – but in the ensuing 80 years only a mere 14,000 assisted Irish passages were paid to Table Bay.[3] And yet, as the century progressed, the Irish became a familiar feature of the South African scene. There were the notorious: the renegade leaders of the 1808 slave revolt in the western Cape; and the ubiquitous Fenian Alfred Aylward – journalist, medical quack, commando leader and political agitator, who led the 'black flag rebellion' on the diamond fields, wrote the excellent treatise *The Transvaal of today* (1878) and joined the Boer forces on Majuba, where he replaced the brain of Dubliner General George Colley back in his skull.[4] Then there was the 'Irish Brigade': these ruffians under 'Captain Moonlight' helped build the celebrated railway from Lourenço Marques in Portuguese East Africa up to the Boer capital of Pretoria in the Transvaal. They also indulged in serious drinking in the low bars of Lourenço Marques, in street brawls, in banditry and, on one occasion, in piracy.[5]

At the opposite end of conformity, the Cape and Natal could boast a host of respectable Irish bishops, doctors, judges, lawyers, merchant princes, newspaper editors and politicians, including two prime ministers.[6] For the ordinary Irish immigrant four occupations beckoned: the colonial police forces, where up to a quarter were Irish;[7] the building and running of the expanding railway network; the diamond diggings at Kimberley; and, most important, the retailing business, where Ulstermen had made good.[8] Yet the Irish remained a minority of a minority of a minority – a minority of the English-speaking population, of the white population, of the total population.

By 1891 it is doubtful whether there were more than between 15,000 and 20,000 ethnic Irish in the subcontinent, of whom only about 6,000 were first generation: mostly young men, as many protestants as catholics.[9] And then came the discovery of gold in 1886 on the Witwatersrand of the South African Republic, or Transvaal Republic. Into this primitive Boer state came the uitlanders keen to make money and to enjoy themselves. Sir William Butler, the liberal and catholic Irish commander of British forces at the Cape, had no doubt as to their qualities: 'probably the most corrupt, immoral and untruthful assemblage of beings present in the world'.[10] And into this assemblage were drawn hundreds of young Irish, little realising the fate which was to befall them.

# CHAPTER ONE

# Storm clouds on the highveld

## 1896—EARLY 1899

In the 1870s a Dublin-based scheme tried to sell farms of up to 6,000 acres in the Transvaal to Irish farmers.[1] Not surprisingly, the venture failed, though a scattering of Irish-owned farms were to be found in the eastern Transvaal (Mpumalanga) in the latter half of the nineteenth century – the O'Gradys of Dullstroom, the O'Neils, founders of the dorp of Belfast, and the Murphys of Barberton.[2] And over on the sun-scorched plateau of the Orange Free State there were the O'Reillys. Most of these families were absorbed into the white community and became Afrikaans-speaking. When the second Anglo-Boer war came, it was the Boer commandos they joined, not the 'Irsche Corps'.

The discovery of the world's biggest gold field on the Witwatersrand in 1886 and the rapid growth of the Johannesburg mining camp inevitably led to an influx of foreigners intent on making good. Among the ragtag community of uitlanders was a limited number of newly arrived Irish. On St Patrick's day 1887 – when Johannesburg was less than a year old – 'scenes of the wildest confusion' heralded the first organized Irish meeting in the Transvaal Republic. In some ways it was an appropriate omen of what was to come – the riot, caused more by drink than political fervour, wrecked the dining-room of Guttman's Hotel. And as the bewildered Boer government guests scrambled out through the windows, the baton-wielding ZARPs (Transvaal police) came through the doors to a 'scene like Donnybrook fair'.[3] All good fun for most of the 100 guests.

Sadly for the participants, for a number of succeeding years the annual St Patrick's day bash was in the hands of Johannesburg's emerging bourgeoisie. Thumping on the table because the soup arrived cold gave way to pious speeches on the virtues of Irish home rule, on the graciousness of Queen Victoria and on the unfair manner in which uitlanders were treated – while, of course, praising the rectitude of Kruger's government.

By 1890 a branch of the Irish National Foresters (Tom Daly branch) existed in Pretoria, an extension of various branches at the Cape,[4] which was now visited by such notables in the Irish parliamentary party as Swift MacNeill and John Redmond. The best that the Transvaal got was the less high-profile, anti-Parnellite MP for King's county, B.C. Molloy.[5]

And then, on 29 December 1895, came the Jameson raid.

## THE JAMESON RAID

The impact on Irish politics of Dr Starr Jameson's notorious cross-border raid into the Transvaal Republic has yet to be fully explored. The Irish nationalist press denounced the abortive incursion as did the parliamentary nationalists, and one of their number, Edward Blake, served on the parliamentary committee of inquiry.[6] There must, however, have been unease in the top echelons of the Parnellites as Cecil Rhodes continued to make substantial and clandestine payments to party funds – to 'square the Irish'.[7]

In the Transvaal there emerged in Irish circles for the first time a rather shadowy figure who was to a large extent the *éminence grise* of Transvaal-Irish politics for the next quarter-century. Little is known of Solomon Gillingham except that he was the son of an Irish soldier. 'Pious Paul's Pal' ran a baker's shop in Pretoria, was said to have a cold-storage monopoly in the republic, was a member of the licensing board, and lived in a mansion in Church Street, flanked by the Transvaal's flag (the *vierkleur*) and by a green Irish flag. Here the 'Irish renegade' entertained the regime's leaders and on at least one occasion was host to President Steyn of the Orange Free State Republic and his entourage.[8] Gillingham was one of the few private individuals in the Transvaal to have a telephone, his number being Pretoria 91.

If M.C. Seton is to be believed, it was Gillingham who offered to raise an Irish brigade to fight for the Boers against Jameson and his column of mounted police.[9] This offer was rejected. Nevertheless, a vigilante group of Irishmen came into being in Johannesburg. Writing home, one Ulsterman in the unit observed:

> The representatives of the various countries have formed themselves into national Brigades. I have joined the Irish Brigade which is formed to protect life and property and if need be to march to the front. Papers speak very highly of us and really we are [a] credit to the old land ... see us drilling and marching in military order through the city wearing badges of green and singing 'God save Ireland'.

One gets the impression that these lads were not quite sure which side they were on. Anti-Jameson yes, but, as H.G. Hasken said, also wanting 'a republic under a good government'.[10] Writing ten years later, John Whelan stated this was a pro-British 'Irish corps', a belief also held by John MacBride. That said, it does appear as if Andrew Gill from Mayo and a nucleus of the 'Irish Brigade' were present at Doornkop when the Boers defeated Jameson's raiders.


## THE WILD GEESE GATHER

The Jameson raid's impact on young advanced nationalists in Ireland was surprising. A small but steady stream of advanced men made their own way to the Transvaal. We do not have numbers but by July 1896, about the time when John MacBride arrived, there were about a thousand Irish in Johannesburg, two-thirds of them male.[11]

In the 1880s Inspector John Mallon of the Dublin Metropolitan Police (DMP) had sent the Invincible-turned-informer, James Carey, to Natal – a British colony where very few Irish lived – to escape a Fenian revenge. But the revenge came all the same, with a bullet onboard the *Melrose* off Port Elizabeth, though this assassination does not seem to have been premeditated and certainly was not Fenian-planned. Now, fourteen years later, on 14 January 1897, Assistant-Commissioner Mallon – 'the man who held Ireland' – wrote the following secret report to the under secretary in Dublin Castle:

> *Subject*: Departure of John R. Whelan for South Africa
> Under Secretary
>
> The above named who is a BA of the Royal University is a prominent member of the INA [Irish National Association]. He held a lucrative appointment here and his departure for South Africa this time is very suspicious.
>     He is the fifth INA man who has gone to South Africa within a recent very short period.
>     McBride – Gill – Briscoe – two members of the Independent staff and now Whelan.[12]

To this list Mallon could have added Arthur Griffith, who had set sail for Lourenço Marques in Portuguese Mozambique twelve days earlier.

Why did these advanced nationalists – members of the Irish National Association and the Celtic Literary Society – leave Ireland at this juncture? Were they deserting their own revolution? The answer is not obvious. Undoubtedly economic hardship was a factor, as was the sterility in contemporary Irish politics. Health, for people like Griffith and MacBride, could have been a secondary cause.[13] And, of course, once underway there was chain migration.

Two other factors seem to have been paramount, however. First, the Jameson raid drew attention to another nationality pitted against the traditional enemy. Perhaps, as was claimed, Gillingham actively recruited young firebrands from Ireland. It should be noted that by no means all Irish immigrants over the years 1896 to 1899 went into the mines. Some, like Whelan worked in Pretoria. Griffith went off to the back of beyond to edit the *Middelburg Courant*. There is no evidence that any of the lads made much money, or indeed that they sought to make money. What they went for – and what they got – was experience.

Linked to this was the second factor. Arthur Griffith freely admitted that going to South Africa was a sojourn.[14] It is doubtful whether many of these young men believed that they were leaving Ireland for ever. Thus there is a complete lack of sentimentality among them – and no songs about leprechauns dying on the highveld. Africa was an adventure.

For the adherents of conspiracy theories, a case can be made out that scheming was underway between Gillingham and the revolutionary Irish Republican Brotherhood. Gillingham was in London in 1896 and met Dr Ryan; they became 'close friends'. The same year John MacBride travelled to London, met Ryan, returned to Dublin, resigned his job as a pharmaceutical chemist ('a fairly good salary'), and – to the surprise of Dublin Castle who expected him to become a paid organizer of the INA – set out for the Transvaal.[15] A further link existed between the IRB activist Fred Allan and MacBride, as indeed it did between Allan and Griffith, who followed MacBride some eight months later.

When the Irish Race Convention met in Dublin in September 1896, South Africa was represented by the relatively moderate Moses Cornwall from Kimberley and H. Haskin from Johannesburg.[16] Back in the Transvaal, however, MacBride was rapidly transforming the Irish community. The respectable Irish gatherings addressed by St John Carr, Dr Croghan and the Chevalier Donoghue and attended by such randlords as De Beer and Robinson were hijacked. There is evidence that at least one home-rule meeting was broken up by the newcomers who, just a month after the Irish Race Convention, were confident enough to hold a march through Johannesburg. MacBride and the boys had had to put up with Dillon, Redmond and co. at home; they were damned if they would stomach the same home-rule mentality in Johannesburg.

[18]

By July 1897 Irish home rulism had been silenced on the highveld. Whelan had taken over the John Daly court of the Irish National Foresters in Pretoria and in Johannesburg MacBride was in charge of the newly established Wolfe Tone court (no. 269). An offshoot of this was an Amnesty Association which, with substantial publicity, sent back to its parent association in Ireland modest sums of money which aided political prisoners.[17]

As if to assert their new-found dominance, that July a letter, with twelve signatories including MacBride, Whelan, Griffith and Gillingham, appeared in *The Nation*. This 'effusion' called for an Irish Majuba:

> Britain boasts that the sun never sets on the English Empire; but it is the proud boast of Irishmen that it never sets on its enemies.

'Poor old John Bull' was the reaction of Major Gosselin of the DMP on reading the letter.[18]

This was not the only letter sent. A renewed and secret offer to President Kruger to raise an Irish volunteer corps was once again politely refused. The time had not yet come.

The St Patrick's day banquets in 1897 and 1898 in Pretoria and Johannesburg were noteworthy for the 'characteristically bitter' speeches in support of Kruger. 'The Transvaal has no more loyal citizens than the Irish,' boomed C.E. O'Driscoll at the Pretoria dinner in 1898.

By the middle of 1898, the new Irish uitlanders were well settled in the republic. There were some like Arthur Griffith who meandered about the place – Pretoria, Middelburg, Lydenburg, Barberton, Johannesburg and even over the border into the colony of Natal to visit the hill of Majuba. His activities in South Africa have recently been chronicled and make interesting reading.[19] For our story, however, Griffith's significance is not in the eighteen months or so that he stayed in South Africa but in the impact his sojourn had on his thinking and especially on his activities in support of the Boers when war came.

Irish haunts in Johannesburg included the Exchange bar, MacKay's music shop in Rissik Street – 'a bit of Dublin' – and John Mitchell's clothes cleaning and pressing shop between Smal and Delvers Streets, at 106 Pritchard Street. Irish meetings were also held on the mines, especially on the J.B. Robinson goldmine at Langlaagte, where MacBride was an assayer and where Griffith ended up as the supervisor of a rather dangerous machine containing a cyanide bath.

In Pretoria the 'Irish centre' was Gillingham's bakery shop:

A hunchback Irishman stood behind the counter, and all his business seemed to be, to pass silently, certain people into Gillingham's sanctum behind the baker shop. This little den was always in semi-darkness; though it looked out on to a dead wall, the blinds were always down for precaution's sake, and was termed the Third Volksraad. The walls were adorned with blood curdling pictures of England's perfidy and cruelty, and the *Irish Freeman* was lying usually scattered about ... It was here the treacherous sons of Erin met in unholy conclave.[20]

How this coterie of conspirators got on with the rest of the population is not clear. They had common political cause with the Boer population, and some Boer officials like von Brandis, Jan Eloff and especially Ben Viljoen, the future Boer general, were to be seen at Irish gatherings, whereas one bitter opponent noted, 'High Boer officials attend these [Irish] dinners, smiling joyfully, when half inebriated.' Yet the distrust of the foreigner, combined with the Irish reputation for riotous living, frightened away some Boers. Even when the Irish proved their worth in the heat of battle, this caution remained in certain quarters. Advanced Irish nationalists' relationship with British uitlanders was generally cool and later hostile, the British looking on the Irish with contempt as being 'the worst sweepings of Johannesburg' and as 'renegade curs'. As the hour of action drew nearer, the Irish found it necessary to meet and to recruit in secret for fear of persecution by British uitlanders, though such secrecy may in part have been due to the thill of covert operations.

Irish relations with the black population are difficult to gauge in the Transvaal of the 1890s as next to no references have come to light – an interesting phenomenon in itself. In the Cape, Irishmen and black women had lived together apparently unmolested in the 1820s but the arrival of the first catholic bishop, Bishop Griffith from Wexford, seems to have put an end to such relationships at least in public: a stark contrast to the church's attitude in the second half of the twentieth century.[21] So-called coloured people with such Irish names as Ogle and Fynn lived in South Africa in the nineteenth century and continue to do so. And it is probable that some Irish lads in the Transvaal in the 1890s did have liaisons with black women. In the late 1980s reports appeared in the Irish press that MK activist Robert McBride was the descendant of John MacBride and a Cape Malay woman.[22]

It is, however, unrealistic to pretend that the Irish advanced nationalists of the Rand in the 1890s did not hold the prevailing, and at best paternalistic, attitude to black people. Arthur Griffith might very well have got on with the black workers he encountered. They called him 'Cuguan', prob- ably meaning a dove, a reference to Griffith's swaying gait caused by a clubbed foot. He denounced English-speaking white South Africans for teaching the black man the Bible, telling him he was a man and a brother, and then treating him like a dog.[23] Griffith, however, following in the footsteps of the Young Irelander John Mitchel, had ideological racist views against Jews – 'the swarming Jews of Johannesburg' – and against black people.[24]

## THE 1798 CENTENARY

The centenary celebrations in Ireland of the insurrection of United Irishmen in 1798 were generally a bit of a flop. None the less several events were a success, and present and prominent at these was the ubiquitous Solomon Gillingham representing the Irish on the Rand. There he was in the Frascati restaurant in Dublin on 9 August at a commemorative banquet with such luminaries as W.B. Yeats, Maud Gonne, Lionel Johnson and John F. Taylor QC. Six days later Gillingham stood alongside the old Fenian John O'Leary and made a speech to a large crowd at the laying of the foundation stone of the Wolfe Tone memorial. Nearby stood his friend, the revolutionary Dr Ryan.[25]

Ten thousand kilometres away that same 15 August a grand Irish parade marched through the streets of Johannesburg. American, French, German, Hollander and Scandinavian uitlanders joined the Irish as did some Boers, including Ben Viljoen who travelled in specially from Krugersdorp on the west Rand. As they marched 'Who fears to speak of '98' was 'lustily sung'. And that night a crowd joined in choruses of 'Volkslied' and 'God save Ireland'. At a packed banquet John MacBride rose to cheers to propose the toast, 'The memory of the dead'. The fervour of Johannesburg had eclipsed Dublin.

A month later Griffith left the Transvaal for home, why we are not sure. Improved health, pressure from Dublin from his close friend, Ireland's forgotten intellectual William Rooney, homesickness, dreams of a young woman back home, a sense that he had achieved what he set out to accom- plish – or perhaps even a realization that the war clouds over the highveld were about to erupt into a storm of hostilities? Griffith was certainly no coward, but he was equally no soldier, be it 1899, 1916 or 1920. By the end of October 1898 he was back in Dublin and soon planning the launch of the *United Irishman*, the offspring of the defunct *Middelburg Courant*.[26]

CHAPTER TWO

# The Irish Transvaal Brigade is founded

## THE AFRICAN WINTER OF 1899

From land to land throughout the world
The news is going round
That Ireland's flag triumphant waves
On high o'er English ground.
In far-off Africa today
The English fly dismayed
Before the flag of green and gold
Borne by McBride's Brigade.

About the time the second Anglo-Boer war broke out, an anonymous and vicious scaremongering pamphlet appeared in South Africa under the title *The great Transvaal Irish conspiracy: Dedicated to all disloyal subjects of Her Majesty the Queen.*[1] The twelve pages were obviously written by a disgruntled former colleague of the inner circle of conspirators, the main target of attack being Gillingham. Half lies, half truth, the document has to be treated with caution. It begins with the words, 'The arrival of P.J. Tynan (No. 1) at Johannesburg and of Gillingham at Delagoa Bay . . .' And on page seven it states, 'the Irish Invincibles could only hurriedly organize Blake's Irish Ragged Brigade . . .'

There seems to be no doubt that the Fenians took a lively interest in the situation in the Transvaal. How deep their involvement was and whether the Invincible Patrick Tynan (No. 1) did come out to organize an Irish fighting unit remains a mystery. Accounts by brigade members are silent on the issue, but they were mainly concerned with boasting of their own role in the heady days of that African winter time. The most reliable account of those days seems to be that of Thomas Byrne, one of the more respectable members of the Irish Transvaal Brigade. Byrne had been born in Carrickmacross in 1882; in late 1896, at the age of nineteen, he emigrated to the Transvaal.

According to Byrne, the idea of an Irish commando came from Belfastman Dan O'Hare: he (O'Hare) and a Kerryman called Dick McDonagh put the idea to John MacBride, who agreed to the suggestion. MacBride said the 'hint' that the Irish nationalists on the Rand should be got together came from Sol Gillingham, who told MacBride of the impending war when it was still secret. From about early August 1899, for some six weeks, on Sundays when the miners had a day off, small clandestine meetings were held in John Mitchell's small cleaners and dyers.[2] In addition, Byrne and McDonagh visited various mines, seeking out Irish lads in their wood-and-iron huts and recruiting their support. Byrne 'with one other' also got the agreement of Thomas Menton, alias Madden, an Irishman who apparently deserted the British army immediately prior to the battle of Majuba in 1881 and was now 'Boer commander in Johannesburg' in charge of the fort and gaol.

The scheme seems to have gone public at a small meeting of the ''98 Centenary Committee' chaired by MacBride on Sunday, 3 September 1899. The following Sunday a larger meeting was held of

> miners and artisans, clerks and merchants, 'new chums' just out and old prospectors who had spent the best part of their lives knocking around Africa.[3]

This gathering of Irish uitlanders approved a proposal by MacBride for the establishment of a brigade to fight for the Boers should war break out with Britain. A delegation was charged with negotiating the brigade's formation with the Transvaal government.

A letter signed by Connolly, Gerraghty, Gillingham, Oates and Stone was sent to President Kruger,[4] requesting permission to raise a military unit of Irishmen to fight in the event of war, as well as to gain burgher status for any such volunteers. At least three of the signatories were from Pretoria, which indicates the influence of the John Daly court of the Irish National Foresters. The authorisation of the establishment of 'het Irsche Corps' of 750 men was made that Wednesday 13 September, four weeks before the outbreak of war.

The Irish were not the only uitlanders banding themselves into fighting units. There was the Dutch, or Hollander corps, under Commandant Jan Lombard. Hollanders also featured in the police's fighting unit (ZARPs), as did a few Irish. A German corps was formed under Colonel Schiel, and an Italian corps, under the dashing Colonel Camillo Ricchiardi, contained Pope Leo's nephew. The small Scandinavian unit was led by Fieldcornet

Flygare, and the Russian corps of the 'gallant playboy' Count Alexis de Ganetzky excluded 'Russian Border Israelites', though there were Russian Jewish pro-Boers in the Transvaal.[5] There were American scouts and Belgian, Dutch, Italian, German and Russian ambulance corps. Probably the most famous of the foreign fighters was the colourful French colonel and later general, the Comte de Villebois-Mareuil of the ill-fated foreign legion.[6]

Several points need to be made about all these foreign units. First they were not mercenaries, though they sometimes numbered freebooters in their ranks. The oath sworn by the Irish and other uitlanders, in translation, ran as follows:

> I hereby make an oath of solemn allegiance to the people of the South African Republic, and I declare my willingness to assist, with all my power, the burghers of this Republic in the war in which they are engaged. I further promise to obey the orders of those placed in authority according to law, and that I will work for nothing but the prosperity, the welfare, and the independence of the land and people of this Republic, so truly help me, God Almighty.[7]

Second, these units invariably fought well and many sustained high casulties, not least at the battles of Elandslaagte and Modder River, and during the retreat through the Orange Free State. Third, these units were few in number. As no complete army lists were later found by British military intelligence, only estimates can be made. Excluding some 7,000 Cape Afrikaners, it is doubtful whether the uitlanders and newly arrived foreigners who enlisted numbered much more than 3,000 men, of whom about 500 would have fought in the two Irish commandos and in Boer commandos.

This number might well have been greater had Kruger been more sympathetic to recruitment outside the Boer republics. MacBride, through the intercession of Gillingham with the Boer government, had tried to encourage Irish-American recruitment and one suspects that, if Tynan was indeed in the Transvaal in September 1899, this is what he, too, was up to. But for a variety of reasons, not least because the Boers did not trust foreigners, recruitment overseas of large numbers of fighting men was discouraged.[8] The words of President Kruger to German volunteers are worth quoting:

> Thank you for coming. Do not imagine that we have need of you. The Transvaal wants no foreign help. But as you wish to fight for us you are welcome.[9]

Of course, foreigners did arrive from abroad, including a unit of Irish-Americans, but only in a few cases was this practice encouraged by Pretoria.

As far as the Irish were concerned, the existence of other foreign units had little impact on them and there was only occasional contact with them. Indeed, it can be argued that as the war progressed, the Irish and the emerging younger Boer leaders developed a special affinity. This is not surprising, for the existence of MacBride's brigade was an extraordinary phenomenon. The Boers were at war against the United Kingdom – and Ireland was an integral part of that kingdom. For this reason it was particularly important that Irish brigaders be granted citizen status and thus avoid the certainty of being court martialled and shot as traitors. That they became burghers prior to the outbreak of hostilities was a critical factor in international law which they probably did not appreciate at the time but which was to have dramatic repercussions some years later.

## THE LAST MONTH OF PEACE

Michael Davitt claimed that the Irish Transvaal Brigade was organized chiefly by the exertions of John MacBride.[10] That is probably true, though Gillingham was always in the background liaising with the authorities, and others, such as Tom Byrne and the Transvaal secret service agent, the Scot, James Bain, worked on the ground to get things organized.[11]

Once news of the establishment of an Irish commando became public there were, in Tom Byrne's words, 'all kinds of "dirty digs" against us' in the Transvaal's pro-British, English-language press. MacBride claimed a couple of the brigade called on the editor of the *Transvaal Leader*, who 'vanished through a back window from the Transvaal'. There was, however, one exception – the pro-government, English-language *Standard and Diggers' News*. This is not surprising as the editor, Alfred Ernest O'Flaherty – an Oxford gold medallist in Sanskrit – came from Galway.[12] Even after O'Flaherty's departure to change sides and fight with the British, his old newspaper kept the Johannesburg public more informed on the exploits of the Irish commando than on any other foreign unit.

It was in the *Diggers' News* that the 'Irish Manifesto' appeared on Thursday, 28 September – or at least one version of the manifesto. For the historian it gives little insight into the Irish on the Rand. Having accused the British government of stirring up race hatred in South Africa, this 'call to arms' concludes:

Vengeance! Irishmen! Away with every mean and selfish consideration. Remember against whom we call you to fight, your oppressor for seven hundred cruel years. Remember what thousands of your dearest friends have suffered by their merciless tyranny. Remember your wrecked homes. Remember Michaelstown. Remember Allen, Larkin and O'Brien!

Every Irishman worthy of the name and every Irish-American in South Africa will be found in the ranks of the Irish Brigade of the S.A.R., under the sacred Green Flag, fighting against the brutal English Tyrant. 'God save Ireland'.[13]

A similar call to arms appeared in *Die Volksstem*.

That Sunday, 1 October, Irish pro-Boer rallies were held: one in Johannesburg's van Brandis Square; the other in Dublin's Beresford Place. At the latter 20,000 people protested in the damp against 'the attack of England upon the liberties of the Transvaal' and cheered with enthusiasm when Patrick O'Brien MP unfurled a large Transvaal flag, the *vierkleur*. Also present were Michael Davitt MP; the old Fenian John O'Leary; Maud Gonne and, of course, W.B. Yeats; T.D. Sullivan MP; and Arthur Griffith.[14]

Ten thousand kilometres away the gathering was considerably smaller, about 300, but the excitement was as great. The manifesto was formally approved and, in the tradition of the Boer commandos, nominations were requested for the brigade's officers. The senior rankings had already been sorted out behind the scenes and MacBride was not prepared to lead. This was probably a mistake, but his natural caution and conservatism came to the fore. At Gillingham's suggestion, MacBride had met in Pretoria an Irish-American called Blake, formerly of the US cavalry. Blake was brought to this Sunday meeting and after MacBride had declined nomination he then in turn nominated Lieutenant Blake, accepting for himself the position of second in command.[15]

In his speech of acceptance, Blake said he took the command under the condition that no brigader took 'one cent of money for his services, and they all would fight purely for their love of liberty and for down-trodden Ireland'.[16]

## THE OFFICERS

The rankings in the foreign Boer units were somewhat bizarre, not least because the commando leaders generally styled themselves colonel. That

*Table 1: Officers of the first Irish Transvaal Brigade*

| Name | Rank | Place of origin |
|---|---|---|
| John Y. Fillmore Blake | colonel | Missouri, USA |
| John MacBride | major | Westport, Mayo |
| Thomas Menton | major | Galway (?) |
| — Molloy | major | n/a |
| Dan O'Hare | major | Belfast |
| Thomas Shenton | major | n/a |
| James Laracy | captain | Kilkenny |
| Malcolm McCallum | captain | American |
| John Joseph Mitchell | captain | Galway |
| P.J. Oates | captain | Kerry |
| — Pollard | captain | n/a |
| — Shea | captain | n/a |
| Charles Francois Coetzee | captain-intendant | Transvaal |
| Michael James Dunville | lieutenant | London |
| Thomas Enright | lieutenant | n/a |
| — Gaynor | lieutenant | Longford |
| John R. Lovely | lieutenant | n/a |
| — Malan | lieutenant | Transvaal |
| Hugh B. Ryan | lieutenant | Tipperary/USA |
| Edward Thornhill Slater | lieutenant | n/a |
| F. O'Reilly | sergeant-major | colonial Irish |
| — Higgins | sergeant | Co. Down |
| Pat Malone | sergeant | Louth |
| Jim O'Keefe | sergeant | Co. Kilkenny |
| — Papillon | sergeant | n/a |
| Joe Wade | sergeant | Balbriggan |
| Patrick Darragh | corporal | Moneymore |
| Dick McDonagh | corporal | Listowel |
| Dr M.S. Walsh | doctor | Swords |
| Fr Alexander Baudry | chaplain | n/a |
| Fr Alphonse van Hecke | chaplain | Belgium |
| Tommy Oates | flagbearer | Kerry |

the Irish took these ranks is interesting for as one contemporary noted, 'commissions in the Boer army were not to be had [by foreigners] for the asking'.[17] One can sympathize with Kruger when he later said:

> All these men are mad after military titles, and we have a regular topsy-turvy condition. There are some men who have seen some real fighting and they have kept with their former titles of Lieutenant or what not, although they are commanding troops, and here is a man [Arthur Lynch] who has never commanded at all, and wants to be Colonel.[18]

So it was that the next day, Monday, 2 October, the officers of the Irish Transvaal Brigade went to Pretoria to receive their commissions – according to MacBride, from Kruger himself. The commissions were signed by State Secretary F.W. Reitz, and Lieutenant Blake became Colonel Blake and Mr MacBride Major MacBride, both 'van het Irsche Corps'.

MacBride, and possibly also Blake, became a special justice of the peace as well so that he could administer the oath to recruits. This presumably made it legal for him to grant burgher status to the Irish lads who turned up over the next four days at the brigade offices, flanked by the flags of America, Ireland and the Transvaal, at the corner of Pritchard and von Wielligh streets.

Who the other officers were at this stage is not clear, but according to various diverse sources those named in Table 1 on page 27 at one time or another over the next year were, or claimed to be, or were later described as, officers in the Irish Transvaal Brigade. This impressive list should be viewed with a jaundiced eye. Some, like Menton, must have had a brief connection with the Irish commando. Further, as Tom Byrne points out, besides Blake and MacBride, the other elected ranks 'were all wiped out some time after the fighting started. Those ranks were not necessary as we were now organized on a Commando basis.'[19] The names of officers which crop up most often, besides Blake and MacBride, are Laracy, Mitchell, Oates, McCallum and O'Reilly.

### BLAKE AND MAC BRIDE

Ironically, neither Blake nor MacBride would have been in charge had the now legendary Alfred Aylward still been alive. Even at the age of fifty-six, Aylward would have willingly and ably-taken to the saddle. In that autumn of 1899 his name was resurrected by Arthur Griffith and crowds in the Dublin pro-Boer rallies cheered loudly for the memory of the Fenian, journalist and captain of the Transvaal's first foreign unit, the Lydenburg Volunteer Corps.[20] Blake and MacBride were then still mere shadows of 'Joubert's Fenian'.

That said, Blake and MacBride are interesting personalities – very different in character. Blake was something of a caricature of Buffalo Bill: six-foot tall, broadshouldered, hail and hearty, a raconteur, a lady's man, an action man and a good soldier – but with occasional fits of morbid depression. As the earl of Rosslyn wrote, 'half wild, yet gentle, the type of adventurer one reads of in a novel yet never expects to meet'.[21] The *Natal Witness*, still living down the time when Aylward was editor ('mud in the streets and mud in the press')[22] spoke of Blake arriving in Johannesburg 'in a destitute condition' and a few months later a letter in the same paper described Blake as 'a good-humoured ass'.[23]

John Fillmore Blake was born in 1856 in Bolivar, Poek County, in the state of Missouri. When an infant, his family moved to Fayetteville in Arkansas and then to a cattle ranch in Denton County in Texas. At the age of fifteen, he was sent to Arkansas State University and from there, when aged twenty, to the US Military Academy at West Point, graduating and being promoted to second lieutenant on 12 June 1880. His time at West Point was not distinguished academically. Of the twelve categories judged over the few years he did well in only French, Spanish and 'Discipline' though the West Point 'Register of delinquencies' cites Blake for such misdemeanours as throwing bread in hall at dinner, smoking, using profane expressions, striking a horse with a sabre at cavalry exercise, and slowness.[24] He was in the bottom quarter of his year, graduating fortieth out of a class of fifty-three.[25] But then Blake, when unstimulated, was lazy. He did not, however, like the star pupil of the class, Captain Oberlin M. Carter, end up eventually in a military prison.

Blake served thirteen years in the US Sixth Cavalry, some of which was spent at the garrison fort of Leavenworth. But for most of his time – eight years in all – he was on active service with the 'galloping Sixth' in the arid lands of the Navaho and Apache, to the south and south east of the Grand Canyon, attached to small forts such as Bowie and Lowell in Arizona, and Forts Bayard and Wingate in New Mexico. He was mentioned in orders for his meritorious conduct when fighting the Chiricahna Indians in Old Mexico and in 1887 was promoted to first lieutenant. The following year Blake was given command of a company of Navaho Scouts. One account claims Blake helped capture the famous chief Geronimo.

But Blake was a restless soul and by 1888 he wanted out of the army. His ambitions now lay elsewhere. For a start there was the southern belle Kit Aldrich, the daughter of a 'pine baron'. As usual Blake got his way and a military wedding took place in St Mark's, Grand Rapids.[26]

In 1889 Blake left the cavalry. The wars against the 'Indians' were all but over and Blake was content for the while to 'live the life of people of wealth' in Grand Rapids. But boredom set his mind to becoming a businessman so he started the Grand Rapids Transfer and Cold Storage Company. It may be that this venture failed or it may have been 'a rift in the marital clouds', but whatever the cause Blake seems to have deserted the beautiful Kit and on 5 December 1894 fled to Britain and then to Africa in search of adventure.[27] From the Cape, where he arrived on 12 January 1895, Blake travelled to Rhodesia where he was caught up in the Ndebele insurrection. But the draw of Kruger's republic and the prospect of a new war soon attracted him to Pretoria.

Though John Blake made the right noises about Irish freedom and the iniquities of the English, despite his Irish ancestry he could not by any stretch of the imagination be called 'Irish'. The reverse was so of his second in command, Major John MacBride. 'Foxy Jack' was a wiry, red-headed man, with grey eyes and a long nose. He was a good six inches shorter than Blake and, at thirty-four, nine years his junior. MacBride was born in Westport, County Mayo, and educated at St Malachy's College, Belfast. He had a decent, lower-middle class Irish catholic background and his divergence from the straight and narrow in involving himself in the GAA and in Dr Ryan's neo-Fenian Irish National Association was, to a man from the west, almost as great an orthodoxy as going to mass on Sunday. MacBride was a conformist, even when a 'rabid Nationalist' in Dublin in the mid-1890s.

MacBride's arrival in South Africa undoubtedly increased the flow of advanced men to the Transvaal and in particular to the Langlaagte goldmine, where his experience as a Dublin pharmaceutical chemist had gained him the job of assayer on the block B mine. And there can be no doubt about the assertion of a contemporary that, 'No Irishman in the Transvaal has ever possessed anything like the influence that he does amongst his exiled countrymen.'[28]

Yet John MacBride was not a polished man. Once a journalist from *Le Figaro* asked him about Kitchener and Roberts. He made a 'significant gesture of contempt and disdain'.[29] Later Roger Casement spoke of MacBride as a 'swashbuckling miles glorious'. The journalist H.W. Morrison also described him as a swashbuckler but qualified this rather damningly by adding that MacBride was 'dissipated, devoid of character'.[30] That is too harsh. John MacBride was a straightforward, perhaps limited man, but he was a good leader of men in the field and a good soldier. One suspects that, given their different characters and coming from two very different wild wests, there was little love lost between John Blake and John MacBride. In Blake's 400-page book on his involvement in the war he mentions MacBride once and then only in passing; no photograph of MacBride is included in the memoir.

## THE RANK AND FILE

The appendix to this volume contains details of 263 men who, it is likely, at one time or another between September 1899 and September 1900 were members of the two Irish commandos: 202 in Blake's unit; forty-seven Irish-Americans who joined Blake's unit, and fourteen in Lynch's unit. This includes the double-listing of three men who served in both units, ten unknown Frenchmen and four men whose membership might have been only by association. No full brigade lists have survived and it is doubtful whether any ever existed after the initial intake. In keeping with the Boer commando system, men seemed to join and leave at will. Then there was a handful of recruits from Ireland, including Dr Walsh, as well as an Irish-American contingent from the USA, both these groups arriving well into the new year. The following table sets out some of the estimates of the corps' strength:

*Table 2: Estimates of the strength of the first Irish Transvaal Brigade*

| Source | Estimated number |
|---|---|
| John Blake's book | 300 |
| Michael Davitt's book | 100/200: average muster 120 |
| Conan Doyle's book | c.250 |
| *The Graphic* (18 Nov. 1899) | c.120 |
| Cecil Rhodes | c.1000 |
| *Times History of SA War* | c.100 |
| *United Irishmen* (19 Dec. 1899) | 1,700 |
| *United Irishmen* (6 Jan. 1900) | 2,000 |

Davitt was probably the most accurate, though the Irish balladers thought otherwise:

> From land to land throughout the world the news is going round
> That Ireland's flag triumphant waves on high o'er English ground.
> In far-off Africa today the English fly dismayed
> Before the flag of green and gold borne by McBride's Brigade.
> Three thousand sons of Erin's Isle, with bayonets flashing bright,
> For Ireland's cause and Kruger's land, right gallantly they fight;
> And Erin watches from afar with joy, and hope and pride,
> Her sons who strike for liberty, led on by John McBride.[31]

The term 'brigade' was, of course, not a military reality but a romantic allusion to the Irish brigade of Wild Geese who had fought as part of the French army in the eighteenth century. The Irish fighting on the highveld were commandos – the Boers referred to them as the Irish corps.

Who the Irish brigaders were is difficult to discern. MacBride claimed there were forty protestants in the unit, probably an exaggeration. The corps had two catholic chaplains in its short history: first the fifty-three-year-old Father Alexandre Baudry; then in early 1900 a Father Alphonse van Hecke, a twenty-five-year-old Belgian priest, joined. We know that there were some Irish-language speakers in the brigade and some Gaelic football players. Indeed, Hugh Carberry had played for Armagh in the Irish semi-finals against Cork in 1890.

Excepting John Blake, only about ten of the men had previous military experience, having formerly served in the British army.[32] Some of the Chicago Irish who came later had fought in the recent American war against Spain. Perhaps one or two brigaders had fought against the Jameson raiders. Most of them, like MacBride, were 'townies' and were unsteady on a horse. Such disadvantages became less significant given that many were miners and as such often expert in the use of dynamite. There was a scattering of 'physical force' men from the Fenian days, like Pat Malone from Louth and probably John Mitchell from Galway. A man named Larissey (Laracy?) was said to be wanted by Dublin Castle.

One interesting example of an Irish brigader was Michael Flynn of Newtown Forbes in County Longford. According to the RIC he was 'a well respected, well conducted boy, who knew nothing about Politics or Secret Society work previous to leaving home'. Flynn's father was the local national schoolmaster but, when he remarried, the eighteen-year-old Michael did not like his stepmother. With John Thompson he left home and about

1897 went out to Johannesburg. When war broke out he joined the Irish commando. The sad part of this story is that Michael's brother, James, joined the Inniskilling Fusiliers, fought opposite Michael at Ladysmith and was killed as the British advanced on the town.[33]

Most of the brigade were Irish born and bred but, even before the arrival of the Irish-American contingent, there were some non-Irish members. It was said that the brigade contained ten Frenchmen. Giovanni Bianes was likely an Italian and Bouwer and Coetzee would have been Afrikaners. Of 202 known brigaders with Blake (excluding the later Chicago recruits), the following is a breakdown of addresses. Most of the South African addresses are usually less than five years old:

*Table 3: Table of known addresses or places of origin of Blake's Irish corps*

| *Place* | *Number* | *Place* | *Number* |
|---|---|---|---|
| Dublin | 14 | UNKNOWN | 49 |
| Belfast | 9 | (Probably Ireland or America) | |
| Kerry | 8 | | |
| Down | 7 | Johannesburg | 13 |
| Kilkenny | 4 | Pretoria | 14 |
| Longford | 4 | Boksburg | 1 |
| Galway | 3 | Middelburg | 1 |
| Tipperary | 3 | Transvaal, place unknown | 3 |
| Armagh | 2 | Cape Colony & Natal | 10 |
| Cork | 2 | SOUTH AFRICA | 42 |
| Donegal | 2 | | |
| Meath | 2 | | |
| Waterford | 2 | USA | 12 |
| Co. Antrim | 1 | | |
| Clare | 1 | GREAT BRITAIN | 9 |
| Kildare | 1 | | |
| Louth | 1 | Australia | 1 |
| Mayo | 1 | Belgium | 1 |
| Monaghan | 1 | France (Names unknown) | 10 |
| Queens | 1 | Italy | 1 |
| Tyrone | 1 | Norway | 2 |
| Wexford | 1 | OTHER | 15 |
| Ireland, co. unknown | 4 | | |
| IRELAND | 75 | | |
| | | TOTAL 202 | |

We know of two fathers and sons who fought in the brigade – Ben Bouwer and his son Pieter from Pretoria, and P.J. Oates and his boy Tommy, who came from Kerry (Mrs Oates lived in Johannesburg and kept the family home going when the men were away fighting). The average age of the Irish brigade seems to have been quite high, probably around thirty. This would tie in with the fact that most brigaders had come out as young men in the mid-1890s and had worked in the Transvaal for four or five years before the outbreak of hostilities. The newcomers who turned up in March and April 1900 would have been much younger.

In addition to the regular fighters, in the early days the brigade seems to have attracted colourful figures to its fringe. These included Solomon Gillingham – it is very doubtful whether he ever fought; Major Menton, who may have been unstable; and the larger-than-life Captain Jack Hindon. One hopeful recruit never made it to Johannesburg. John Whelan was telegraphed in Mafeking by MacBride and invited to join the brigade but, like fellow Irish nationalist James Quinlan, he was arrested and imprisoned in the besieged town by the British. Reports of their execution proved false.

The men who joined the Irish Transvaal Brigade did so out of a variety of motives. For most, though, their thinking was simple enough: they were fighting the traditional enemy, they were supporting the Boers and they were having an adventure. The argument, sometimes tentatively raised in Ireland, that the Boers were calvinists who had penal laws against catholics was not a consideration for the brigaders, who knew that theory and what they themselves had experienced did not tally. The general attitude of the Irish to the Boers was, if anything, slightly paternalistic and well summed up by John MacBride after the war:

> My general impression of the Boers is that they were a decent, kind, chivalrous, hospitable people, passionately devoted to their freedom and religiously intent, without being intolerant of the beliefs of others.

On the other hand, there were a few who freely admitted, 'it was not for the love of the Boer we were fighting: it was the hatred of England'.[34] MacBride also made it plain that he would have rather fought in Ireland.

Maybe it was particularly such comments which led to a sharp division amongst the Irish in South Africa, between the Irish separatists fighting for the Boers and the moderate home rulers and unionist Irish in the Cape and Natal colonies. This divide is nowhere more vividly illustrated than by quoting two newspaper reports both from the *Standard and Diggers' News*:[35]

Grahamstown, 9 October. A meeting of local Irishmen is to be called shortly for the purpose of repudiating the action of Irishmen at the Rand in forming a corps, and also to express strong and unswerving loyalty to Britain.

10 October 1899

The Barberton Irishmen heartily sympathize with the Transvaal and decline to believe that the Durban Irishmen will join the cry of the capitalist.

28 October 1899

A comment needs to be made concerning those Irish who did not join Blake's Irish corps. There was, of course, a rival Irish corps established early in 1900 which will be looked at later. But in addition there was an unknown number of Irishmen scattered in various Boer commandos. The names of a few of these are contained in the appendix to this volume. Michael Davitt estimated their number at 1,200, but this is probably an exaggeration. President Steyn told Davitt, 'all the Catholics and Irishmen of the Free State were loyally with the Federal cause from the beginning'.[36] De La Rey, de Wet and Smuts all had Irishmen under their command. Of Smuts' famous raid into the Cape, Deneys Reitz noted:

> There were two Irishmen with us, Lang and Gallagher, members of [Commandant] Bouwer's commando, and, with the Irish love of explosives, they had ferreted out a quantity of dynamite and fuses from some outlying mine the day before, with which they had half a dozen hand-grenades.[37]

Michael Davitt confided to the Irish nationalist leader John Dillon in April 1900 that the Irish who did not join the two Irish brigades 'have the good sense to remain with their Boer Officers'.[38]

CHAPTER THREE

# The road to Ladysmith

EARLY OCTOBER 1899

### THE EVE OF WAR

From Monday, 2, to Thursday, 5 October 1899, frantic preparations were made to get the Irish Transvaal Brigade prepared, not that any drilling or military discipline was imposed. 'It was an anxious time,' wrote MacBride. 'Many recruits wanted to leave immediately.' John Mitchell's house was used as a brigade headquarters and store. Thanks to Gillingham's intervention with the government, their wish was soon granted and on Friday, 6 October, the brigade marched through Johannesburg to the railway station.[1] The artist Frank Dadd made a sketch of the scene from a photograph by Emile Andreoli which was reproduced by *The Graphic* and *Leslie's Weekly*.[2] The caption in *The Graphic* under the caption 'Traitors: The Irish Brigade serving with the Boers' ran:

> The men of the Irish-American Irish mainly Brigade who left Johannesburg on the outbreak of the war to fight the British are described as 'some of the worst sweepings of Johannesburg' and as 'all loafers'. They were about 120 strong, and were led by an American adventurer called 'Colonel' Blake. Their avowed object was loot, and probably that is all they would be any good for. The Boers themselves had the poorest opinion of them and were very anxious to keep them out of the way to prevent their doing anything disgraceful. When they left Johannesburg no rifles or cartridge belts had been served out to them. The Irish flag bears the motto 'Remember Michelstown'.[3]

If it was anti-Irish propaganda which was intended, Dadd should have found another photograph. The men shown 'marching' across a road all look very respectable – certainly not loafers.

The flag mentioned did exist and was one of several the Irish were to have. This first one had been worked by a Miss Butler of Harcourt Street in Dublin and had been made for the Fenian rising of 1867. When the insurrection petered out, it was given to Bridget Gill of Westport and it was she who had entrusted it to her nephew, John MacBride, on his departure for the Transvaal,[4] suggesting that he already saw stirrings of anti-British feeling beyond the sheer adventure of being in Africa.

As a defiant gesture to what remained of the British uitlander community, Blake wrote a strong letter to the *Diggers' News* which was published the day after the brigade had been mobilized and set out for the frontier. 'The Irish Brigade,' he wrote, 'will do its duty because its members have felt the lash of slavery at the hands of the English soldiery.'[5]

At Johannesburg's Park Station 'young Boer ladies' lavished gifts of flowers, fruit and cigars on the brigaders. With such a send-off, morale must have been high as the brigade's train steamed across the veld. At one of the stations between Johannesburg and Sandspruit Colonel Blake and a few of the men had got off to 'stretch their legs'. While they were so occupied, the train moved off and they were left behind. When they caught up with the brigade next day, there was much merriment caused by this incident. The train offloaded the Irish at the railway siding of Sandspruit on the afternoon of Saturday, 7 October. That same afternoon in Dublin, Arthur Griffith, Maud Gonne, W.B. Yeats and John O'Leary founded their Irish Transvaal Committee in the rooms of the Celtic Literary Society.

After a few days at Sandspruit the brigade was moved the fifteen kilometres on to the small town of Volkrust on the border of the Transvaal Republic and the British colony of Natal. Tom Byrne's account of their exciting days went as follows:

> As every man was mounted, there was no such thing as drilling. We marched to Park Station, Johannesburg, where we were mobilized. We entrained for the Transvaal and Natal border. On our arrival at a town on the Transvaal side [Volksrust] we were given horses. Most of us had no previous riding experience. The next fortnight was spent learning to ride, and this created a great deal of fun as well as painful memories. We were supplied with Martini rifles, which were only single shot weapons, as there were not enough Mausers to go round.

The lack of experience on horseback proved to be a problem for many brigaders, but provided much merriment for the Boers.[6] The weather was not good and it was especially cold at night, for snow was falling on the nearby Drakensberg mountains. But the men squeezed into their twenty tents and morale was high and there was lots of gossip to talk over. One rumour had it that the British had withdrawn from Natal the Dublin Fusiliers and Royal Irish Regiment for fear they would desert.

Kruger's birthday fell on Tuesday, 10 October, so that afternoon Commandant-General Joubert reviewed his forces, including the Irish corps.[7] A few days earlier the old Boer general thanked the Irish for joining his army, expressed his support for the Irish nationalist cause and granted them permission to fly the Transvaal flag alongside their Irish emblem.[8]

War broke out on Wednesday, 11 October 1899.

In the west a Boer army crossed into the Cape colony, cut the railway line south of Kimberley and proceeded to invest both Kimberley and the more northern outpost of Mafeking in Bechuanaland. In the east Joubert's army was divided in three, of which the Irish, Hollander and German corps were with the main body of some 11,000 mounted men, which had sixteen field guns and three heavy 155mm French Creusot fortress guns or Long Toms.[9]

Some confusion exists about the movements of the Irish commando on its advance down the Laing's Nek pass. MacBride says Blake waited behind for fifty new recruits expected from Johannesburg and that he, MacBride, was ordered to encamp at the pass but 'seemed to have forgotten' the order and to have ridden on to Newcastle. Blake, on the other hand, makes no mention of waiting behind.

Whatever the truth, at least most of the Irish brigade seems to have set off shakily on horseback into the Laing's Nek pass. There was driving rain with a severe lightning storm thundering above their heads. And as with the Boers, when the Irish passed under the shadow of Majuba mountain they cheered the Boer victory of eighteen years before. Near the bottom of the steep hill, on their left, they, probably unknowingly, rode past the graves of fellow countrymen General Colley and the Liberator's grand-nephew, Lieutenant Maurice O'Connell. Ahead through the mud and the rolling mist lay the green hills of Natal with its Irish governor, its Irish prime minister and its large continent of Irish soldiers. Even 10,000 kilometres from home nothing was simple for the Irish.

The dividing line between commandeering and looting is very thin. Apparently at some point in the war the ever-controversial Commandant Schutte illegally gave the right to commandeer goods to both Irish commandos, which powers they appeared to have used with alacrity.[10] The diary entry for a Red Cross member, Dr Raymond Maxwell, for 23 October recorded:

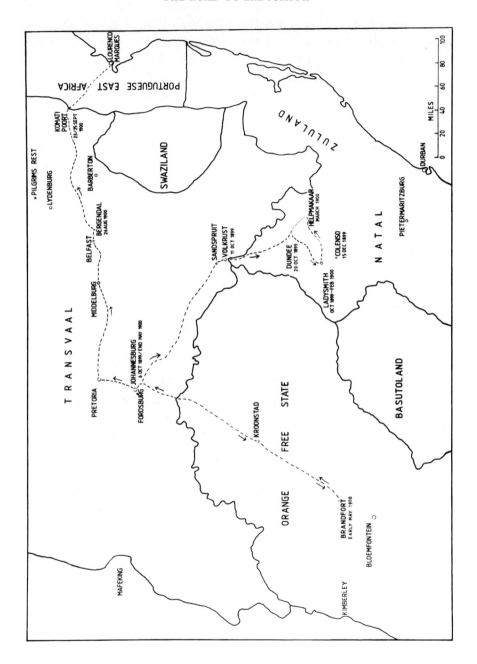

Map 1: South Africa, showing the areas of operation for Blake's commando.
(D.P. McCracken)

[39]

We outspanned for the night at the top of the Glencoe Valley [in Natal], and had a very wet time of it. All the farm-houses are cleaned from top to bottom, and what cannot be carried away is smashed up. About the worst offenders in this line are the Irish corps, and I can safely say I have never seen a bigger lot of blackguards in my life.[11]

It was the Irish who hauled down the union jack in the northern Natal town of Newcastle and hoisted the *vierkleur*. Cabling *The Times*, the Irish former editor of the Johannesburg *Star*, Dungannon-born William Monypenny noted, 'Reports state general drunkenness, laxity discipline, Boer corps Newcastle.'[12]

When exactly the Boers began to rein in the Irish is not clear, but it is likely that it was at Newcastle. The corps was placed in charge of guarding the artillery pieces of Commandant Stephanus Trichardt's Transvaal State Artillery. MacBride was introduced to the commandant by Gillingham the day prior to their entering Newcastle. Trichardt would have known Aylward in the 1870s, and possibly Arthur Griffith, too, for his home had been in the Middelburg district in the mid-1890s. Trichardt seems to have got on well with the Irish corps as, indeed, did several other Boer leaders such as General Botha and State Secretary Francis Reitz.

On the other hand, a prejudice continued in certain quarters for some time. Kruger, it was believed, thought John MacBride was mad and to be kept at arm's length, while State Secretary Reitz's famous son, Deneys, said that Blake's 'roystering habits and devil-may-care method suit his own'.[13] When Deneys Reitz's own seventeen-year-old boy wanted to join the Irish Transvaal Brigade – an interesting preference in itself – Deneys Reitz advised against with the words, 'The members of the Irish Brigade do their work well, my son, but they are not gentle in their manner.'[14] That Blake, MacBride and some of the brigaders were heavy drinkers and that there were internal divisions within both Irish commandos did not help their reputation. And yet, in fairness to the Irish, once they had settled down, they rendered good service to the Boers and perhaps of all the foreign units grew closest to their calvinist, Afrikaans-speaking allies.[15]

On Sunday, 15 October, four days after crossing into enemy territory, the Irish brigade was in the van of the Boer army which entered Newcastle. But they were not there for long. That evening, as part of the force under General Erasmus ('General Maroola'), they followed the railway line and pitched camp some two hours out of town. Here, according to MacBride, Colonel Blake and his section caught up with the brigade. On Wednesday,

18 October, they set out again in 'the mist and clouds'. The brigade established a new camp near the small village of Dannhauser, about twelve
kilometres from the coal-mining village of Dundee. Very close by were
4,000 professional British troops, including the First Battalion of the Royal
Irish Fusiliers and the Second of the Dublin Fusiliers.

## THE BATTLE OF DUNDEE

To say that Irishman fought Irishman at the battle of Dundee or Talana
Hill on Friday, 20 October, is in part true. The Dublin Fusiliers formed the
front line of the assault on the hill. The Irish Transvaal Brigade, however,
was not involved in this pitched battle when – at great loss – the British
captured the 200-metre-high Talana Hill, only to vacate it. It was said the
hillside grass was dyed with the blood of Irish soldiers. According to the
*Natal Mercury*, the Irish regiments lost twenty killed and eighty-one
wounded.[16] One of the saddest losses was Captain O'Connor, 'the giant of
the Fusiliers', mortally wounded in the stomach.[17] His grave stands at the
north-west of Talana where Erasmus' force waited. But the thirty or forty
brigaders were certainly involved in the fight against Colonel Möller's
force, containing eighty-one Dublins, which had tried unsuccessfully to cut
off the Boers behind Talana Hill, and which finally surrendered in a cattle
kraal on the farm Adelaide.[18]

J.G. Dunn, an Irish-American, claimed that the Irish troops in the kraal
surrendered when they saw the brigade's flag and were 'sort of tickled' to
be captured by Irishmen. He also said that they surrendered to Major
O'Hara and Captain Pollard of the Irish Transvaal Brigade. This may well
be true. What is controversial was the claim that of 196 Irishmen captured,
eighty-five of these troops begged to join the Irish corps, but were
prevented from doing so by the Boers.[19] Later the then imperialist Roger
Casement denounced the Boers for allowing Irish prisoners-of-war to enlist
in the Irish brigade. 'Tampering with men's loyalties' was a game he himself
was to play when in Germany during World War I.[20]

According to Winston Churchill's account of his own capture in Natal,
Irish brigaders showed open hostility to their fellow countrymen who had
been captured:

> He [the Irishman] addressed himself to Frankland, whose badges
> proclaimed his regiment. What he said when disentangled from

obscenity amounted to this: 'I am glad to see you Dublin fellows in trouble.' The Boers silenced him at once and we passed on.

Be that as it may, the Irish corps had been in its first battle and in the tradition of the Wild Geese had come up against their own people. Far away in Dublin the Irish capital was in an unsettled state as pro-Boer fever swept through the nationalist community. The same day as the battle of Talana was fought, part of Dublin was proclaimed by the authorities a no-go area for British troops after dark.[21] Maud Gonne was doing a good job.

The news of the battle in South Africa that Friday prompted one anonymous balladeer to compose one of the best of the Irish Boer war verses. It is worth quoting in full:

On the mountain side the battle raged, there was no stop or stay;
Mackin captured Private Burke and Ensign Michael Shea,
Fitzgerald got Fitzpatrick, Brannigan found O'Rourke;
Finnigan took a man named Fay – and a couple of lads from Cork.
Sudden they heard McManus shout, 'Hands up or I'll run you through'.
He thought it was a Yorkshire 'Tyke' – 'twas Corporal Donaghue!
McGarry took O'Leary, O'Brien got McNamee,
That's how the 'English fought the Dutch' at the Battle of Dundee.

Then someone brought in Casey, O'Connor took O'Neil;
Riley captured Cavanagh, while trying to make a steal.
Hagan caught McFadden, Carrigan caught McBride
And Brennan made a handsome touch when Kelly tried to slide.
Dicey took a lad named Welsh; Dooley got McGurk;
Gilligan turned in Fahey's boy – for his father he used to work.
They had marched to fight the English – but Irish were all they could
    see –
That's how the 'English fought the Dutch' at the Battle of Dundee.

The sun was sinking slowly, the battle rolled along;
The man that Murphy 'handed in' was a cousin of Maud Gonne,
Then Flanagan dropped his rifle, shook hands with Bill McGuire,
For both had carried a piece of turf to light the schoolroom fire.
Then Rafferty took in Flaherty; O'Connell got Major McGue;
O'Keefe got hold of Sergeant Joyce and a Belfast lad or two.
Some swore that 'Old Man Kruger' had come down to see the fun;

> But the man they thought was 'Uncle Paul' was a Galway man named
>     Dunn.
> Though war may have worse horrors, 'twas a frightful sight to see
> The way the 'English fought the Dutch' at the Battle of Dundee.[22]

Perhaps not of that quality but more poignant was Arthur Griffith's 'The song of the Dublin Fusilier'. This tells of an Irish soldier left to die by the British when they retreated from Dundee. Three stanzas run as follows:

> Me father – Heaven rest him! – died twelve years ago in jail,
> A Fenian – and they used him like a hound.
> Still I took the English shilling; though I knew me mother'd wail –
> God curse him! when the sergeant kem around.
>
> 'Charge up, boys,' sez the colonel, and I charged straight to the hill
> To strike down freemen battling for their right.
> To make myself a murderer – for England's sake to kill,
> The patriots standing out agin her might.
>
> Yes, the curse of God is on me, an' I broke me mother's heart.
> An' me father's curse is on me, too, as well,
> But wan thing cheers me still when me life tonight I part,
> I'll meet the man that 'listed me in hell.[23]

Whether any Irish on the British side actually took such a view is doubtful. Private Francis Burns of the Royal Irish Fusiliers was full of excitement when he wrote home to his father:

> The papers say the Dublins were first on the hill, but it was the Royal Irish. It does not matter anyhow, for we were all Irish. Tell my mother England's first battle was won by the Irish Brigade.[24]

It was a pyrrhic victory, however, for young Private Burns and his regiment. Talana Hill once captured was soon vacated and the British retreated leaving their commander, Major-General Penn-Symons, mortally wounded. His force had been depleted by 546 men. Sixty kilometres to the south in Ladysmith things looked grim for the newly arrived commander-in-chief, Natal: Antrim-born General Sir George White.

The Boers occupied – and looted – the village of Dundee, with its store of provisions. Tom Byrne commented:

We were not long in the field until we got Lee-Metford English service rifles and dum-dum ammunition, captured at the town of Dundee, also food stores, and I personally had a Lee-Metford two or three days after the war started.

Blake and MacBride made the same controversial claim about dum-dum bullets, Blake adding that:

> I had the pleasure of supplying the whole Irish Brigade with these dum-dum bullets and split bullets, and the English Lee-Metford rifles captured at Dundee … We gave the English back their own medicine in big doses at Ladysmith.[25]

Fortunately for the Irish Transvaal Brigade they were not at the British victory the next day at the railway halt of Elandslaagte, when Donegal-man Captain Robert Johnson of the Imperial Light Horse won his VC. The behaviour of the British Lancers including the Fifth (Irish) Lancers – 'like a lot of Sioux' – at Elandslaagte did, however, annoy the Irish corps and they were put down in 'our black book'. Two brothers named Ryan were said to have fought that day with the Boers, attacking the Lancers with the butt ends of their rifles; they were wounded and captured.

The British victory was short lived and soon White was consolidating his forces preparing for a siege at Ladysmith. The Irish brigade now worked its way slowly south helping move the heavy guns of Trichardt's artillery. A week after Talana, at four o'clock in the afternoon of Friday, 27 October, they came in sight of the garrison town of Ladysmith.[26]

# CHAPTER FOUR

# Ladysmith and the Tugela

OCTOBER–DECEMBER 1899

And I met with White the General,
    And he's looking thin enough
And he says the boys in Ladysmith
    Are running short of stuff.
Faith, the dishes need no washing,
    Now they're left so nice and clean;
Oh! it's anything but pleasant
    To be starving for the Queen.

But if he gave in tomorrow,
    I would not think it right
To throw the least disparagement
    On a man like General White.
He is making a bold resistance
    As great as could be made,
Against their deadly Mauser rifles,
    And their tremendous cannonade.[1]

The Irish Transvaal Brigade was not involved in the battle of Rietfontein, the British rearguard action before retreating into the nearby military garrison town of Ladysmith on the brown, sluggish Klip river. According to one source some brigade members were intent on blowing up the railway bridge at Colenso, twenty kilometres south of Ladysmith on the mighty Tugela river. This scheme, however, foundered, probably because the British army still held a corridor between Ladysmith and the Tugela. MacBride claimed he could not get a Boer escort for his 'dynamitards'. But the scheme may also have been dropped because of an incident in a nearby coalmine. Intent on finding explosives, three members of the brigade – Halley, McCormick and McDonagh – entered the mine with a naked flame. An explosion occurred and all three were blasted and lucky to have escaped with their lives.

On Saturday, 28 October 1899, Blake and his men arrived at Pepworth farm in the company of the Ermelo commando, a Long Tom, two field guns and two pompom rapid-firing guns. Soon the low-lying ridge of Pepworth Hill had been established as a stronghold with Long Tom pointed at Ladysmith, some six kilometres to the south and clearly visible from the hill.[2] In Ladysmith itself, among the 13,500 troops and 7,800 civilians, was the First battalion, Royal Irish Fusiliers, the Second Royal Irish Regiment and the Fifth Royal Irish Lancers and, before they retreated south on 31 October, the Second Royal Dublin Fusiliers. Half a company of Dublins remained in Ladysmith. Trichardt remained in overall command of artillery, but the Pepworth site fell under Blake's friend Major J.F. Wolmarans, and the general line from the Modderspruit in the east to the Bell Spruit in the west was controlled by General 'Maroola'.[3]

The Irish camp was initially established on the back of Pepworth Hill looking north away from and, as they thought, protected from Ladysmith. Not far off, to the rear of the Irish camp, was that of the police commando (ZARP) and some distance to the north-east of the Irish camp just across the Natal Government Railways track at Modderspruit siding, was Commandant-General Joubert's headquarters. The sharp-tongued de Villebois-Mareuil observed:

'Headquarters' staff is composed of relatives of General Joubert … They are all very friendly and easy of access, with the exception of Mrs Joubert. As a whole headquarters, with its animals, negresses and large tents, is more fair-like than military.[4]

### THE BATTLE OF MODDERSPRUIT

All was quiet that Saturday, 28 October, and the next morning confession was heard and communion given in the Irish camp. But the lads were anxious for action. An unofficial sortie to a now-derelict farm house near the town (possibly Bell's farm) flushed a pig, which was shot. Unfortunately, from behind a wall emerged some British tommies and an exchange of fire occurred as the Irish made a speedy retreat with their pig. It was all great fun.

Later that Sunday evening some brigaders spotted the great, dark shape of a British military reconnaissance balloon gently drifting up from

Ladysmith and slightly towards their direction. Late that night British troops began to file out of Ladysmith: some went north-west toward the Tchrengula, or Hogs Back, and Nicholson's Nek, others went east towards Lombard's Kop and the Modderspruit stream and one column, under Colonel Grimwood, north then veering east towards Long Hill, with the intention of proceeding on to storm Pepworth. So it was in the early hours of Monday, 30 October, that the battles of Nicholson's Nek and Modderspruit, collectively known as the battle of Ladysmith, began.

For the British, 'Mournful Monday' was a disastrous attempt to prevent encirclement by the Boer forces. For the Irish corps, it was their first full-scale battle. Once Long Tom roared into life, it was soon engaged by a 120mm Royal Navy gun which had recently arrived in Ladysmith. As the commandos and the British forces battled it out among the plains, the dongas and the hillsides, Pepworth Hill was enveloped with smoke and became a dangerous place to be:

> Shells were bursting over our heads,
> on the ground among us, and great
> chunks of iron were whizzing about
> from stone to stone.[5]

By seven in the morning, the cooked but uneaten pig still lay by the camp fire and the Irish brigaders were in a state of great excitement. When Long Tom fell silent, Commandant Grobler came up to Blake and requested four volunteers to carry up 44kg shells across the open, sloping and stony hillside to the great gun. So many of the Boer gun crew had been killed that no one remained for this unenviable task. But in the Irish brigade, of course, everyone wanted to volunteer and Blake ended up sending seven men, two of whom were not to return from that heavy field of fire.

An hour later a pellet from an exploding shell hit Colonel Blake, 'smashed both the bones of my arm near the elbow, cut the tendon, nerve and artery and completely paralysed my whole arm'.[6] In a state of shock and in great pain, with blood flowing from him, Blake found his horse and, with the help of a young Boer lad, managed to mount and made it to the military field hospital. As Blake freely admitted, 'it was a close call,' but the Boer doctors pulled him through. Now Major MacBride was officer commanding the Irish Transvaal Brigade.

By lunchtime the great battle had been fought and lost by the British, who retreated behind their defences. Losses in men killed, wounded and captured had been great. Not least were the casualties suffered among the Royal Irish Fusiliers at Nicholson's Nek. Approximately 950 prisoners were taken by the Boers that day, about 500 of whom were fusiliers.

Conan Doyle painted a sad but striking picture of the scene among the Irish Fusiliers when they surrendered:

> Haggard officers cracked their sword blades and cursed the day they had been born. Privates sobbed with their stained faces buried in their hands. Of all tests of discipline that ever they had stood, the hardest to many was to conform to all that the cursed flapping handkerchief meant to them. 'Father, father, we had rather have died', cried the Fusiliers to their priest.[7]

Back on Pepworth Hill the scene was no happier. The Irish camp itself was destroyed: 'Every pot, kettle, blanket and tent etc., in the Irish camp was simply riddled by shells ... a total wreck.' All that remained of the tents were 'flying ribbons from poles'. A flying rock splinter had even knocked a stone from a ring John MacBride was wearing. But there was a lot worse.

Dominic Cox and the young flagbearer, Tommy Oates, were dead. Oates, the brigade's first casulty, had had his skull smashed by the casing of a shell. At first they had thought he had fallen asleep and only when Frank Dunlop offered him some food did they realize he was dead. As the brigade buried Cox and Oates on the side of Pepworth Hill that night, Tommy's father stood over the grave. Like Tom Byrne, he was one of the more respectable members of the corps. Ahead for him now lay the journey back to the Rand to tell Tommy's mother; no doubt he wished they had never left Killarney.[8]

Thomas Hawney and Pat Fahey made a wooden cross and carved the names of their dead comrades on it and placed it above the grave. Soon Fahey would rest under his own cross.

Estimates of the number of Irish brigaders wounded at the battle of Modderspruit vary, but there seem to have been at least eight in addition to Blake, including brigaders called Barnes, A.G. Boer, Hugh Carberry from Armagh city, Lieutenant Gaynor from Longford, Andy Higgins from County Down, Kepner, Olsen, a Norwegian, and a man called Tinen. Some of these, but not Blake, were evacuated to the Rand by special ambulance train under the care of Doctors Lingbeek and Veale.

The thirty-two-year-old Hugh Carberry received a bullet in the centre of the forehead. This was extracted by Doctors Mehliss and Lilpop and within three days Carberry was walking around the field hospital. Invalided out of the brigade, Carberry was sent to Pretoria where he appeared to be making good progress. But about three months later he collapsed with a stroke and died.[9] It is also possible that an Irishman named A. Murphy may have died of wounds received on Pepworth Hill on 'Mournful Monday'.

According to Blake, over the next ten days he urged the Boers to storm Ladysmith but his pleas were dismissed as nonsense by Generals Jacobus Erasmus and Schalk Burger. Be that as it may, the Irish had won their battle colours. First Trichardt and then no less a figure than Commandant-General Joubert had ridden up to congratulate and thank the Irish corps. One can well believe that, as reputed, Colonel Trichardt said on one occasion: 'To get my guns the English will first have to kill my Irish troops.'

The next day, Tuesday, 31 October, a duel opened up between the British naval guns and the Boer artillery. It was to become a regular occurrence for the Irish corps who were soon to guard the Pepworth guns both night and day, though in truth the Long Tom on Lombard's Kop did more damage to the besieged town than did that on Pepworth Hill. Amery's *The Times history of the war in South Africa* is worth quoting on the Boer artillery:

> Both on Pepworth and along the Modderspruit, the Transvaal artillery fully justified the expectations the Boers had formed of it, and reversed the contemptuous estimate in which the British authorities had hitherto held it.

And at the battle of Modderspruit *The Times history* is also complimentary of the Irish corps:

> But for the rest of the morning the actual summit of Pepworth was unoccupied save for the men of the "staats Artillerie" and for a handful of burgers and of Blake's Irish Brigade, who remained and indefatigably helped in dragging up ammunition under the hail of British sharpnel.[10]

### LADYSMITH BESIEGED

Three days after Modderspruit a contingent of Fifth (Royal Irish) Lancers was turned back at Tatham's farm, north west of the town and the 23 kilometres encirclement of Ladysmith was complete. The Irish corps now settled down to its guard duty with a new camp further back from Pepworth Hill in the Modderspruit valley near the Modderspruit railway siding, nearly opposite Joubert's headquarters.[11] On the same side of the railway track the Irish had as neighbours General 'Maroola's' section of the Pretoria commando, van Dam's police unit and Ben Viljoen's Johannesburg commando. It is possible that they also still occupied Pepworth farm house. On 29 October it was reported:

> By means of slow trekking we reached Pepworth's farm, and found the homestead in the hands of the Irish Corps. Mr Pepworth's house is completely looted and all the furniture, etc., is smashed.[12]

The brigade seems to have been divided into shifts, with about fifty members spending each night on the hillside surrounded by millions of empty cartridges as they guarded Long Tom and the howitzers. They invented a game called 'mumble peg', the details of which are now lost save that they used captured British lances.

The brigaders seem to have led a pleasant enough life. They had a few African servants, or at least African grooms. Sundays were usually free and there were occasional trips to Johannesburg where some commandeering might be done. They were not ignorant of events in Ireland as Transvaal newspapers were sometimes available and occasionally a letter from home made its way to them via France, Lourenço Marques and Pretoria. The brigaders would have known about the clash in the British House of Commons on 17 October when the Irish parliamentary party united in opposition to Joseph Chamberlain. And they would have read of Michael Davitt's resignation from that chamber eight days later. Even the big Irish Socialist Republic Party pro-Boer rally in Dublin on the day before the brigade sighted Ladysmith would have come to their attention.

Colonel Blake was off duty for six weeks with his injured arm, from 30 October to 12 December. He did not leave Natal but seems to have enjoyed himself: this tall broad-shouldered man got on very well with the Boers.

From various photographs of Blake, his attire seems rarely to have changed. He wore a large hat, a white silk handkerchief around his neck, 'a claret-coloured sort of tunic, displaying a gorgeous vest. Corduroy breeches and huge boots and spurs.' In his breast pocket was a handkerchief and on his left lapel a green ribbon. It is said he also carried a lasso round his body or on his Mexican saddle.[13] Blake's horse was as impressive – a large grey hunter. A trophy of the siege, this fine animal carried two brands: '5 D.G., B136' and 'J.H.' – the Dragoon Guards were at Ladysmith.

Blake was able to handle General Joubert better than MacBride could. MacBride freely admitted:

> General Joubert, I know, did not like me. I spoke rather hotly and impatiently to him after the battle of Modderspruit, when he refused to allow us to follow up an undoubted advantage and smash the flying English enemy, and I fear he never forgave my hastiness.

But even Blake did not always get his way with the old general. He tells us that he tried to persuade the Boers to drop bombs on the British from kites but that Joubert had rejected this unusual suggestion on the grounds that the British did not use their balloons for such practices and besides there was no justification in scripture.[14] Blake also says that when he was away the Boers 'were making fools' of the brigaders, who now tried to persuade Blake to return to them.[15]

One aspect of Blake's character was recounted by a Dr Mate in the *Natal Witness* that November. 'Judging from the number of expletives in his vocabulary,' wrote Mate, 'I should say that the American-Irishman is richer in this line than any three languages combined.'[16]

While one does not doubt that Colonel Blake was able to find himself a drink, there were periods when alcohol was in short supply in the Irish camp. Without a drink, the lads got bored and when that happened diversion had to be found elsewhere. In the weeks following the battle of Modderspruit this took the form of somewhat foolhardy raids by Irish brigaders on the outposts of Ladysmith.

This practice of raiding was greatly encouraged by the animosity which existed between the Irish brigaders and the Irish troops in Ladysmith, mainly Dublin Fusiliers and Royal Irish Rifles and Royal Artillery. Using African messengers, notes of a threatening and, one suspects, obscene nature were on occasions exchanged. Part of one reply from the Dublin Fusiliers asserted that when they caught up with the Irish corps, they would go through them 'as the devil went through Athlone'.

Michael Davitt recounts an incident when a column of Royal Irish were enticed into attacking a small group of Irish brigaders on Pepworth Hill. As they panted up the hill after the 'flying Fenians', there emerged a hidden block of brigaders and the Irish troops had to take to their heels.[17]

The *Ladysmith Bombshell* was prompted into verse by the Irish Transvaal Brigade:

*Maloney*

I was a rolling blade of the Irish Brigade
Of Joubert's, and fond of orating,
I'm hungry for foight, shoore
I'm kill 'em all right
I'm hungry for want of a bating
Have a hoult au me head
Let me at 'em he said,
Put me up on a horse or a pony.
An I'm sthrong an I'm talk talk
I'll slaughter thim all
For there's no such a man as Malony.

I was a bombadier gay of the gallant RA
I'm the pride of the force and they know it,
Went out for a walk, heard that orator talk
His answer was simply ''ere stow it'
He slipped in a shell and he rammed it home well
It burst on a ridge bleak and stony
It grieves me to say, when the smoke cleared away
There was no such a man as Malony.[18]

Equally as exciting as baiting Irish troops were the raids for horses and mules on the outposts of Ladysmith. The Boers had the Irish corps in mind when they proposed offering £100 to any volunteer who blew up a British gun and £200 to the person who captured a gun. It is not known if this idea was ever implemented.[19]

Sergeant Major O'Reilly, 'an Afrikaner born, but an Irishman to the backbone', was said to be particularly expert at rustling. The practice, however, was very dangerous and at least one brigader was shot dead in such an expedition. Eventually the Boers put a stop to these acts of bravado.

This did not, of course, bring to an end military raids on the British, in some of which the Irish corps participated. It is doubtful, though, that brigaders were part of the Boer force which ambushed near Chieveley the famous armoured train – Wilson's death trap – which contained Winston Churchill and a variety of troops including some Dublin Fusiliers.[20]

In his *Four Months Besieged*, the journalist Henry Pearse recalled an attack on Ladysmith on about 9 November 1899 which included a column of Irishmen with a red flag as a standard. The attack was soon put to flight.[21] More significant was a military operation on Thursday, 30 November. Captain Jack Hindon, who seems to have a tenuous connection with the Irish brigade, then had scouted the eastern defences of Ladysmith opposite Lombardskop. His plan to storm the British forts on Devonshire Hill did not excite the cautious Boers. But John MacBride and some forty brigaders expressed themselves game as did Lieutenant Koos Boshoff and twenty-seven burghers.

There are various accounts of this attack and where it took place. What is clear is that it was unsuccessful with the force being surprised and nearly overwhelmed by the British. But the Irish brigaders fought well and Foxy Jack's actions were particularly noteworthy. MacBride himself was in real danger, not least because he stopped to help the wooden-legged Frank Dunlop mount his horse. MacBride's own horse, Fenian Boy, bolted but was brought back through the firing line to the major by Pat Darragh.

Some time later the secretary to General Blignaut wrote to MacBride in Paris, 'Your attack with six or seven men on the little Red Fort of the British at Ladysmith was such that those who saw it wondered.'[22] Unpleasantness, however, seems to have resulted from a claim by MacBride that Captain Mitchell had not given covering fire to the attackers.

It is little wonder that occasionally an Irish brigader fell into the hands of the besieged. Stories of a member of the Irish Transvaal Brigade being captured at Ladysmith and then killed by a British soldier circulated to such an extent that knowledge of the incident was denied in the British House of Commons on 9 February 1900.[23] One brigader captured was a twenty-four-year-old Belfast man called McLade. His story ran as follows:

> I sold my public house in Belfast and left only six weeks ago. I went straight to Pretoria, took the oath of allegiance to the Republic and was made a burger on the spot. At the same time I renounced my allegiance to the Queen, and that did without shedding a tear.[24]

On the other side of the coin, Irish troops fell into the hands of the Boers and, before being sent up to the Transvaal, sometimes had encounters with Blake's men. Such experiences could vary. Captain Haldane, the hapless officer in charge of the famous armoured train, recalled a visit after his capture, from 'a member of the Honourable Artillery Company, an Irishman'. He told him, probably inaccurately, that as a burgher he had been forced to take up arms. Some weeks later he returned bringing with him large quantities of cigarettes for the POWs. Haldane, however, also

[53]

recounts an incident when an Irishman used insulting language against captured Dublin Fusiliers. This is possibly the incident also recalled by Winston Churchill and mentioned earlier.[25]

The *Natal Witness* reported in early December 1899 that an Irish man named O'Neill had left the Boers forces and come into Ladysmith: his story was the same as Haldane's visitor with the cigarettes, that he had been forced to join the Boer army. Perhaps he was the same man.[26]

Two weeks earlier, on 12 November, one notable thing happened in Ireland and two notable things happened in Ladysmith. In Ireland a large Irish Transvaal Committee rally was held in Cork. In Ladysmith the first siege baby was born and an Irish-American deserter arrived in the town. The deserter, whose name is not known, spoke of the Irish raid three days previously. As might be expected in the circumstances the story, in Henry Pearse's words, should not be 'swallowed without salt':

> The deserter said that the Irish brigade that day [9 November] lost heavily, having now only seventy three left of the original three hundred and fifty, and that ten Irishmen were killed by one of our shells.[27]

On 16 November 1899 Captain James Laracy of the Irish brigade and three Boers set off to Pretoria with fifty-six POWs, whom they delivered safely to the authorities. He returned to the Irish camp with fourteen new recruits he had got in Johannesburg.

## COLENSO

By November 1899 something of a stalemate existed in the war. To break this the British despatched to South Africa an expeditionary force of 45,000 infantry and 5,000 cavalry. The commander was the Devon man, General Sir Redvers Buller. About 8,100 of Buller's men were drawn from Irish regiments and of these 130 officers and 4,402 men were grouped into the Fifth (Irish) Infantry Brigade under the command of Major-General Fitzroy Hart. This was constituted as shown in Table 4 (opposite).

In addition the Second Battalion, Royal Irish Fusiliers, and later the First Battalion, Royal Irish Regiment, joined the ranks of Major-General Barton's Sixth Infantry Brigade. Thus six Irish infantry battalions took part in the push to relieve Ladysmith. In addition many Irishmen were members of other regiments, some of them as senior officers.[28]

Buller finally arrived in Durban on Saturday, 25 November, and slowly began to move his army inland towards the Tugela river, 200 kilometres to

*Table 4: Fifth (Irish) Infantry Brigade*

| | |
|---|---|
| First Battalion, Royal Inniskilling Fusiliers | 998 men |
| Second Battalion, Royal Irish Rifles | They disembarked at East London to join Sir William Gatacre's ill-fated brigade and many of the Rifles become POWs. They were replaced in the Fifth Brigade by First Battalion Border Regiment (987 men), First Battalion, Connaught Rangers (883 men) |
| Second Battalion, Royal Dublin Fusiliers | 1,002 men |
| No. 8, Bearer Company | |
| No. 15, Field Hospital | |

the north-west. With him went five batteries of field artillery and sixteen naval guns from HMS *Terrible*.

The Boers had been wise to choose the Tugela as their line of defence. An undulating plain led up to the broad and, at this time of year, fast-flowing grey river. Beyond its banks lay a deep ridge of hills which dominated the land to the south. To relieve Ladysmith twenty kilometres beyond, Buller would have to hammer his way through this fortress.

Before he was in a position even to attempt this, two of his armies in the Cape had been repulsed, one at Stormberg on Sunday, 10 December, where the Irish Rifles had over 200 men captured, and the other next day at Magersfontein.

In Natal the Boers were all too aware of the seriousness of Buller's presence to the south. Quickly they began to drain men away from Ladysmith down to the Tugela. This was no time to be lazing in a hospital camp, and on that Tuesday Colonel Blake cast off his convalescent lethargy and returned to the Irish camp behind Pepworth Hill. On Thursday, 14 December, Trichardt ordered Blake to send thirty men to Colenso where, it was clear, the British were soon to attempt a crossing of the Tugela. It is interesting that Blake choose to send MacBride with the men. Perhaps his injury was still a problem or maybe he was glad of an excuse to get rid of his second in command for a few days. Or maybe Botha wanted Blake at Ladysmith. The successful disabling of a Boer gun by the British in a night raid meant that there would have to be a twenty-four-hour watch kept.

It was about midnight on 14 December when MacBride and his men arrived on the heights overlooking the Tugela. At 2 a.m. Trichardt took them to his two fifteen-pound Creusot guns. By now the ranks of the Irish at the Tugela had risen to sixty, thirty men having left their camp behind Pepworth Hill against orders to come down for the fight. When MacBride upbraided them, Joe Tully replied: 'Sure we may be all dead before evening and then you will be sorry for saying anything to us'[29]

At 3.30 a.m. General Hart had his Fifth (Irish) Brigade up and out for drill practice. It was in quarter-column, as if on the barrack square, that he later sent his men into the fight. W. Baring Pemberton has written of him:

> This dashing Irishman might have stepped straight out of the Crimea for all his apparent ignorance of what had been achieved in gunnery and small arms over the past Fifty years.[30]

At 5 a.m. MacBride saw the enemy on the undulating plain across the river, thousands upon thousands of men and cavalry moving towards them. It was a spectacular sight.

At about 5.30 the British naval guns began a bombardment of what they thought were Boer positions. MacBride's men were on the right of General Botha's centre and as such had a good view of the military disaster which ensued after General Hart's decision at 6.30 a.m. to march his men into a pronounced and unprotected loop in the Tugela river in search of a non-existent drift.

The Dublins led the advance, followed by the Inniskillings, the Connaughts and the Border Regiment.[31] A Boer shell smashed into the Dublin Fusiliers. Shortly after, another sent the Connaught Rangers flat on the ground. The grass was long, but even so it gave little protection, for on the far bank of the river was the Swaziland commando and parallel to the east side of the loop on a slight elevation across the river was the Middelburg commando. 'Like the hissing of fat in the pan' came 'the monotonous crackle and rattle of the Mausers'.[32]

Some of MacBride's men, including MacBride himself, came down and were positioned first to the rear of the Middelburg commando. Not 200 metres away their fellow countrymen were in a killing field. Though there was no panic, there was chaos in the ranks of Hart's Irish Brigade.

The Irish soldiers broke rank and the Connaught Rangers under Colonel Brooke surged forward to take the place of those Dublins who had fallen. When they reached the south bank, there occurred one of several heroic incidents which were later widely reported in Ireland. The soldiers were massed beside the steep-banked river but were uncertain what to do next. Against orders, the bugle boy of the First Battalion Royal Dublin Fusiliers, Bugler John Dunne, had stayed with his regiment. At the river he sounded the advance and was immediately struck down by a bullet.[33] Later Queen Victoria was to present Bugler Dunne with a new bugle to replace the one he lost at the Tugela.

The Dublins waded into the deep, fast-flowing river, with their rifles held over their heads. Five metres from the north bank they were stopped by barbed and netted wire hidden under the water. A few of the Dublins actually made it to the far bank but soon retreated. One was overheard quipping to a comrade, 'This beats Athlone on a Saturday night.'

On the heights, back to the right of the British forces, Buller could see the battle. 'Hart has got into a devil of a mess down there,' he said to General Lyttelton, 'get him out of it as best you can.'

Four hundred men had been mown down in forty minutes. When the order to retreat finally arrived, the troops pulled out under protest. A group of about ten Connaught Rangers and twenty Inniskillings under a Colonel Thackeray were surrounded by the Boers. When he refused to give up his arms, the Boers told him he was a brave man and let him go, telling him if he came to Pretoria there would be a bottle of brandy waiting for him. It was reported that when the old colonel returned to camp, 'the whole Irish Brigade hurried out and cheered him again and again'. On the Boer side, General Botha observed, 'They were men of pluck and no mistake.'[34]

If the battle was now over for Hart's Irish Brigade, it was still very much in full swing for MacBride's Irish brigade. General Botha decided to concentrate fire on some British guns which foolishly had been brought in front of the British infantry lines, just to the east of the village of Colenso and only a few hundred metres from the river and the Krugersdorp commando beyond. To reinforce his position at Fort Wylie, opposite Colenso village, Botha ordered reinforcements from his right flank. Some of the Middelburg commando and about twenty Irish brigaders mounted and made a dash across an area of open ground raked by British fire.

The sun was now well up and it was getting hot. Crossing this no-man's land MacBride's horse (not Fenian Boy) was killed by a shell and MacBride was thrown to the ground. Thirteen-year-old Willie Smith, who had attached himself to the brigade, rode up and offered the major his horse. MacBride's language was such as to send the boy galloping off at speed. Then Sergeant-Major O'Reilly wheeled his own horse round and placed himself between MacBride and the enemy. Quickly MacBride tore across the veld as fast as he could run to safety with O'Reilly sheltering him from enemy fire. Michael Davitt was not far wrong when he said that had O'Reilly done such a thing on the British side he would have received a Victoria Cross.[35] Soon three VCs would indeed be won by two Irishmen and one son of an Irish field-marshal.

Many years later Maud Gonne wrote that the capture of the guns at 'the Tugela was thrilling': she had received a first-hand account of this famous incident from John MacBride. Colonel Blake said that the Irish were among the first to seize Long's guns. Minutes earlier Corporal Nurse from Enniskillen managed to hitch up and drag out a cannon. A similar, but unsuccessful, brave attempt was made shortly afterwards by Dublin-born Captain Hamilton Reed. Both men later received VCs, as did Freddy Roberts, who was mortally wounded at the site of the guns; MacBride said he saw young Roberts fall. When MacBride left South Africa he took with him as a memento a sight from one of Long's guns.

There is some controversy about what exactly happened when Colonel Bullock's small group of men were captured and the remaining guns seized. Cheere Emmet had members of the Krugersdorp and Johannesburg police commandos with him as well as some Irish brigaders; it is to be hoped that it was not one of the Irish brigade that slammed a rifle butt into Bullock's mouth breaking his teeth.[36] MacBride said it was a young Boer. MacBride himself walked back to camp with Bullock, who offered him one of the two dry biscuits in his pocket, "sharing a soldier's fare". When MacBride told the colonel who he was, 'he became remarkably silent'.

BACK TO CAMP

The battle of Colenso was the last great battle of the nineteenth century. For the nationalist press in Ireland the heroic (if misplaced) action of the Irish regiments and the presence of some members of the Irish corps fighting the British all made for good copy. Two days after Colenso a pro-Boer crowd marched through Dublin behind a wagon carrying, among others, Maud Gonne, Arthur Griffith and James Connolly, though lacking several MPs who discreetly kept away. The decision of Trinity College, Dublin – 'a horrible sink of anti-Irish feeling' – to award the colonial secretary Joseph Chamberlain an honorary degree had particularly annoyed the Irish Transvaal Committee. The inevitable riot occurred, dramatically covered two weeks later by *Le Petit Journal* in Paris.[37] Later that day the Dublin Metropolitan Police sabre-charged the crowd in the region of Parliament Street and Grattan Bridge,[38] injuring several people. James Connelly was charged, rather ludicrously, with driving without a licence. As W.B. Yeats was to write a few days later, 'The war has made the air electrical just now.'[39]

Excitement in Natal had given way to excitement in Ireland. But now life in the camp of the Irish Transvaal Brigade settled into a routine. The replacement of Buller by Lord Roberts as commander-in-chief of British forces in South Africa meant nothing to them; besides, Buller was not removed from his post in Natal.

There were occasional visitors to the Irish camp during the 118-day siege. Journalists often called. The crack was good, as was the copy, and perhaps some brandy might be found and shared. The American writer B. Webster Davis turned up one day and a photograph of himself with the brigade was published in his book *John Bull's crime* (New York, 1901).[40]

Eight days after Colenso, on Saturday, 23 December, Mrs Fannie Trichardt presented the Irish corps with a new flag which had been sent out from Ireland by the Irish Transvaal Committee, mainly on the initiative of Maud Gonne. This had been made by two women who were soon to be closely associated with Maud Gonne's Inghinidhe na hÉireann (Daughters of Erin). This flag (1.73m x 1.22m) was made of green poplin with a gilt braid border and fringe. It had a gilt harp with the centre cut away and with six golden strings traversing the harp. On one side above the harp was inscribed 'Irish Transvaal Brigade' and below the harp was 'Ar dTir, Ar Muinteár, Ar dTeanga' (Our country, our people, our language).[41] The occasion of the presentation of this fine flag was a lively one. Many cheers and hurrahs were offered up, 'God Save Ireland' and 'Volkslied' were sung and no doubt toasts were also drunk.[42]

MacBride later told Maud Gonne how they had this flag up in camp, 'and at night I often saw one or other of our lads go up and kiss its folds'.[43] Later the following year a reporter for *Echo de Paris* visited the Irish camp and saw MacBride, who spoke 'in queer French':

> He says nothing, but I see that he is much affected. His hand trembles as he touches the bunting, and so does his voice when he calls for three cheers for Green Erin. In the calm air the patriotic cry rises like an appeal to heaven.[44]

[59]

The first and last Christmas the Irish Transvaal Brigade spent on the veld was a memorable occasion. Its little camp behind Pepworth Hill became a hive of activity. A half-mile racetrack was prepared, the camp was tidied up and at least six different national flags – but not, of course, the union jack – were flying when the Boers arrived:

> generals, commandants and veldtcornets were there; young ladies and old ones too, from Pretoria, Johannesburg, Dundee and other towns, were entertained by the Irish boys.

The Irish won all the horse races as one of their number had commandeered a proper racehorse when visiting Pretoria. The Boers came out tops in athletics – running, jumping and weight throwing. Much fun was had.

The sports over, an Irish banquet was laid out by the men – 'meats, cakes, pies etc.' – for the crowd of men, woman and children. The Irish may very well have been behind the firing of a plum pudding into Ladysmith that day.

The only problem was that the banquet was 'painfully dry'. The Irish had been caught out at their own game. Some cunning Boers had appropriated several cases of their liquor at nearby Modderspruit station. Colonel Blake regretted not being able to offer his guests a drink or two, 'and besides I wanted a drink or two myself'.[45]

Serious as it was not to have anything but coffee to drink, Irish spirits were high and the day culminated in Tom Byrne rising to sing the 'Song of the Transvaal Irish Brigade', specially written and sent out to South Africa by Arthur Griffith:

> The Cross swings low, the morn is near –
> Now comrades fill up high;
> The cannon's voice will ring out clear
> When morning lights the sky.
> A toast we'll drink together, boys,
> Ere dawns the battle's grey,
> A toast of Ireland – dear old Ireland –
> Ireland far away!
> Ireland far away! Ireland far away!
> Health to Ireland – strength to Ireland!
> Ireland, boys, hurrah!

Who told us that her cause was dead?
    Who bade us bend the knee?
The slaves! Again she lifts her head –
    Again she dares be free!
With gun in hand, we take our stand
    For Ireland in the fray –
We fight for Ireland – dear old Ireland!
    Ireland far away!
        Ireland far away! Ireland far away!
           We fight for Ireland – die for Ireland!
    Ireland, boys, hurrah!

O Mother of the Wounded Breast!
    O Mother of the Tears!
The sons you loved and trusted best
    Have grasped their battle-spears.
From Shannon, Lagan, Liffey, Lee,
    On Afric's soil to-day –
We strike for Ireland – brave old Ireland!
    Ireland far away!
        Ireland far away! Ireland far away!
           We smite for Ireland – brave old Ireland!
    Ireland, boys, hurrah!

The morning breaks – the bugle calls!
    Now, comrades, for the fight!
A hero's grave be his who falls
    Ere comes again the night.
For Freedom's flag – for Ireland's cause –
    Strike stout and swift to-day!
Hurrah for Ireland – brave old Ireland!
    Ireland far away!
        Ireland far away! Ireland far away!
           God guard old Ireland – dear old Ireland!
    Ireland, boys, hurrah![46]

# CHAPTER FIVE

# The new century

## THE AFRICAN SUMMER OF 1900

When the Lion shall lose its strength,
And the brachet Thistle begin to pine,
The Harp shall sound sweet, sweet at length,
Between the eight and the nine.[1]

On 6 January 1900 at the battle of Platrand the Boers made their last serious attempt to capture Ladysmith. Here, south of Ladysmith on Wagon Hill and the adjoining Caesar's Camp, the British held back a determined Boer assault. The Irish commando was involved in the battle, but from afar. With four field guns they seem to have been positioned on the hills to the north-west of Ladysmith shelling Observation Hill as a diversionary tactic and, according to Blake, providing covering fire for the 'Pretoria boys'.[2] But MacBride said the Irish did not use their rifles all day. The Boer assault failed and the Irish returned to their camp behind Pepworth Hill.

The weeks that followed were dull enough for Blake and his men, with Sundays being particularly grim. It is likely that this was when dissension started to grow within the ranks. Certainly it would not be long before several leading brigaders would move elsewhere. We do know that it was in January 1900 that Captain James Laracy of Kilkenny left the commando for a military exercise in the Orange Free State and the northern Cape. Years later he and MacBride would be at each other's throats in the Irish press.[3] Of this period outside Ladysmith, MacBride said he and Blake had the hardest time of their lives trying to keep the men 'in countenance and check'.

To relieve the boredom of camp life, individual brigaders were granted short periods of leave to go to Johannesburg or Pretoria. Others gained permission to go round the battle area visiting commando camps and battle sites. One evening MacBride and the colonial Irishman Frank O'Reilly visited a burgher campfire near the Tugela. Some Boers were placing unexploded British shells in the hot ashes and watching 'the sparks fizzle up something like a small display of fireworks.' Sensibly O'Reilly pulled MacBride away just in the nick of time before an explosion killed one man and wounded several others. MacBride's comment was that shrewd and experienced as they were, in some respects the Boers were 'like a lot of big children'.[4]

Mishap was not avoided, though, when Sergeant Papillon set out in a wagon to fetch a commandeered stove. The vehicle went into a donga and the driver – who possibly was not completely sober – was lucky to get away with a broken foot.[5]

A handful of brigaders took part in the hard-fought battle of Spioen Kop on Wednesday, 24 January. Opposite them once again were the Dublin Fusiliers. During the heat of battle Winston Churchill, recently escaped from imprisonment in Pretoria, came on the Dublins' senior officers behind a two-foot stone wall. The conversation ran as follows:

> 'Very few of us left now,' said the colonel, surveying his regiment with
>     pride.
> 'How many?'
> 'About four hundred and fifty.'
> 'Out of a thousand?'
> 'Well, out of about nine hundred.'

Churchill added:

> This war has fallen heavily on some regiments. Scarcely any has suffered more severely, none has won greater distinction, than the Dublin Fusiliers – everywhere at the front ... Half the regiment, more than half the officers killed or wounded or prisoners.[6]

Back in Ireland, however, the political balladeers chose to celebrate the British defeat:

> Have you heard of Warren's victory –
>     It was at Spion Kop;
> It was not long in his hands,
>     He had to let it drop.

The summit was taken so easy,
    He suspected he was sold;
And the position he had taken
    He found too hot to hold.[7]

Colonel Blake was later to write that at Spioen Kop the whole atmosphere was laden with yellow, sulphurous-looking lyddite fumes and the men who emerged from the trenches, 'looked like so many Chinamen.'[8] Three days later the young Father van Hecke – who had recently replaced the infirm Father Baudry as brigade chaplain – visited the battle site with MacBride, Coetzee and O'Reilly:

> we almost became physically sick at the abominable stench which came from the numerous half-buried corpses ... It was an appalling and a disgusting scene!

More devastating for the Irish corps than Spioen Kop was the nearby battle of Vaalkrantz nearly two weeks later. With General Ben Viljoen and his small force was a group of Irish brigaders. The fighting was hard and when the battle had been fought and a British breakthrough halted four Irishmen lay dead: Mat Brennan, Jim Lasso, Australian-born Pat Richardson, and Pat Fahey from Clare. Fahey, in particular, was singled out by the Boers for praise. He had set up a remorseless covering fire for the retreating Boers and 'hurling abuse at the storming British until, riddled with bullets and bayonet stabs, he was stilled forever'.[9] Sadly in 1979 the remains of Patrick Fahey, 'the bravest of the brave', were taken from where he fell and reinterred in the bleak burgher memorial on Wagon Hill – within British lines.

The *Standard and Diggers' News* reported in mid-February:

> The Irish camp is in a mournful frame of mind owing to the reported death of two or three of its members, who broke away and fought in the latest Tugela affair. One of them, who started the singing of 'God Save Ireland' when the colours were presented, is said to have been found with his head completely severed from his body.[10]

Back in camp day followed day. On Friday, 16 February, there was some excitement when Mevrou Schultze, the wife of a well-known artillery officer, presented the Irish brigade with yet another flag, 'which now floats proudly above the Colonel's tent'. It was made of green cashmere and had a harp worked in gold silk thread. On Sundays Father van Hecke would use the flag as an altar cloth. And it was to the priest that the flag was given when he was about to sail back to Europe, as a memento of his days with the brigade. Though he did not know it, even then his role in this unusual story was not finished.

Horse-rustling continued to be a favourite sport for the brigaders. This had been dangerous at times, but occasionally it also had its amusing side. One brigader on the prowl outside Ladysmith one evening ran into an African lad sent out by the British to spy. The Irishman took his prisoner direct to General Joubert, who promptly ordered that he guard the prisoner until morning. It was a very disgruntled brigader who stumped into camp for breakfast, swearing that was the last prisoner he would take.

Brennan, Lasso, Richardson and Fahey were not the only brigaders to die that summer. Another danger stalked the Irish camp at Pepworth Hill – disease. In the middle of February James Murphy of Patrick Street, Kilkenny, was taken to the nearby Russian ambulance field-hospital with fever. Here he was attended by Father van Hecke. Despite efforts to save him, young Murphy died on Monday, 19 February. The next day the entire brigade attended the funeral:

> . . . standing with arms reversed while the coffin was lowered into the earth. And there we left him, sleeping very peacefully before the waving grasses of the hillside, till the last bugle shall sound 'reveille'.[11]

A few years later Colonel Blake wrote, 'the Tugela Valley is now renowned as an Irish graveyard'. He was referring to the heavy casualties in Irish regiments, but the comment also applies to some of his own men.[12]

## THE TIDE TURNS

On 15 February General French and his cavalry broke the Boer line and relieved Kimberley. Twelve days later General Cronje surrendered to Lord Roberts, who with General Kitchener had arrived in Cape Town the month before to take command from Buller. Now the Orange Free State lay open for invasion. In Natal General Buller stirred himself and prepared to bludgeon his way through the Tugela Heights to the east of Colenso on the 'Back Route'.

For the Irish there was at last some action. The news from Kimberley was depressing, as was the letter received from Gillingham in which he told them that an Irish-Australian called Arthur Lynch was to set up a second Irish Transvaal brigade. This was immediately and correctly perceived as a rival unit.

The week James Murphy died, unbeknown to Blake and his commando, a handful of men set out from Ireland to join them. Also already on the high seas was a larger contingent of Irish Americans. And that same week there arrived at Lourenço Marques Dr M.S. Walsh from Swords, County Dublin, the representative of what it had been hoped would be a full-sized Irish ambulance corps sponsored by the Irish Transvaal Committee. Within days a lone American, Ernest William Luther, would also set out from New York on a romantic quest to join the brigade – an odyssey from which he would not return. But they were all coming too late.

On Friday, 23 February, the Inniskilling Fusiliers, followed by the Connaught Rangers, the Dublin Fusiliers and the Imperial Light Infantry, led the assault on Hart's Hill, soon to be renamed Inniskilling Hill. While the valley of the Langverwacht Spruit and the Tugela-facing slopes of the hill were captured, the summit remained in Boer hands. To break this stalemate, both sides determined to draft in new forces. Among those ordered south from the besieging army were seventy members of the Irish corps under Major MacBride, Captain McCallum and Sergeants MacDonagh and Higgins. There were unpleasant scenes in the Irish camp caused by those not selected for this adventure and some men 'had even to be placed under temporary arrest to prevent them stealing out of camp to join those selected'.[13] One brigader who was selected but who had been excluded from the Colenso expedition was Tom Byrne.[14]

Following inspection from Commandant Trichardt, the column rode out of camp and made its way east of Ladysmith down to the Tugela Heights. The journey took four hours. They spent the night at the artillery camp behind the Boer lines. Then at 4 a.m. on Saturday, 24 February, the Irish moved forward on foot taking up a firing position on Horseshoe Hill, to the right of the defence line adjacent to Wynne's Hill. They appear to have been attached to Hans Grobler's Ermelo commando and were also in close proximity to their old friends in the Middelburg commando.

The stalemate continued that Saturday with the Irish regiments huddled behind hastily constructed walls on the side of Hart's Hill. There was a great deal of sniper firing in which MacBride's men indulged with relish.

For most of Sunday, until 9 p.m., there was an armistice to allow stretcher parties to collect the wounded. We are told that British tommies chatted amiably to burghers. Tobacco was exchanged. MacBride's men, however, were not involved in such niceties with the English army and its 'Irish mercenaries'.

With British troops withdrawn from Wynne's Hill, an assault on Hart's, Railway and Pieter's Hills was underway on the 26th. The Irish corps, slightly to the south west of the main action, kept up their fire at the enemy.

Tuesday, 27 February, was to be the decisive day. A message from Queen Victoria was relayed to the Irish regiments in the British army:

> I have heard with the deepest concern of the heavy losses sustained by my brave Irish soldiers. I desire to express my sympathy and my admiration of the splendid fighting qualities which they have exhibited throughout these trying operations.[15]

The Inniskillings, the Dublins, the Connaught Rangers and the Irish Fusiliers were in the thick of the renewed fighting.[16] MacBride's men were also busy that Tuesday. MacBride claimed the British pushed their line within 200 metres of his men:

> for hours the roar of the heavy guns, the bursting of shells, and the splintering of rocks made up a deafening noise, while the fumes of the lyddite were absolutely sickening.

There appear to have been no Irish corps deaths in the action though there was at least one brigader wounded. 'For God's sake, Major', cried one lad standing up, 'let us get at them with the butt of the rifle.' A moment later a bullet smashed his arm. Despite this setback, Irish morale was high and MacBride spoke of 'the merry joke and laugh which went from rock to rock even after those three days' hard work in the active fighting line'.[17]

That Tuesday was the anniversary of the battle of Majuba – Majuba day. It was now the Revenge of Majuba day, for Pieter's Hill was captured and far away on the highveld General Cronje surrendered to General Roberts at Paardeberg. With defeat staring them in the face, the Boers south of Ladysmith began to withdraw. The news of Cronje's surrender turned the retreat into a dash. Rout it might have been had Buller not been so cautious.

For MacBride's men the order to withdraw came at 2 a.m. on Wednesday, 28 February. It was a surprise and an annoyance to them, but the retreating cannon had to have an escort. As later in the retreat across the Orange Free State, the foreign elements proved reliable and determined.

When the Irish column hit the Klip river near Bulwana Kop, south-east of Ladysmith, a welcome was awaiting the downcast brigaders. Here was Father van Hecke with 'a trolley-load of good things' for the men. On the column rode the couple of miles to the foot of Lombard's Kop. Here, with a Boer force of about the same size, a defensive position was taken up for the expected British advance. Howard Hillegas believed that by this time Blake had rejoined the men, but this is doubtful.[18]

Perhaps it was now that the Irish Transvaal Brigade gave its best service to the cause of the Boer republics. There is little doubt that for several vital hours they held the way to the south and in particular discouraged a breakout from the besieged town. Indeed, a cavalry force did emerge from Ladysmith only to wheel about when the Irish Mausers opened up on them. This was largely a bluff, in fact, and it is likely that the small force at the bottom of Lombard's Kop could have been easily put to flight.[19]

By now Major Hubert Gough had made his famous dash into Ladysmith, beating Dundonald and Churchill for the prize. 'Hello, Hubert, how are you?' inquired the worn-out General White of his liberator.[20]

As the Natal Carbineers and the Imperial Light Horse rode into Ladysmith, a few miles away the Irish brigaders waited. It began to rain. Soon there was a heavy downpour. Up on Lombard's Kop Major Wolmarans was having difficulty raising and manouevring the Long Tom gun. In the middle of the night the Irish decided to return to their camp behind Pepworth Hill: 'We could scarcely mount our horses, and the poor brutes from cold, wet and hunger, were nearly as bad as ourselves.'

They had barely set off north when they met General Botha and his staff. The general displayed 'grim determination, and a sad sternness that almost brought a lump to one's throat'. MacBride explained what they were doing. Botha replied, 'We and our horses are nearly finished too. But there are so very few to look after the guns.'

The Irish turned their horses and in the driving rain, with terrifying thunder crashes and lightning bolts illuminating the night sky, they returned to the hill. They helped manhandle the great gun slowly down to level ground where it was hitched to the great span of oxen, 'and during the night crawled with it past Ladysmith almost within earshot of the British outposts'.[21] Only now did the Irish, exhausted, hungry and drenched to the skin, make their way slowly through the mud towards Pepworth Hill. Years later Tom Byrne recalled that it was 'only by means of the vivid lightning flashes that we could see our way on the road round Ladysmith'.

One last shock awaited MacBride and his men early on that Thursday morning. Colonel Blake had wisely decided to strike camp. But there was now neither food nor provisions. In desperation they rushed the few hundred metres to the railway just in time to unload some supplies from what must have been the last Boer train out. The men sat on the veld and ate their tinned beef and bread. Beside them their horses munched away at their mealies. Man and beast were exhausted. The 118-day siege was at an end.

On Saturday, 3 March 1900, the relieving British army made its triumphal entry into Ladysmith. In far-off Fermanagh the Church of Ireland bells rang out across the lakes in salute. The Catholic bells remained silent. Of the march through the dusty streets of Ladysmith, Conan Doyle recorded:

> For their heroism the Dublin Fusiliers were put in the van of the procession, and it is told how, as the soldiers who lined the streets saw the five officers and small clump of men, the remains of what had been a strong battalion, realising, for the first time perhaps, what their relief had cost, many sobbed like children.[22]

# CHAPTER SIX

# The Irish pro-Boer movement

## 1899–1900

The River Liffey separated the offices of the *United Irishman* at 17 Fownes Street, off Dame Street, from the rooms of the Celtic Literary Society at 32 Lower Abbey Street. The sight of Arthur Griffith, the newspaper's editor, making his rolling way across O'Connell Bridge to the society's rooms must have been a common enough one in Dublin at the turn of the century.

Arthur Griffith had emigrated to the Transvaal Republic in December 1896, probably at the suggestion of John MacBride. Griffith had enjoyed an adventurous life in the old Transvaal: he had worked in a printing house; edited his first newspaper, the *Middelburg Courant*; been a surface worker on a goldmine; and generally involved himself in Irish separatist politics in the political hothouse of the South African Republic in the heady days after the Jameson raid and prior to the outbreak of the second Anglo-Boer war.[1]

Why Griffith returned to Ireland in early 1899 is not certain. An appeal from his friend William Rooney to return, attraction to Maud Sheehan, improved health – all might have contributed. Whatever the reason, his African sojourn was central to Griffith's political development. The Transvaal was the only foreign country he was to live in for any length of time, and he never wavered from his support of the Boer cause.

Indications are that he learnt both from Boer tactics in handling the British and from their ultimate defeat. That Europe's most influential and indeed violent pro-Boer movement was in Ireland was mainly the result of the activities of 'MacBride's Brigade' as it was, and in Ireland still is, invariably called, and of the pro-Boer fever whipped up by Griffith and his associates. While the full story of the Irish pro-Boer movement is told elsewhere in book form, a synopsis of its activities needs to be laid out, especially when it linked up with the Irish corps.[2]

## THE IRISH TRANSVAAL COMMITTEE

The *United Irishman* was first published on 4 March 1899, two days before Anna Johnston and Alice Milligan's *Shan Van Vocht* ceased publication. The new weekly was in some respects a continuation of the old, not least in the prominence it gave to the members of Dublin's Celtic Literary Society. It was a fringe nationalist paper, more literary than Connolly's *Workers' Republic*, but with an equally small circulation, which necessitated an input of outside cash. At first this came from Maud Gonne to the tune of twenty-five shillings a week. Later the IRB would help out. That upwards of 2,000 copies a week of the *United Irishman* were sold at all in the first couple of years was in no small part due to the copy produced from the war in South Africa and the trouble stirred up by the Irish Transvaal Committee.

The Irish Transvaal Committee (ITC) was founded on Saturday, 7 October 1899. The last entry in its poorly kept minute book is 6 March 1900, five months later. Though the Celtic Literary Society continued to exist, the ITC was largely made up of its members.[3] The ageing John O'Leary was president and its secretaries were Arthur Griffith and Peter White. The committee's travelling agent was Henry McAteer, 'a drunken fellow altogether unfit for his position'.[4] The chair of the committee varied from meeting to meeting, with the thirty-three-year-old Maud Gonne usually prominent. Other notables included James Connelly, Michael Davitt MP, George A. Lyons, Pat O'Brien MP, Willie Redmond MP, William Rooney, Thomas O'Neill Russell, and T.D. Sullivan MP. Chief Commissioner J.J. Jones of the Dublin Metropolitan Police considered them 'Fenians of the worst type.'[5] Ramsey Colles, the unpleasant editor of the unionist *Irish Figaro* went further:

> Now, without wishing to make a mountain out of manikin, for that is all Mr Arthur Griffith is, I may say that this Griffith is only a specimen of a crowd of reptiles known as the Transvaal Committee.[6]

Of course, W.B. Yeats appeared at some committee meetings but it is likely he was more interested in one of Colles' reptiles – Miss Gonne – than in the Boer cause. None the less the young poet was to prove useful to the cause the following spring.[7]

The activities of the ITC can be briefly summarized. In October 1899 they had 25,000 hand bills and 1,000 double-crown-size pro-Boer posters printed.[8] These were put up and distributed around the capital and caused Dublin Castle and the DMP some unease.

The weekly meetings of the Irish Republican Socialist Party in Foster Place were used as platforms to whip up pro-Boer fever. Soon the Dublin populace was familiar with the names of the dead Irish pro-Boer fighter, Alfred Aylward, and the very much alive pro-Boer soldier, John MacBride. The Transvaal Republic's flag also became a common sight for them as did the pictures of Boer generals on lapel buttons. As the autumn progressed, scuffles with the police gave way to pro-Boer riots, one of which, on the occasion of Trinity giving Joseph Chamberlain an honorary degree, was graphically described by Sean O'Casey in his autobiography.[9]

Local government councils were urged to pass pro-Boer anti-war resolutions. The most widely adopted of these was that initially passed by the Limerick Corporation, which ran as follows:

> That we consider it a great sign of National weakness and decay that the various organizations in Ireland have not in a more determined manner expressed their sympathy with the plucky Boer farmers in their fight against the English, and this especially when the Englishmen themselves are protesting against the contemplated slaughter at the instance of Chamberlain and the other English Capitalists, and we express a hope that if a war takes place it may end in another Majuba Hill.[10]

There was the odd exception. When the Limerick resolution was tabled at a meeting of the Rathmines Urban District Council, one councillor shouted, 'Throw it in the waste paper basket.' Another, on asking its contents, was told, '"It is asking us to go out and fight for the Boers." (Laughter).'[11]

None the less such resolutions did have an impact, especially helping the ITC in its campaign against Irish recruitment into the British army. For a number of months, outside Ulster, there was a marked drop in recruitment, though news of heavy Irish casualties in South Africa must also have had a sobering impact on potential recruits.[12] On 17 October 1899 the ITC minute book recorded the following:

> A discussion arose as to the practicability of utilizing local ballad singers in singing appropriate songs against enlistment. A list of gentlemen was made out to be written to for the names of ballad singers in their districts.[13]

Certainly some very fine Irish pro-Boers ballads were written, many by Arthur Griffith himself.[14]

# ENLISTING IN THE ENGLISH ARMY IS TREASON TO IRELAND.

Go—to find, 'mid crime and toil,
  The doom to which such guilt is
  hurried!
Go—to leave on Afric's soil
  Your bones to bleach, accursed, un-
  buried!

Go—to crush the just and brave,
  Whose wrongs with wrath the world
  are filling!
Go—to slay each brother slave—
  Or spurn the blood-stained *Saxon
  Shilling!*

## FELLOW-COUNTRYMEN—

The Irishmen in England's Service who are sent to South Africa will have to fight against Irish Nationalists, who have raised Ireland's Flag in the Transvaal, and have formed an Irish Brigade to fight for the Boers against the oppressor of Ireland.

## REMEMBER NINETY-EIGHT.
## REMEMBER THE PENAL LAWS.
## REMEMBER THE FAMINE.

Think of the ruined homes and of the Emigrant Ships. Within sixty years our population has been reduced by one-half as the direct result of English rule. The Boers are making a brave fight against this rule. Let no Irishman dare to raise a hand against them, or for our enemy and their enemy, England!

England's Army is small, Englishmen are not good soldiers. England has to get others to do her fighting for her. In the past Irishmen have too often won battles for England, and saved her from defeat, and thus have riveted the chains upon their motherland. Let them do so no more.

In all our towns and villages we see the recruiting-sergeants trying to entrap thoughtless Irish boys into joining the British army. The recruiting-sergeant is an enemy, and it is a disgrace to any decent Irishman to be seen in his company. But he should be watched and followed, and the boys whom he seeks to entrap should be warned and reasoned with.

In preventing recruiting for the English army you are working for Ireland's honour, and you are doing something to help the Boers in their Struggle for Liberty.

By order,
IRISH TRANSVAAL COMMITTEE.

Dublin, 12th October, 1899.

DOYLE, Trade Union Printer, 9 Upper Ormond Quay, Dublin.

Anti-Boer war recruitment leaflet, 1899. The Irish Transvaal Committee paid the printer Bernard Doyle to run off 25,000 of this anti-recruitment call as handbills and a further 1,000 as posters, which were plastered up all over the Irish capital, quickly to be removed by the police.

Money was also raised and a flag sent out to the Irish brigade. A fund was also established to send out an Irish Transvaal ambulance corps, rather along the lines of the Franco-Irish Ambulance Corps which served in the Franco-Prussian war of 1870–1.[15] No ITC ambulance ever left Ireland though, as will be seen, a small number of men did travel to the Transvaal at the committee's expense, including Dr M.S. Walsh of Swords.

Outside Dublin the war also stirred up emotions in the nationalist population. Professor Foster has pointed out that during the Boer war branches of the Gaelic League increased nearly four-fold from 107 to 400 and that in Belfast catholic gangs took the names of Boer generals. And in County Roscommon the police were worried by reports that a group of young men were trying to buy Enfield rifles:

> The county is in a very excited state over the war and all the people generally are greatly in sympathy with the Boers so much so that if any enemy of England landed in this county the disaffected portion of the population which is by far the larger part would receive them with open arms.[16]

Cork city could muster a substantial pro-Boer demonstration when Griffith arrived by train and Limerick was equally fervent. But perhaps the most touching pro-Boer sentiment came from country folk who, though largely removed from the political scene, had a genuine sympathy for the underdog. Stories of Boer victories against the English were told in small cottages and listened to with excitement by people who were very different from the Boers, both in culture and religion. But both were country folk, both had limited worlds and both disliked the English.

Later in the war when Lady Gregory returned to Coole Park after a period away she presented Mrs Farrell, her retainer, with a side of bacon. The old lady in thanking Lady Gregory sighed, 'It will rise his [Mr Farrell's] heart after the bad news that is after coming.' 'What bad news?' inquired Lady Gregory. 'The Boers being beat,' came the reply. Lady Gregory also recounted the attitude of an old miller to the British army and the war:

> They thought to go shooting them [the Boers] just as if they were snipe or woodcocks. And it wasn't long before they were stretched in the field, and the Royalty of England along with them, and not a knocker in London town without a bit of crepe on it.[17]

## THE BATTLE IN WESTMINSTER

While the Irish Transvaal Committee was stirring up trouble at home, the disparate groups of Irish nationalists in the House of Commons were quickly realizing that the Boer war presented them with a common cause. After nearly a decade of internecine warfare Parnellite, anti-Parnellite and even the Louth jackdaw, Tim Healy, could at last stand shoulder to shoulder.

Irish nationalist MPs gave sterling service to the Boer cause, much more so than did English radical MPs. That the home-rule cause was damaged is obvious but as home rule was never going to be granted by Salisbury's conservative administration, the sacrifice was worth the loss.

The much-heralded resignation of Michael Davitt as member for South Mayo on 25 October 1899 must be viewed in isolation from other events at Westminster. Davitt was genuinely pro-Boer, perhaps the most genuine pro-Boer in Ireland, Griffith excepted. But Davitt detested the House of Commons. He hated the life of being an MP and he had little time for many of his nationalist colleagues; he would have left anyway in the not-too-distant future. As it was, the Boer war gave him the exit he wanted. After a powerful speech Davitt left the chamber for the last time. Stopping at the bar of the house he turned and shouted, 'I wish you joy in your plundering of the Boers.'[18]

Soon Davitt would be on the high seas bound for Lourenço Marques en route for the Transvaal Republic. Back in Westminster the Irish move to unity grew apace.

Negotiations on unity under the auspices of the United Irish League took place in January 1900. Then on 6 February, as the battle of Vaalkrantz was raging in Natal, John Redmond was elected leader of the Irish parliamentary party. Of course there was still little love lost between many Irish nationalist MPs – T.P. O'Connor would not even sit in the same railway carriage as John Redmond – but a start had been made and for the next eighteen months the common neutral cause helped build up some measure of trust.

The men of the late-Victorian Irish parliamentary party were perhaps the most educated and literate parliamentary political group that Ireland has produced. One need look only at the amount of erudite books they produced. They were able speakers as well as writers and anyone who now bothers to read their speeches against the Boer war cannot but have admiration for the style and turn of phrase. Healy's speeches are, of course, the most readable and at times very witty. He painted the joyous picture for the Boers of 'a band in Potchefstroom garrison playing "God save the

Queen", to remind them of old times'. He also said that one of the secretary of war's speeches should be 'taken as a manual for De Wet's horse'.[19] The Irish were not popular at Westminster.

## SOUTH MAYO

The resignation of Michael Davitt resulted in a by-election in his rural constituency of South Mayo. As Davitt had applied for the Chiltern Hundreds on account of the war and as John MacBride was a Mayo man, the opportunity was too good a one to miss for the ITC. So without consulting the United Irish League or the parliamentary party, MacBride was nominated for the seat. They were too clever by half.

William O'Brien was not going to be blackmailed into supporting one of the advanced men outside his circle. An undated letter in the Leyds archive signed 'William' runs as follows:

> We were both entirely exhausted yesterday but after a day's rest have today been busily engaged with preliminary correspondence by wire preparatory to going down as I explained to you to engage and I think defeat my old enemy in the west – whom you know of already – I am well supplied with munitions of war and as you can imagine on personal grounds I shall give no quarter.

This very well might be William O'Brien writing. There were personal scores to be settled. The *United Irishman* was not slow to point to 'the Gold of the Jews' behind the opposition to MacBride in South Mayo and it was rumoured that O'Brien had a jewish wife.

A nonentity called John O'Donnell, then languishing in Castlebar goal, was put up against MacBride. It was a dirty fight: intimidation, mudslinging in the press and at least one stoning incident. Poor O'Donnell was bewildered and tried to withdraw his candidature, only to be cabled by O'Brien, 'Fight MacBride to the end.'

Only a quarter of the electorate voted on a wet and bleak election day. O'Donnell polled 2,401 votes and Major John MacBride a mere 427. It was a bitter blow for Arthur Griffith, perhaps more so than the Sinn Fein defeat in South Leitrim in 1908.[20]

## 'A SET OF FARCEURS': THE PARIS CLIQUE

The South Mayo defeat was an object lesson for Griffith. Nationalist Ireland may have been overwhelmingly pro-Boer but that did not mean conservative nationalism had lost control of the national movement. Griffith also recognized that though Dublin had experienced the most serious riots in a generation, armed revolution was a non-starter in 1900. Not only had Assistant Commissioner John Mallon and the DMP kept the lid on things, but Griffith himself had firmly ruled out a rising, a matter over which he and James Connolly had rowed. Griffith correctly prophesied that if an insurrection occurred in Dublin the British would bring a battleship up the Liffey and shell the city. Connolly would have none of this and went off in a huff, vowing never to have anything further to do with what he termed the 'Nationalists'.[21]

The nearest thing Griffith got to revolution in 1900 was a punch-up with Ramsey Colles in the offices of the *Irish Figaro* in early April, after the paper had likened Maud Gonne to Herodotus, 'the father of lies'. Griffith's sjamboking of Colles gave Griffith his first gaol experience – a fortnight.[22]

Of course, while revolution might be on the back burner, this did not rule out violence. Mallon acquired a letter addressed to 'Dear Arthur' and signed by J.F. McCarthy, an ITC member. On the back of it, written in pencil was the following:

> Bank of Ireland
> 24 ft. 2 in.
> Within 2 flags from wall
> ??
> Acknowledge same (him?)
> Meet McCarthy and McBride corner Essex Bridge, tobacconist's side, give the usual sign. Get Colles' address (private).

A guard was put on the Bank of Ireland and on Colles' home. It may have been a plot, but more likely Griffith playing a practical joke on Dublin Castle.[23] Maud Gonne, however, was not into practical jokes; instead she had a plan.

In November 1899 Maud Gonne had been behind the foundation of the grandly titled 'Boer Franco-Irish Committee'.[24] One of the leading lights of this small gang of conspirators was a thirty-eight-year-old Irish-Australian called Arthur Lynch. Lynch was bright and had sailed through Melbourne University gaining an honours bachelor in civil engineering (1883), a BA

(1885) and an MA (1887).[25] By 1888 he was studying science in Berlin, from where he progressed to medicine in Paris. A doctor, engineer, scientist, man of letters and a journalist, Lynch had great talent, but he also had an ability to alienate people. Davitt liked the 'tall, handsome and accomplished' young man but many felt otherwise.

In the early 1890s Lynch was a journalist in Britain, having been given a break by T.P. O'Connor. In 1892 Lynch stood as a Parnellite for O'Connor's old Westminster seat of Galway City, but was defeated by fifty-one votes by the anti-Parnellite John Pinkerton. Nine years later, in very different circumstances, Lynch was to win the seat, the consequences of which nearly cost him his life.[26]

From August 1896 to December 1899 Arthur Lynch lived a pleasant enough life in the Pigalle district of Paris, at 22 rue Chaptal, ninth arrondissement. The immediate area was populated by arty types and just off rue Chaptal was the newly opened Théâtre du Grand Guignol. Lynch was Paris correspondent for the *Daily Mail*[27] and though on the periphery of Irish revolutionary politics, he was a close associate of Madame Maud Gonne. He was probably involved in the production of Maud Gonne's *L'Irlande Libre*, which appeared in Paris monthly from May 1897 to October 1898. Maud Gonne's lover, the right-wing French politician, Lucien Millevoye, had no illusion about this whole set-up – 'your Irish revolutionists are only a set of *farceurs*'.[28]

Lynch considered himself to be a renaissance man. As such, he must, in addition to his many academic achievements, be a soldier. He made contact with the Boer consul-general in Paris, J. Pierson. Dr Leyds, the Boer emissary in Europe was consulted. On the back of Lynch's card left for Dr Leyds was written, 'credentials will speak for themselves, and absolute confidence may be reposed in his words'. In November Lynch wrote to Leyds in Brussels: 'I have completed the arrangements which will enable me to go to the Transvaal by the next boat. I am extremely anxious to do good work there.' On 29 November 1899 Pierson paid Lynch 500 francs to cover his expenses. Even in his autobiography, published in 1924, Lynch remained quiet about this arrangement.[29] His cover was that he went to the Transvaal with journalistic commissions from *Black-and-White*, *Collier's Weekly* and *Le Petit Journal*. He even bought a camera to prove the point. There can be little doubt, however, that the Boers paid his fare on the *Herzog* to acquire a trained engineer who might be useful in the war effort.

With Lynch away in Africa, Maud Gonne also went travelling – on a lecture tour to the USA. She was there when the South Mayo by-election took place. On her return to Paris she set to work on an audacious new plan: a terrorist attack to blow up British troop ships on their way to South Africa. This crazy scheme was to disguise bombs as lumps of coal, which would explode when used to stoke the boiler, blowing the bottom out of the ships. Money would be needed to activate the plot. Lynch had squeezed money out of the Boers, why should not Maud Gonne? She told Griffith and Mark Ryan her scheme and set off for Brussels.

The saga of Maud Gonne's attempt to extract £500 from Dr Leyds is not easy to unravel. This is partly because Maud Gonne invented a face-saving story to explain her failure and partly because, unwittingly, she blundered into the realm of spying and intrigue.

By January 1900, and probably for some time before, the Boers had decided that the best way to stir up trouble for the British in Ireland was through the IRB. As mentioned earlier, the IRB chief, Mark Ryan, was chummy with Pretoria's Solomon Gillingham. The Boers seem to have used an IRB man as a secret agent in Ireland. This was probably the eccentric Frank Hugh O'Donnell, who had championed the cause of the Transvaal in the House of Commons back in the 1870s.[30] But Ryan himself and others also appear to have sent Leyds reports on Ireland. In the state archives in Pretoria is a volume entitled, 'Ierse Geheime Korrespondensie'. The tone of many of these anonymous reports to Leyds, often in French, is somewhat hysterical, which would point to O'Donnell as the author. W.B. Yeats certainly believed O'Donnell was the spy: 'the mad rogue'. Yeats also believed O'Donnell to be 'driven on by an insane jealousy' of Maud Gonne.

By the time Maud Gonne got off the train in Brussels, Dr Leyds had been forewarned by Ryan of her coming – 'Don't say a word to inform this woman or everything could possibly go wrong.' Another report to Leyds ran:

> I have always warned you against letting yourself being any way connected with this notorious woman. Any good she may do is outweighed by the evil of her conduct and the grossness of language. When she poses as Friend of the Transvaal at the head of a meeting of Social-Democrats, the news is sent by the English diplomacy to St Petersburg in order to show that the friends of the Boers are the revolutionary scum of Europe.
>
> You can easily understand the effect upon the military circles in Germany and Russia of this 'friend of the Boers' advising soldiers to shoot their own officers. This shameless woman is a disgrace and a danger to every cause to which she attaches herself.

Maud Gonne explained her plan to Leyds. She would organize the bombings but she needed £500 to pay for the escape of the bombers to America. Leyds was genuinely horrified: "But this not a recognized means of warfare," he exclaimed. Maud Gonne left on the Paris express empty handed.

But the story did not end there. Maud Gonne claimed that next morning she was visited by Dr Leyd's secretary and told that the envoy had changed his mind and that £2,000 would be forwarded on the morrow. The next day came and the secretary returned with the news that another member of 'your party' had come to Brussels and taken the money on her behalf.[31]

We know that on 9 March 1900 £2,000 was paid by Dr Leyds to an Irish agent. Maud Gonne must have got wind of this fact and used it to authenticate her farrago. Certainly she turned up in high dudgeon, with Yeats in tow, on Dr Ryan's doorstep at 13A Gower Street in London. O'Donnell's account of the incident is worth quoting:

> The 'Millevoye's young lady' came to our chief's house, quite furious at not having received what she demanded. She was accompanied by one named Yeats who it is said is the latest successor to Millevoye, and before this young man she said all she had heard at your house, and further ... She declared that you had claimed to be in communication with Irish revolutionaries 'through a person who did not belong to their organisation'!!! Without doubt, within twenty-four hours all Dublin will know she has not had success because, and because, and because, etc, etc.
>
> If she is not a spy, she is almost one and her bragging is more dangerous than treachery itself.
>
> Except among the common people, she has the most detestable reputation. Stories are being circulated of 'three children put out to nurse in Paris', but she shows herself everywhere at our Meetings, and we are obliged to put up with her. But one could not be too prudent when she is near.[32]

The chronology of events is hard to pinpoint. The payment of £2,000 to the IRB was in March, yet it is possible the whole affair took place in early January 1900 or even in December 1899 and that an earlier payment of £2,000 was made. An anonymous letter from the Chancellerie de la République Sud-Africaine in the Leyds archive, dated 20 January, is worth quoting, though this may be 1901 and not 1900. It was addressed to Arthur Griffith:

Sir,

While thanking Mademoiselle Gonne for her warm sympathy with
the Republics of South Africa, I am instructed to request you as
quickly as possible to point out that both in Brussels and Paris our
diplomatic representatives inhabit neutral territory and we cannot
allow ourselves to be accused to neutral governments as abusing their
hospitality by entering into relations with the indiscreet advocates of
insurrection in Ireland or elsewhere. We have already declined the
services of M. Cipriani and similar gentlemen for related reasons ...
we should accordingly wish Miss Gonne to cease sending telegrams
and paying visits to our chancelleries and consulates. We shall
continue all the same to be grateful to her and all other Irish ladies
for expressions of their good wishes.

Whatever the chronology of events, Maud Gonne resigned from the IRB
in disgust and on 30 June 1900 the *United Irishman* denounced Frank Hugh
O'Donnell and apologized to its readers for having published his writings
in the past.

What Maud Gonne did not realize, and what might have abated her
pro-Boer ardour had she known, was that Dr Leyds was already making
substantial payments to the IRB. The following payments were made
between March and September 1900 and no doubt monies were supplied
before and after these dates:

| | |
|---|---|
| 9 March 1900 | £2,000 |
| 23 May 1900 | £1,000 |
| 8 August 1900 | £ 500 |
| 8 September 1900 | £1,000 |
| *Total for the six months* | £4,500 |

In January 1900 Dublin Castle was aware that Ryan was 'flush' with
money and by October 1900 the police had heard 'whispers' of Boer money
coming into the country.[33] They need not, however, have been alarmed for
the IRB was singularly unsuccessful in instigating unrest. One wonders
what the IRB did with the money and indeed why the Boers continued
supplying them with cash. Whatever O'Donnell said, if it was trouble they
wanted in Ireland, the money would have been far better invested in
'Madame Gonne Mad'.

## THE PRO-WAR LOBBIES

There were those in Ireland who supported Britain in the Boer war, but they were a minority and they were diverse groupings. Unionist Ireland was overwhelmingly behind the British in the war effort, though the northern unionists had a greater measure of respect for the enemy than did their southern allies. The Anglo-Irish were heavily represented in the officer corps out in South Africa and they were proud of the fact. Generals Roberts, Kitchener, White and Kelly-Kenny were all of ascendancy stock. The protestant clergy were also generally behind the British campaign with the usual exception of the Revd J.B. Armour of Ballymoney. Bishop Alexander of Derry was compelled to compose verse:

> They say that 'war is hell', the great accursed,
> The sin impossible to be forgiven –
> Yet I can look beyond it at its worst,
> And still find blue in heaven.

Letters home from Irish troops in the field, catholic and protestant, often painted a fairly sympathetic picture of the Boers. This did not stop various branches of the Orange Order offering the War Office many hundreds of 'marksmen and good riders' as volunteers. In fact, many orangemen did serve in the northern regiments and in the militia units that went out to South Africa. One prominent orangeman, Colonel R.H. Wallace, penned the following additional verse to 'The South Down Militia':

> When Kruger heard the regiment was landed in Cape Town,
> 'De Wet,' says he, 'we're bate,' says he, 'They've sent out the South
> Downs'.
> Says De Wet, 'If that's a fact, me son, we'd better quit the Rand,
> For them South Down Mileeshy is the terror of the land.'

Predictably the war took on a local sectarian stance in working-class parts of the north of Ireland, with catholic pro-Boers pitted against protestant anti-Boers. The absurdity of this was not lost on all in nationalist Ireland. There were those like D.P. Moran, the pugnacious editor of *The Leader*, who openly stated that support for the Boers 'turned the mind of Ireland away from evils at home'.[34] As well as these 'little Irelanders' there were a few catholic priests and especially some of the catholic hierarchy who were distinctly and not unnaturally worried at the road Irish nationalism had chosen to follow on the issue. Not all of the clergy had forgotten that penal laws had existed in the Transvaal Republic where the 'Roomse gevaar' still very much held sway.[35]

Finally there were those nationalists who supported the war because they had relatives in the British army. One correspondent to the *United Irishman* wrote of poor people in his area:

> to whom it would be dangerous to say a word derogatory of England's invincibility. They have relatives among the Fusiliers etc. who are at present fighting in South Africa, and they are proud of the fact.[36]

Sean O'Casey recalled one Dublin woman in a large brown shawl shrieking at a pro-Boer demonstration:

> Listen to me – in about as much time as it 'ud take a clever hand an' a sharp knife to peel an apple, England'll put the sign o' death on Kruger an' his gang ... General Roberts, General French, an' General Kitchener, three Irishmen – remember that! ... ah!, me faithful darlin' Dublin Fusiliers![37]

### THE FAMINE QUEEN

Henry II, King John, Richard II, James II and William III had all visited Ireland, but it was not until 1821 when George IV came that the English monarch arrived without an army behind him. George's visit was a great success, as was Queen Victoria's in 1849. On this latter occasion, the young activist John O'Leary denounced 'some Dubliners' as 'a pack of school-girls'. The queen visited in 1853 and 1861, and then kept away. 'For health and relaxation no one would go to Ireland,' she told Disraeli. But she did return, thirty-nine years later, a small old lady, and stayed from 4 to 26 April 1900.[38]

In March 1900, at General Wolseley's suggestion, members of Irish regiments were granted permission to wear shamrocks on St Patrick's day as a mark of the queen's admiration for their prowess on the Natal battlefields. In response to a patriotic Kipling re-write of 'The wearing of the Green', State Secretary Reitz penned the following:

They tell me that good honest Pat,
By favour of the Queen,
Has got the right as well he might –
To wearing of the Green.
Patrick Atkins, how your breast
Must swell with pride and joy
To think that Mr Chamberlain
Has found his Irish boy.
...
But if you say, now tell me pray,
What may this difference 'mane'?
Listen to me and you will see
The matter is quite plain.
It means that Paddy now has got
This 'favor' from the Queen,
Because – and that's a fact – because
He is – so very green!39

Back in Ireland the advanced nationalists had their noses put out of joint by the royal visit and became more and more abusive as the twenty-three-day visit progressed. It was then that Maud Gonne penned her famous article, 'The Famine Queen', which led to the punch-up between Colles and Griffith and also to a libel suit which Maud Gonne won, albeit with a token award. Maud Gonne took the occasion of the queen's visit to issue in Paris a '*numéro exceptionel*' of her *L'Irlande Libre*, which had long since ceased publication. And of course Yeats, foolishly, could not resist writing to the press: 'the reason [for the visit] is national hatred of our individual national life'. John O'Leary was as incensed as he had been in 1849 and ITC-member George Lyons publicly spoke of, 'this senile relic of royalty'.

Why were they all so annoyed? The answer is simply that the British had trumped their pro-Boer card. There was an ambivalence to the monarchy in Ireland. Many nationalists were proud of what Irish soldiers had done in the war. The main Irish nationalist party was not republican, and tried to play down the political aspects of the visit. Writing to John MacBride in South Africa, Anna Johnston in Belfast stated:

> The Queen's visit has upset all the snobs in the country. They are like mad people with loyalty. Miss Gonne has been very ill in Paris and I do believe she would have headed an insurrection here.40

By then Dublin was only sixteen per cent protestant, so it was more than just a sectarian manifestation. There can be little doubt that the visit was both a move to counter the Irish pro-Boer movement and to promote recruitment. The announcement on 5 April 1900 of the formation of an Irish regiment of foot guards and a later children's treat in the Phoenix Park, attended by the queen, were just too much for the advanced lobby. Incidents of violence were reported by the police, who took obvious delight in baton-charging an ITC torchlight procession. The *United Irishman* was suppressed for the first time in its existence, but this was to be the first of four bannings that year alone.[41]

On 1 July 1900, when the queen had long returned to Britain, Maud Gonne and her women's movement organized a 'Patriotic children's treat' in Clonturk Park for those patriotic children who had not gone to the Phoenix Park events. While the police considered the children were given 'moderate refreshment and unlimited treason', the Clonturk festival was a great success. Whether some Dublin children had lax political morals and went to both treats is not known. Certainly, years later many Dubliners claimed with pride to have been a 'Patriotic child'.

The RIC report for April 1900 noted, 'Secret societies are very languid and the pro-Boer sentiment received a severe blow from the loyal enthusiasm evoked by the Queen's visit.' That was probably true. In fact, those who had initiated the pro-Boer agitation were beginning now to think more of Ireland and less of Africa. That Easter Maud Gonne had established Inghinidhe na hÉireann, Daughters of Erin, and in September, from the nucleus of the Irish Transvaal Committee, Griffith founded his new political movement Cumann na Gaedheal, the Confederation of the Gaels. Just as the Celtic Literary Society had continued to exist after the formation of the ITC, so in turn the ITC was not immediately eclipsed. Indeed in 1901 the ITC had its own youth league in the guise of the John MacBride Club which met at 18 High Street in Dublin. As late as November 1901 the police considered the Irish Transvaal Committee to be the most dangerous group in Dublin, openly treasonable and capable of anything that would further their ends.[42]

Be this as it may, there is little doubt that advanced nationalism, having been put back on its feet, was now beginning to drift away from concentrating only on the war. Strangely enough as this happened, mainline Irish nationalism became more genuinely pro-Boer. Tales of the evictions, farmhouse burnings and concentration camps could not but strike a chord in Ireland. Alice Stopford Green and Mrs Lecky, the Dutch wife of Professor

W.E.H. Lecky of Trinity College, Dublin, strove hard to publicize the civilian suffering in the South African war.[43]

The daring activities of the young Boer commanders, de Wet, de la Rey, Botha and Smuts, with their hit-and-run tactics later in the war increased the respect of ordinary Irish people for these 'simple farmers' – and, as time would prove, presented them with the model of a new form of warfare against the English. A cartoon in the *Weekly Freeman* showed a bulldog holding on to a springbok's nose and being kicked by a Russian bear. A verse beneath ran:

> The bull dog bold
> Might loosen his hold,
> If he could, and he dared to do it,
> But he needs no tip to stick to his grip
> Or turn – and live to rue it.
>
> For the springbok's wild
> And he's awful riled,
> While the bear is a great strong beast.
> So the dog feels sick,
> But prefers the kick
> To being a dog deceased.[44]

In the streets of Dublin the manifestation of sympathy and support for the Boers shifted in 1900 away from rally and riot. Of that summer George Lyons later wrote:

> The rather dazzling colours of the South African Republic – red, white, blue and green – became everywhere evident. We wore them in our summer hats; personally I went so far as to wear them in my neckties, to the horror of all 'refined people'. Portraits of Boer Generals were largely on sale and pendants, 'buttons', and badges were everywhere to be seen.[45]

# CHAPTER SEVEN

# Reinforcements and rivalry

## FEBRUARY–MAY 1900

The Irish Transvaal Brigade retreated northwards from Ladysmith in a leisurely fashion, living off the local farmers' mealies. The Irish brigades were not popular with Natal's colonial farmers. On reaching the mountainous protection of the nearby Biggarsberg, MacBride turned round and surveyed the scene below:

> I beheld the famous trek of the whole [Boer] army, one of the most remarkable sights that it is possible to imagine. Across the seemingly illimitable veldt hundreds and hundreds of wagons, laden with provisions, tents, medical appliances, and all the innumerable appurtenances of an army on the march, were struggling along in a procession of colossal and most imposing dimensions. Above the lumbering of the ponderous, heavily-laden vehicles was to be heard the cracking of innumerable long whips, and the voices of Kaffir boys expostulating with or cheering on the mules or bullocks under their care.[1]

First the Irish commando reached the small settlement of Glencoe, not far from where the battle of Talana Hill had been fought four months previously. It was at Glencoe that the now-dying Commandant-General Joubert established his new headquarters.

St Patrick's day was celebrated at Glencoe in fine fashion. No doubt the brigaders were later greatly amused at State Secretary Reitz's parody of the 'Wearing of the green' written that day. Down at the coast no St Patrick's day dinner was held in Durban that year because of the heavy casualties in the Irish regiments. One of the leading lights in Durban's Irish community, Patrick O'Hea, did, however, attend a 'pro-British' Irish congress in Port Elizabeth on St Patrick's day. O'Hea, a former Irish parliamentary party MP, had once been Parnell's parliamentary secretary.

Blake and his commando enjoyed themselves at Glencoe. They made new friends with Ricchiardi and his Italian scouts. The South Mayo by-election caused great excitement in the Irish camp. The *Standard and Diggers' News* reported: 'the "boys" have noticed a distinct accession of dignity in the part of the gallant Major since he has become a candidate'. The defeat of MacBride prompted the same paper to proclaim 'Ungrateful Mayo'.[2] Later, with some understandable bitterness, MacBride noted that the news of his defeat was 'proclaimed in every British camp in Africa with joy'. But he added that the arrival of reinforcement for the Irish commando gave the lie to the claim that Irish did not support the Boers.[3]

Quite which Irishmen arrived in Natal when is not certain. It would appear that two small parties came out. Tom Byrne claimed many years later that ten Irishmen arrived when the siege was still on. This may be so, or he may be confused with those who came shortly after Ladysmith was relieved.[4]

The problem with sending men out from Ireland to the Transvaal was the cost, which seems to have been £40 to £50 a head. The attempt to raise funds to send an Irish ambulance corps had limited success. First proposed by the Irish Transvaal Committee on 2 November 1899, by 12 December £230 had been raised. A list with twenty-six names of possible corps members, including at least six women was drawn up. This included doctors Walsh, Blewitt and Quinn.[5] We do know that Dr Walsh was sent out with Red Cross accreditation, arriving in Lourenço Marques on 23 February 1900. While nominally with Blake's unit, he was attached to a military hospital and by early April 1900 was working in a veld hospital at Fourteen Streams in the Orange Free State.[6]

In one of his outpourings to Dr Leyds, Frank Hugh O'Donnell stated:

> At a time when every penny is wanted to watch the attempts to kid-nap the Irish Militia, this reckless cabotine [Maud Gonne] is wasting the money of the public, just as she wasted £300 of the Transvaal Committee money on sending six useless boys to South Africa.

Those six 'useless boys' were Mickey Dalton, Martin MacDonnell D'Arcy, Jack McArdle, Owen O'Kelly, James Harold and a man named Matthews. These were ordinary Dublin lads. O'Kelly, for example, was a shop assistant in Egan's of Talbot Street. They were ITC men and Dalton had made his name by defiantly brandishing the Transvaal *vierkleur* during the pro-Boer riot in Dublin on 17 December. One source claims that one of the things brought out to Natal by Owen O'Kelly was the song composed by Arthur Griffith, entitled 'Song of the Transvaal Irish Brigade'; however, it does appear that this was in fact the song sung at the Irish camp at Christmas 1899.[7]

When Michael Davitt set sail to Lourenço Marques on Sunday, 25 February 1900, on board the *Oxus*, he found five Irish volunteers on their way to join the Irish brigade.[8] They were members of Féis Ceoil in Belfast, 'boys of the Falls Road'. One source lists Jack Daly, Jack Donnelly, Jim McGuigan, Charles Mallon and F. Raw; however, it is known that Mallon did not leave Belfast until April 1900. With them, Donnelly carried some shamrock and a letter for John MacBride from Anna Johnston. Part of it read:

> Lisuancave, Antrim Road
> Belfast                                                    Feb 21, 1900
>
> Dear Major MacBride
>
> May I recommend the bearer and his companions to you. They will acquaint you with their [business?]. I trust you may find them of service. Any favour done them (and others who will follow shortly) will be greatly appreciated by your friends here.
>         We could send a large number – hundreds in fact if the means to do so were forthcoming. But you know how it is with us.[9]

It was about this time that MacBride went on a mission to Pretoria. His quest was that of Sir Roger Casement some years later: to recruit Irish prisoners-of-war into the Irish brigade. According to MacBride, the Boers would no more countenance such a proposal now than they had outside Ladysmith in late October 1899. On the eve of his return to Natal, MacBride received a telegram from Solomon Gillingham telling him that the ex-MP Michael Davitt was about to arrive in the Transvaal capital. A meeting was arranged.

MacBride must have got quite a shock when Davitt told him that he did not approve of his nomination for his old constituency. However, Davitt did concede that though the nomination had not followed procedure, it was a pity MacBride had been opposed. In fairness to John MacBride, it is doubtful if he had much or any say in his nomination.

In Pretoria MacBride also heard that a contingent of some forty Irish-Americans were on the way to join them. After setting up a provisional arrangement for Davitt to visit the Irish camp in the Biggarsberg, MacBride caught the train back to Natal. It is not known whether he realized that Davitt was not over-impressed with his fellow Mayo man.

While in Pretoria, Gillingham showed MacBride the draft of a letter he was sending to Dr Ryan in London. It criticized Ryan for publishing in the press (he says Durban, but he probably meant Dublin) an incorrect version of what Gillingham had written to Ryan in a letter dated 30 November 1899. With the British on the Boers' back doorstep, this was indeed an irresponsible action and may well have contributed to the later British decision to pack Gillingham off to Ceylon as a prisoner of war. Not that Gillingham held this against the IRB chief. MacBride advised Gillingham against sending the letter; this advice was ignored.[10]

The Biggarsberg sweep south from Glencoe. To hold this bastion, the Boers had secured the Helpmekaar Pass some fifty kilometres south. It was to this beautiful part of the Natal marchlands that the Irish Transvaal Brigade was ordered by the area commander, General Lukas Meyer.

The new Irish camp seems to have been at the top of the long three-kilometre climb of the Helpmekaar Pass behind some low hills. Even today the area is remote, not far from Rorke's Drift on the Zululand border. Both James Rorke and Alexander Biggar, after whom the range was named, had been hardy Irish frontiersmen fifty years earlier.

The Irish brigade arrived at Helpmekaar in the last week of March 1900 and remained there about a month. An announcement in the *Diggers' News* of 27 March announced that the Irish brigade had left the 'Biggars Bergen for Helpmekaar Pass', and went on:

> Major MacBride wishes members of the Irish Brigade at present on leave to be ready to depart for the Natal Front this evening. The major, also is returning, will be pleased to meet members of the Corps at the American Hotel this afternoon.[11]

The American Hotel in Johannesburg was owned by Dave Norris, an American, and was a popular meeting place for Irish brigaders when in town.

The men from Belfast had brought news of Queen Victoria's imminent visit to Ireland. On Wednesday, 4 April, the day she touched Irish soil, some Irish brigaders and a handful of the Germans set off on a 'tommyhunt'. Riding south to near Tugela Ferry, they scoured the veld for British soldiers to shoot. But none as yet had ventured that far east, where still buffalo and the occasional lion might be seen. The posse returned to camp without firing a shot in anger.

Another day the Irish and the Germans had a horse race between a representative steed of each corps. Ireland was represented by the 'gallant little' Fenian Boy, MacBride's pony. MacBride was still no horseman so the brigade's colonial boy, Frank O'Reilly, took to the saddle and put paid to the German challenge.

Preparations were made to receive Michael Davitt in the Biggarsberg. Lieutenant Gaynor from Longford, recovered from being twice shot in the arm at Modderspruit, and twenty brigaders rode up to Glencoe to welcome the famous Irishman. They waited – but he did not appear. A few kilometres from Helpmekaar Blake and MacBride also waited to receive the entourage. Why Davitt choose instead to go to the Orange Free State is not known. Though he wrote of the brigade in his book, the fact is he never visited it. The lads must have been disappointed.


## MICHAEL DAVITT'S AFRICAN SOJOURN

Though Davitt had invested unsuccessfully in a southern African mining syndicate in 1896, he had never been to Africa prior to 1900. His decision to go to the Transvaal at his own expense was determined by a number of factors. He was bored by politics at home and needed some adventure. Besides his doctor had recommended he winter in a warmer climate. Then there was the question of employment. The *Freeman's Journal* was amenable to paying for reports and the idea had occurred to Davitt that if he got a book on the war out quickly, he might make some money. The chronology of this much-publicised tour can be summarized as follows:

| | |
|---|---|
| 25 October 1899 | Davitt's resignation speech from House of Commons |
| 20 February 1900 | Arrives in Amsterdam from London |
| 25 February | Sails from Marseilles on the *Oxus* |
| 21 March | Arrives in Beira |
| 25 March | Davitt's 55th birthday |
| 26 March | Arrives in Lourenço Marques and catches train to Pretoria, 'a most tiring journey'. Met there by State Secretary Reitz |
| 27 March | Visits President Kruger |
| | In Pretoria – meets John MacBride |
| | Catches train to Kroonstad in OFS, where interviews Colonel de Villebois-Mareuil |

| | |
|---|---|
| 3 April | Returns to Pretoria |
| | Visits POW camp |
| | Evening in Reitz's home in Sunnyside, Pretoria: 'an ordinary comfortable house' |
| 4 April | Writes to John Dillon, 'this war has scarcely yet begun'. Predicts it will be two years before the British flag flies over Pretoria |
| 8 April | Driven round the mountain road by Gillingham. Meets Colonel Blake with two ladies on horseback |
| 10 & 11 April | Leaves for train to Kroonstad |
| | Meets President Steyn |
| | To Smaldeel |
| 12 April | To Brandfort |
| | Meets Generals de la Rey and Philip Botha |
| 13 April: (Good Friday) | Visits camps of American Scouts, Hollander corps and the state artillery. Hears Boer ballad: 'When they near the Transvaal Hills' |
| 16 April | Views huge British camp outside Bloemfontein from top of kopje |
| | Meets General Kolbe and Colonel Maximov |
| 21 April | 20 minutes with President Steyn |
| | Returns to Pretoria |
| | Meets Colonel Lynch |
| | Meets Irish-American Ambulance Corps |
| 25 April | Writes to Dillon that this is 'the most interesting experience of my whole life' |
| 26 April | Tea in Johannesburg with Captain and Mrs Oates |
| Early May | Visits Lynch's second Irish brigade in Natal |
| 7 May | Attends last sitting of the Transvaal Volksraad in Pretoria: 'the dying session of a murdered nation's Parliament' |
| | Meets General Viljoen |
| 15 May | Train for Lourenço Marques |
| 22 May | Sails for France on SS *Gironde* |
| 25 May | Arrives in Marseilles |
| 1 July | Back in Dublin |
| 10 July | *Freeman's Journal* publishes Davitt's letter: 'man for man, gun for gun, the Boers would have driven their foes into the Indian Ocean in a month' |

How much Davitt really learnt about South Africa in his two-month visit is unclear. In his reports he depicts the Boers as a fine people much maligned for their treatment of the black population. He was undoubtedly regarded as a very important visitor, much feted, and met most of the leading figures in the Boer armies. He appears to have got on especially well with Generals Tobias Smuts and Philip Botha. He stayed in comfort in the Grand Hotel in Pretoria, but had to rough it in a tent in the Free State.

Davitt had only one arm and the sight of him on horseback must have been a subject of comment by the Boers. Colonel Lynch described Davitt as a kind of 'Spanish hidalgo'. Davitt was sternly straitlaced where the peccadillos of the Rand lords were concerned but obviously greatly enjoyed the smutty stories of Piet Retief's nephew.

And that is the problem with Davitt. One does not know what he really thought. His diaries are only source notes and drafts for his book and for his articles for the *Freeman's Journal*. He does not say much in them about his own impressions, being more concerned to record information about the Boer forces, their officers whom he encountered and any anti-English gossip he could pick up. They are all a bit chaotic.[12] Take, for instance, his entry for 15 May 1900:

> Farewell Pretoria! You will soon cease to be capital of a Nation. The enemy of nationhood will make you another of his 'centres of civilization'. Brothels, paupers, hypocrites, gospel mongers in the pay of British mammon, and all the other inseparable [sic] accompaniments of Anglo-Saxon rogers will replace the kind of life you have been familiar with; not a perfect life, not a blameless one, but one infinitely better, cleaner, and more truly civilized than the one which will begin here the day the ensign of England will float once more over a defeated Nationality.[13]

One source states that Davitt left the Transvaal disillusioned with the Boers: that he had advised the Boers to surrender. Baptist minister Henry James Batts accosted Davitt as he stood alone in Pretoria station waiting for his train out to Lourenço Marques. Batts was an imperialist and also something of a crawler, who later gleefully told Lord Roberts his version of what had transpired on the station platform. 'I go away,' Batts reported Davitt as saying, 'broken and sick at heart, thoroughly disappointed. I would give £100 to withdraw what I have written.' Batts was soon to publish his account of this encounter, which not surprisingly led to an acrimonious correspondence between him and Davitt.[14] That Davitt was depressed when he left Pretoria is probably true, that he had turned against the Boers is doubtful.

As far as Davitt's relations with the two Irish commandos are concerned, he certainly gave them very good publicity back in Ireland. But he did not go out of his way to be with them. He briefly visited Lynch's camp at Glencoe, but as mentioned earlier he considered it more important to venture to the Free State front line than pay a visit to Blake's men. This did not stop him pestering MacBride for some mementos of the war for a 'national bazaar' in Dublin in support of the Wolfe Tone memorial. A Mauser rifle and an English shell were provided but Davitt was unable to take them home, probably because the Portuguese would not allow such items across the frontier at Komatipoort. On 30 April 1900 Davitt wrote a note to MacBride apologising for not having met the brigade.

The *Natal Mercury* informed its readers of Davitt's departure:

> His Boer friends may have expected him to fight for them, but they will have to be content with his moral support.[15]

## THE SECOND IRISH TRANSVAAL BRIGADE

Even by the time Michael Davitt got off the train in Pretoria in late March 1900, exhausted by the voyage from Dublin, serious division had already taken place in South African-Irish ranks. The earlier arrival from Paris on 13 or 14 January of Arthur Lynch served to emphasize and publicize the division.

It appears that there had already been desertions from Blake's unit, several of these being prominent members. Then one suspects that there were others like Captain Oates who, having left for a visit home to Johannesburg, decided enough was enough and never returned to Ladysmith. One, not very reliable, source states that some of the lads in the new rival Irish commando had been 'fired bag and baggage out of the old commando'.

Lynch took the oath of citizenship and became a burgher on Thursday, 18 January 1900. About a fortnight later MacBride received a letter from Solomon Gillingham in Pretoria telling him of Lynch's arrival and of the scheme to establish a second Irish brigade.[16] The news must have come as quite a shock to Blake and MacBride. They wired Gillingham to bring Lynch and Oates down to Natal to discuss the matter as they felt 'a second brigade an unnecessary and a foolish move at the time, as in reality we had not enough of men for the first'. Lynch ignored the invitation.

It is likely that from the start the Boers intended Lynch to fight for them. Lynch's story that General Louis Botha vetoed his proposal to act as a war correspondent does not hold water, especially as Lynch did send despatches overseas.[17] However, the idea of him serving in a second Irish commando was possibly the idea of Gillingham.

Gillingham remains a shadowy figure. It is difficult not to link his being in Pretoria's commissariat department with stories of Irish involvement in theft and fraud. It appears that the scheme was for Gillingham to lead the new commando which he proposed 'to direct from Pretoria'. Indeed, Lynch seems to have turned up when Gillingham's scheme was already being hatched. The concept of Lynch joining the first Irish brigade was a non-starter as Lynch already knew MacBride disliked him. They had met in London in the mid-1890s. Lynch was self-opinionated and undoubtedly looked down on MacBride and Blake. When the three men finally met, Lynch tried to show off with his horsemanship, which did not help him to improve relationships.[18]

Gillingham's attempt to lead the new commando was blocked by President Kruger, who 'struck him out with a gesture of impatience'. Lynch got in as second choice. Though Kruger initially opposed Lynch getting the title of colonel, he did not press the point and Lynch became Blake's equal.

Michael Davitt liked Lynch. In his diary he recorded he was:

> Tall, soldierly looking and much more presentable than either Blake or MacBride. Is much smarter also in other respects. Appears to be well-educated, gentlemanly young fellow. Height 5'10" age thirty (about), handsome regular features dark complexion and smartly dressed in kind of light uniform. Says his brigade is 130 strong offered to amalgamate with Blake but latter would not agree. Counter charges!! We are Irish anywhere.

In his book Davitt merely says the second Irish commando was formed with 'the laudable ambition of increasing the number of bodies with Irish names'.[19]

In his diary Davitt quotes Lynch as putting the brigade size at 130. In Davitt's book it is 150. Other sources state forty and between fifty and sixty. A photograph of the commando has forty men in it.[20] The truth is it probably started at about 150 but soon was reduced by desertion to fifty or sixty men. The composition of Lynch's corps is something of a mystery. We know the names of only thirteen of the men:

Joseph Hayes, M.F. Heron, Gerry Kidmey, Dr Leach, Colonel Arthur Lynch, James McElroy, Albertus Meintjes, Major John Mitchell, Patrick Mooney, Captain P.J. Oates, William O'Connor, a man called Terpend who was known as 'Turpin' [presumably because he was a thief], and E. Viljoen.

Oates and Michell were respectable Irishmen and their decision to join up with Lynch's outfit is an interesting comment on what was going on in Blake's camp. McElroy was also formerly in Blake's commando. Tom Byrne claimed these men had personal grievances against MacBride.

What is clear is that the second Irish brigade was a cosmopolitan unit, 'every nation in Europe except Turkey' – even one Englishman. Lynch himself spoke of his men as 'the backwoodsman hunter type, or men of Irish descent, inured to the hard life of the South'. His detractors in the rival camp were more colourful with their language: 'fifty or sixty sore-heads, greasers, half-breeds and dagos ... a gang of hobos'.[21]

Lynch was in no hurry to get to the front line. The corps' headquarters were in Pritchard Street in Johannesburg. There was already rivalry between the two Irish units. On 14 February *Die Volksstem* noted: ' ... it is no secret that they [Lynch's corps] will do their utmost to place themselves on an equal footing with the Brigade under Colonel Blake which has already so distinguished itself'.

February came and went and it was only on Thursday, 1 March, that General Buller sent a ciphered despatch to Lord Roberts:

> Affairs here are not shaping very pleasantly. The enemy is said to have been reinforced by 4,000 Transvaalers, who came from the Orange Free State through Brandon's Pass, and by a 3,000 Irish-Hollanders-German commando from Johannesburg. Probably these numbers are exaggerated, but I think it is certain that a good reinforcement has arrived. The enemy have fortified the Biggarsberg, and seem to be trying to work slowly round my right, and, they have strengthened their forces at Helpmekaar.[22]

Why Lynch came to Natal, so close to the rival Irish commando, is not known. He set up camp beside the railway junction at Glencoe, a few kilometres to the west of Dundee. Their neighbours were the Krugersdorp commando. They also made contact and were friendly with the Vryheid and Italian commandos. Here at Glencoe in late March Lynch's Irish commando was visited by General Louis Botha and his wife Annie. Lynch was quick to point out to his men that Annie Botha was an Emmet and of Irish extraction.

The second brigade was still badly understrength and Lynch was prompted to place an advertisement ('To Irishmen!') in the *Diggers' News*:

> The Events of the War are daily becoming more critical and important. We (Irish) Burghers of the two Republics are fighting not only for the country, but for liberty, honour, and all that men hold dear ... Irishmen rally to the Green Flag ... Remember that Irishmen who fall in this War will be joined in Irish memories for ever with Sarsfield, with Wolfe Tone, and with Robert Emmet ... Communicate with M.F. Hogan care of H.S. Lombard Fieldcornet, Johannesburg, or direct to me.
>
> ARTHUR LYNCH,
> (Colonel Irish Brigade II)
> By Krugersdorp Laager, near Glencoe.[23]

Three days after this piece appeared we find Solomon Gillingham writing to Mark Ryan in London, 'I have been greatly deceived in Mr Arthur Lynch.' Things were not working out as planned.

The criticism against Lynch's commando has to be treated with caution, for a concerted campaign to discredit Lynch was undertaken in various Irish nationalist and Irish-American circles for some years after the war. None the less it does appear that there were serious problems in Lynch's unit. By his own admission there were times when he had to maintain discipline with the help of his fists. He gives a graphic description of his laying flat one of his men who had molested a twelve-year-old black girl. He also admits to there being a plot from within the commando to overthrow his leadership.[24]

That said, many contemporaries admitted that Lynch did go to the utmost pains to look after the welfare and comfort of his men. Perhaps too much so. *The Times history of the war* speaks of 'cosmopolitan rascality, gathered together for the opportunities of loot and swindling'. It does appear that horses were stolen for the Boers and resold to them time and time again.[25] According to Andy Higgins from County Down, he was seconded from Blake's brigade by the Boers to investigate the wholesale horse thefts and other looting then going on. His account reads:

> I traced the horse thefts to Lynch and I found rolls of silk, tweeds, jewellery and other goods in Lynch's tent at Dundee. I met Lynch at

the Glencoe railroad station, and charged him with stealing horses and threatened to shoot him if I found him stealing any more. I made a full report of what I had found to the Boer Government. These things occurred about a year after Lynch got to SA.[26]

The last statement is definitely false, but the main body of the text may contain elements of truth. What it does firmly establish is the hatred that must have existed between the two camps. And there were others who did not like Lynch's men. The *Natal Mercury* recorded the brigade being on the Neville farm on the Biggarsberg:

Part of the Irish Brigade came past. They were composed of Irish-Americans and Irish-Argentines, men who had served in the Argentine army, and had spent most of their time beach-combing. The Irish Brigade were found to be a mixture of every race, and of the lowest types.[27]

Fifty kilometres south at Helpmekaar, the first Irish Transvaal Brigade was not only annoyed by having Lynch so near but was bored as well. Blake was the first to clear out of this beautiful spot, his excuse being that he must meet the Irish-American contingent that would arrive soon in Pretoria. Once more MacBride was in charge. He took the initiative and on Saturday, 28 April, he telegraphed Pretoria requesting a transfer of the commando to the Free State front. Buller remained cosy in Ladysmith but it was clear that Lord Roberts was about to advance out of Bloemfontein. Blake was consulted by the Boer military and agreement reached. On the Wednesday Blake wired MacBride to strike camp and come to Johannesburg en route to the Orange Free State. Great excitement followed. Farewells were made to General Lukas Meyer and to their old commander, Commandant Trichardt, and on Wednesday, 25 April 1900, a special train steamed out of Dundee. MacBride and his men were on their way out of occupied British territory.

The Irishmen were granted a few days' leave in Johannesburg. Half a dozen of them without homes there booked into the Langham Hotel. The first evening James Harold of Dalkey was hammering 'The boys of Wexford' out on the hotel's piano when to his surprise Arthur Lynch came up to him and asked him to play 'The rising of the moon'. Fourteen years later Harold was to write a vitriolic attack on Lynch saying his commando was 'the laughing stock and contempt of every Commando in the neighbourhood'. Laughing stock or not, Lynch's men were soon to prove their worth.

Lynch returned to Glencoe junction and in early May entertained Michael Davitt. Davitt had been philosophical about the split in Irish ranks, 'inevitable in every Irish concern'. He relaxed in the well-equipped camp and lectured Lynch on the evils of Parnell, 'a cold-blooded sensualist'. Major Mitchell, 'a quiet and somewhat diffident man', was present, but Captain Oates, reluctant always to return to the field of battle, was back home in Johannesburg. Davitt had written that Oates was a 'tall, sinewy, strong, grizzly type, a tower of strength'. It was a pity he was not at Glencoe for on Tuesday, 8 May 1900, General Buller at long last began his advance out of Ladysmith.

While the Boer army was ensconced in the natural fortress of the Biggarsberg, Buller had several choices. He could push north from Elandslaagte through Khupe's Pass to Newcastle. But that would leave his rear exposed to Meyer's forces concentrated in the eastern Biggarsberg. Alternatively, Buller could attack Dundee via Wasbank and Glencoe junction. What, however, he chose to do was to outflank the Boers by moving east to Pomeroy, attacking them up the Helpmekaar Pass and then advancing north through Beith towards Dundee.

When it became clear to Lukas Meyer that the area where the German corps was and where Blake's men had been was the focus of attack, he sent down Lynch's commando and the Italian unit. Ricchiardi, the Italian leader, turned to Lynch and said, 'Here, Colonel, we will hold this between us.' Also present in the rearguard were the Piet Retief and Johannesburg commandos as well as the Swaziland Police unit and parts of the Zoutpansberg and Boksburg commandos. The official war history says there were in all about 1,500 men.

On Sunday, 13 May, the assault on the Biggarsberg fortress was underway as Buller's army battled its way up the Helpmekaar Pass. *The Times history* of the war condescendingly conceded: 'In the general confusion of the Boer retirement there was one corps which, for the first and probably the last time, achieved some slight distinction.' Both *The Times history* and the official history point out the temporary nature of the delay of Dundonald's cavalry by Lynch and his men – 'nearly an hour,' states *The Times history*.

In fact, on Monday, 14 May, Lynch earned his free passage out. At a remote place called Beith he made a stand on a 'natural redoubt'. He claimed this was for the best part of the day. This allowed Viljoen to move his guns away from the nearby van Tonders Nek and onto the Dundee road.

A British horse battery was brought up and started shelling Lynch, and the cavalry began to move along to outflank the Irish. At this point, with the Boer guns trundling north, Lynch decided to withdraw. The tall veld grass was on fire. Although Lynch denied this, it was probably set alight by the Irish or by the Boers: fire threw up a dangerous barrier for the enemy to cross as well as destroying future grazing for their horses.[28]

Lynch found himself on the wrong side of the blaze and by jumping from boulder to boulder crossed the hazard and found his and Major Mitchell's horses in the care of a young Boer. There was no sign of the Galway man. Lynch waited amidst voluminous clouds of smoke, the crash of shells nearby and the crack of bullets ricocheting off rocks. He recalled:

> Suddenly, round the corner, I saw a figure, utterly spent with fatigue, and wearing an air of complete discouragement. It was Mitchell.
>
> He had lost his way and thought that his horse had gone. I called out to him. He looked up electrified, and then came running on, sprang on to his horse, and we were off.[29]

The excitement was not yet over, though. The Irish retreated, probably with losses, along the line of hills, with the cavalry not far behind. And in front of them the Irish brigaders drove the Boer cattle, terrified and bellowing, along the track through a tunnel of smoke. As Lynch said, 'It was a picture of Hell worthy of the pencil of Gustave Doré himself.'

Some kilometres further on, near the ridge of Endumeni, Lynch's men stopped and faced the foe again. Another hour of delay for the enemy that late afternoon before the Irish 'slipped away into the smoke'. The story is finished by *The Times history*:

> ... so that it was not until four o'clock in the afternoon that Dundonald, straining every nerve in the pursuit, reached the long ridge of Blesboklaagte, a spur of Indumeni Mountain, which blocked the road to Dundee some twenty-five miles from Helpmekaar. But Lynch's rearguard action had enabled the Boers to cross the ridge with all their guns and wagons, and as Dundonald approached he was met by the fire of two or three guns upon the ridge. Again the horse battery was brought into action, and again the long line of mounted troops extended and felt for the enemy's flanks. But it was not till after five o'clock, with night fast coming on, that the Boers withdrew their guns and continued their retreat towards Dundee. Cheated of any tangible fruits of the pursuit, Dundonald withdrew his tired and smoke-begrimed men to camp a few miles back within the infantry outposts in accordance with the bad habit of the Natal army. Touch

was thereby lost with the enemy and was not regained by Dundonald until he came in contact with them nearly a week later at Laing's Nek.[30]

The Boers had reason to thank Lynch and it was probably this action which led the Boers to be circumspect when commenting on his alleged misdemeanours.

The second Irish brigade retreated to Laing's Nek, near where Lynch was concussed by a British shell. Quickly recovering, he left the Natal battle zone with his men and rode for Johannesburg. What happened there is not known but it seems likely that the unit disintegrated and it was only Colonel Lynch and a handful of his men who made their way down to the Transvaal-Orange Free State border on the Vaal river. They can not have stayed there for long for on 26 May 1900 Lord Roberts had reached the Vaal river and the town of Vereeniging.[31]

# CHAPTER EIGHT

# 'Paying an instalment on the Irish debt'

## MAY 1900

### THE YANKS ARE COMING

In 1879 there had been talk of Irish-Americans supplying arms either to the Zulus or to the Boers.[1] Nothing had come of these suggestions save to set in people's minds the idea that Irish America was opposed to British imperialism in South Africa. Later the American uitlanders on the Rand tended to be sympathetic to the Boer cause and it is said 'Kruger's eagle' on the wall of the president's Church Street house in Pretoria was presented after the Jameson raid by John Blake on behalf of the 'Committee of Americans'.[2]

At the time of the raid there was also a rumour that 5,000 Clan na Gael men were prepared to sail to South Africa to defend the Transvaal. Kruger consulted Solomon Gillingham who advised against accepting the offer.[3] Another rumour circulated in 1899 that the Transvaal postmaster, I.N. van Alphen, was in cahoots with the Invincible leader, P.J. Tynan, No. 1, to bring out Irish-American volunteers to fight in the war. Irish America was certainly pro-Boer and demonstrated that support not only in New England but as far afield as Montana and Seattle. Bourke Cockran was particularly eloquent in his espousal of the Boer cause.

By 10 January 1900 the British embassy in Washington had got wind that something serious was afoot. Five days later the news had reached Natal.[4] The question was what was going to happen? An invasion of Canada? No, Governor Roosevelt of New York would have none of that. The militia would be called out 'and clap them all in jail'.[5] Luke Dillon's attack on a lock of the Welland Canal was all that happened in north America in that line. Even the widespread purchasing of mules and horses in the United States and their shipment to South Africa went on without molestation.

Plans for an expedition of 5,000 men had been suggested to Dr Leyds in Brussels. In the end the Ancient Order of Hibernians collected funds for a much smaller 'filibustering expedition'. There really was little alternative. US law would not permit the recruitment of its citizens for such foreign adventures. And even if they got away, the Portuguese dared not allow them to land in their east African territory.

The deceit was simple. The men formed the Irish-American Ambulance Corps and swore affidavits that they would not take up arms in the Transvaal. They received recognition from the American Red Cross. Red Cross insignia were worn. True enough, there were medical doctors in the outfit: James P. McNamara (chief surgeon); A.D. Alderholt, A.F. Conroy, E. Ederholt, Ross D. Long, Herbert R. McAulay and James J. Slattery. Apart from these, there appear initially to have been 51 others, some of whom had fought in the recent American-Spanish war and some who were National Guardsmen. Captain Patrick O'Connor, the unit's military leader, had been a sergeant in the regular US army and had served in the recent war.

Some of the men were not American-born: Captain Patrick O'Connor came originally from Moylough in County Galway, Hugh Ryan was from Tipperary and both Thomas Naughton and Mike O'Hara from County Limerick. Most of the men, though, were recruited in Chicago by an old friend of Lieutenant John Blake, Colonel John Finerty of Arizona.[6] A few were signed up in Boston by Patrick J. Judge of Holyoke. The United Irish Societies of Chicago bought and equipped what appears to have been a first-class ambulance unit.[7]

On Thursday, 15 February 1900, the day Kimberley was relieved, the *Chicago Daily News* announced the sailing of *La Gascogne* from New York harbour. The fifty-eight ambulance men had marched to the French line pier behind Edward T. McCrystal and Patrick Egan. They were according to the paper off 'to aid the sick and wounded of the Boer army'; the Chicago Irish-American Ambulance Corps had other ideas.[8] *La Gascogne* seems to have sailed to Le Havre, from where the corps moved to the south of France and sailed, probably from Marseilles, on the *Caravelas*.

John MacBride was the first member of Blake's commando to hear that the Irish-Americans were on the high seas. That was in late March when he was in Pretoria seeing Gillingham and Michael Davitt; on his return to Helpmekaar camp, he told Blake, who was very excited. Some time in the first few days of April Blake and a few of the brigaders set out for Pretoria. On 12 April they caught a train west for 160 kilometres to the dorp of Middelburg, where Arthur Griffith had edited the *Middelburg Courant* three years earlier.

On descending from the railway carriage onto the dusty platform that Thursday, Blake must have groaned inwardly to see the figure of the Revd

Batts. No doubt to annoy the self-righteous cleric, Blake told him that a great fight would soon take place at Fourteen Streams in the Free State and that 20,000 British troops would be lost. 'Indeed!' said the clergyman indignantly. 'Yes,' replied Blake, 'it will last three weeks and then be all over.'[9] This depressed Batts.

Down at Delagoa Bay the vessel carrying the Irish-Americans dropped anchor that evening or the next morning. It was a strange passenger list with people on their way to fight for both sides. One British passenger recorded: '... there were so many inebriated Irish ambulance men on board ... it isn't safe to talk here although nothing but French and Irish is understood on this ship'.[10]

Lourenço Marques was notorious as a place for spying and intrigues. A confidential list mainly of undesirables in the old seaport drawn up by the British four months after the Irish-Americans passed through included the following:

| | |
|---|---|
| Miss Daniels | Bar-keeper Irish. Her bar is the meeting place for every Fenian and Secret Service Man. |
| Samuel Menton | Irish, chief detective in Johannesburg. |
| A. Russell | British, member of the Irish Red Cross, afterwards fought for the same Brigade. |
| — Smith | Formerly Irish Brigade, wounded in one arm, has previously deserted from British Army. |

At other times the name of Solomon Gillingham or of Dr Walsh could have been added.[11]

No one wanted the Irish-Americans in Lourenço Marques. The Portuguese, ever fearful of a British blockade, were keen to keep up the appearance of neutrality.[12] They would not let them in as Red Cross members, but only as US citizens who had sworn oaths not to fight. The American consul, Stanley Hollis, had no illusions about what was going on, but as British military intelligence could do nothing so too the American authorities were powerless to act.

By chance the American writer Richard Harding Davis was in Lourenço Marques that morning. He noted that the town was 'invaded' by the Irish-Americans, 'the Portuguese officials were much upset in consequence'. They had reason to be. The ambulance's medical supplies were made up mainly of quinine and whisky. In truculent mood, the customs official charged two shillings before clearing an American flag. Harding Davis goes on:

The ambulance corps expressed itself rather freely in consequence, and for the good of all, the American consul persuaded the Portuguese railway officials to speed the corps on its way in a special train before, as he significantly expressed it, in the phrase of Jameson raid memory, they 'upset the apple-cart'.[13]

This was not the first time the Irish had caused trouble in the town. Back in the 1880s an 'Irish brigade' of railway navvies had gone amok, seized a Portuguese gunboat and run it onto a sandbank.

The train crossed the great railway bridge and entered the South African Republic. Great waving and cheering occurred and 'snapping their fingers at United States secret service officers, British consuls and Portuguese governors'. Across the lowveld and up the passes to Nelspruit and through to Belfast and finally in to Middelburg steamed the train. It was Friday, 13 April 1900 – Good Friday.

Blake claimed he was disappointed that there were not a thousand Irish-Americans, but it is unlikely he had not been forewarned of the size of the unit.[14] Of course, he was pleased to see 'the good boys from free America', and the people of Middelburg, led by Landdrost du Toit, gave them a warm welcome. All but the doctors seem to have torn off their Red Cross bandages. It is said even some of the Boers were a bit shocked. 'It is a pity they came so,' said one. But as Harding Davis wrote, 'the Boer women were paying for the sons of the women of the city of Chicago, of Cook County, State of Illinois'.

From Middelburg, Blake and his new recruits took the train to the Boer capital. The following Wednesday the American consul in Pretoria, Adelbert Hay, cabled his father, Secretary of State Colonel John Hay, in Washington, 'Irish American ambulance almost all preparing to fight'. He seems to have had a row with them and took away the unit's Red Cross flag. The British *Daily Mail* drily commented that the ambulance men were carrying revolvers.[15]

To say that this incident created 'a scandal of international proportions' is perhaps a bit of an exaggeration. After all, there was nothing the American government could have done, though, it certainly did not want gun-toting citizens dashing across the globe to fight the English. The people who had most reason for complaint were the Red Cross. This was as outrageous an action against them as it was for the British to set up a propaganda photograph on Hampstead Heath purportedly of Boers firing on a Red Cross tent on the veld.

Michael Davitt was still in the country. He considered the American imports as 'the finest looking body of men that had yet reached the Transvaal capital from abroad'. He was probably right. Yet again Pretoria's Grand Hotel served as a headquarters for Irish commandos. It was from here that the Irish-Americans marched to President Kruger's home a week after they arrived in the country. And who should be skulking behind the marching men but the Revd Batts.

In front of the presidency the Irish-Americans lined up. Oom Paul emerged from his house accompanied by State Secretary Reitz, who acted as interpreter. Colonel Blake introduced the troop to the president. There was no high oratory from Kruger. He said that he knew they had come in the cause of righteousness, and those who fought for righteousness would be saved. He told them they would be attached to General du Toit's commando and sent to Fourteen Streams. Finally he told them to take special care of their horses. The lads seemed both puzzled and rather 'scared' of the old man. Captain O'Connor stood forward and said they had come to fight their old enemy, the English. A great cheer was raised and then one of the lads, named O'Shea, cleared his throat and in a tenor voice sang 'Jerusalem'.[16]

The whole event attracted much attention in Pretoria. School children on bicycles pressed against Boers to see this strange event and the men who had taken two months to cross the globe to fight for them. The Revd Batts' comment was that he would not like to meet the newcomers 'alone on a dark night'. It is just as well for him that never happened.

The medical doctors seem to have been assigned to various veld hospitals. For the rest of the newcomers, the Irish brigade would meet up at Elandsfontein just east of Johannesburg. The new united Irish commando of Blake's and O'Connor's men came together in the last week of April 1900. And as Colonel Blake wrote, 'What a rollicking, joyful good time all these jolly Irish boys had!'[17]

THE WRECKERS CORPS

Had the French adventurer de Villebois-Mareuil not been killed near Boshof on 5 April 1900, it is possible that Blake's commando would have joined the count's European Legion. Certainly MacBride thought this. However, it is doubtful whether the Irish would have fitted into this unit, especially as Blake does not seem to have been mentioned as one of the proposed commando's officers. With the gallant Frenchman now dead, all

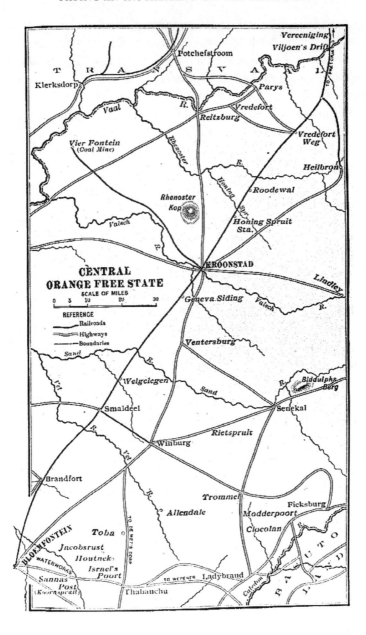

Map 2: of the Orange Free State. Across the vast and flat expanse of the Orange Free State retreated Blake's commando. From Brandfort to Kroonstad, Heilbron and finally crossing the Vaal at Viljoen's Drift, the Irish brigaders were usually in the rear of the Boer retreat.

foreign units were placed under the direct command of General de la Rey in the Orange Free State.[18] As the Irish wanted to be there anyway, this suited them fine. As things turned out, the brigade would probably have enjoyed themselves more fighting Buller in the Biggarsberg and around Laing's Nek.

Dr Walsh found himself working in a veld military hospital at Fourteen Streams (*Veertienstrome*) north of the Vaal and just inside the Cape boundary. From here he had written home to Ireland, 'You can take my tip they have not got the Transvaal yet.'[19] By the time the Irish brigade had entrained at Johannesburg in late April 1900, the advance of Lord Roberts and his juggernaut army of some 45,000 men was poised to move out of Bloemfontein on the way to capture Johannesburg and Pretoria. With a reference to one of the Anglo-Irish generals, a loyal Irish-Natalian had quipped, 'For French is on the veld, says the Shan van Vaught'.[20]

The Irish train from Johannesburg steamed south-west over the undulating plains of the Orange Free State, passed fields of mealies and vast stretches of grassland, interrupted periodically by flat-topped kopjes which rose steeply out of the veld. Finally, at the railway junction of Smaldeel, near present-day Theunissen, fifty kilometres north-east of the Boer frontline at Brandfort, the Irish corps climbed down and organized the offloading of their horses. Everyone was in good spirits.

The brigade camped here for a few days before finally, on the afternoon of Tuesday, 1 May 1900, the long-expected order came. The Irish brigade was to move down to join de la Rey's forces at Brandfort. There was a 'holiday atmosphere' as the lads saddled up and set off, riding throughout that cold night.

By the afternoon of the following day the Irish brigade was encamped in the bush on the banks of the Keeromspruit. Both the Irish-American contingent and especially the original brigade had had dropouts in Pretoria and Johannesburg. The new combined force must now have numbered about 100, possibly as many as 120. They were part of de la Rey's force of some 4,000 men which held the Brandfort line and of the larger Boer army of 8,000 or 9,000 men stretched out across 350 kilometres of open veld.

For the Irish brigade the war recommenced on Thursday, 3 May 1900, over two months after they had retreated from Ladysmith. But it was to be a very different war now for them: what Michael Davitt described as the 'disheartening retirement'.[21] The Irish brigade gave good service to the Boers in the next three weeks, playing a cat-and-mouse game with the British cavalry. Unfortunately, it was the Irish who were the mouse.

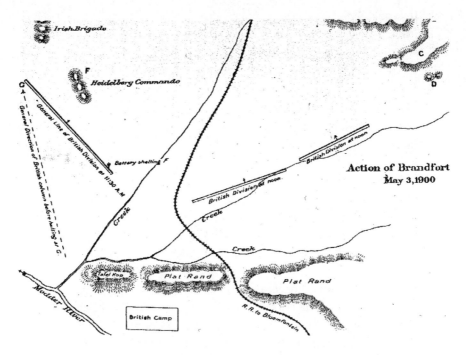

Map 3: Front-line, Orange Free State, May 1900. In early May 1900 a few Boer commandos, including the Irish brigade, held the front line against Lord Roberts' renewed and massive advance. The position of the Irish on the kopje can clearly be seen on the map. It was here the Irish found themselves alone against the British army, when the Boers retreated apparently without telling the Irish. (*Military operations in South Africa …*)

Things got off to a good start for the Irish brigade that Thursday. With the Heidelburg commando, the Irish brigade rode out to a line of kopjes. The Boers were ascending one hill to the south-west of Brandfort and the Irish another to the west, with a central rise blocking the view between the two, or at least that is what the Irish claimed.[22] The day was chilly but the fight was hot. The Irish-Americans 'were in great glee' at being under fire for the first time. Shells burst around them and bullets 'were chipping stones and singing in the air'.

The fight lasted all morning and only at 2 o'clock in the afternoon did a messenger ride up to the Irish and shout, 'General Spruit says get your men away as quickly as possible.' Colonel Blake claimed later that he had no idea the Middelburg commando had already pulled out and that the Irish were holding the line alone, but this behaviour was to be the norm over the next few weeks. The Irish brigade revelled in these dare-devil tactics. They very nearly did not get out of that first scrape.

First, the Irish brigade had to dash across an open plain and then make its way in single file along a path through a low line of hills. Behind it and to the right were General Edward Hutton's troops. Blake shouted to his lads that they would never take him alive. Soon the brigade was forced to veer up a path to its left. Up and up they climbed. Though still a cold day, they sweated heavily. And then they were over the summit and descending quickly. They were safe.

It has been claimed, and Blake seems to support the theory, that Hutton was nervous about firing indiscriminately at the Irish brigade because he thought the Irish-Americans in their Chicago brown serge were colonials whom the commando had captured.[23] It was sundown by the time the exhausted Irish brigade stumbled on the deserted Heidelberg camp. But there was coffee, sugar, bread and meat there, which was welcome, and mealies for the poor horses. Colonel Blake sensibly ordered the brigade to remount and as darkness fell, they hit the main road to Brandfort. They took a supply of oats from one farmhouse and camped finally at another isolated homestead. About 10 o'clock at night a messenger rode up. De la Rey wanted to see Blake in the morning.

Early on Friday morning Blake, his African groom and two Boer scouts set off to find the general. They avoided seven men on horseback whom Blake thought were British in Boer clothing. Blake was worried and sent one of the scouts, Hendrik Slegkamp, back to the Irish camp to tell them to clear out. Perhaps it was just as well for the colonel that de la Rey was not in his camp when Blake arrived. But there was a pleasant surprise. His friend Colonel Trichardt was there and the two men had a good chat before Blake remounted and rode off to rejoin his men.

On his return journey Blake and the scout came under fire from a mealie field. They rode hard for a kopje to which the brigade was also dashing, but wire fences blocked Blake's way and he had given his wirecutters to Slegkamp. They raced to a small farmhouse and a 'little Dutch woman' showed them a sheep path. Still under fire, Blake's 'boy's horse' was slightly wounded. They found a small gate and were through and up to the kopje and safety. Blake firmly believed the seven riders had been part of a British detachment hidden in a deep kloof.

The fighting was over for the day and that evening the Irish brigade quietly rode north and crossed the Vet river just before Smaldeel. Camp was made. Their exploits had not gone unnoticed. Next morning's *Diggers'*

*News* reported, 'There were no burgers to oppose their entrance [the British into Brandfort] – only the Irish Brigade and 10 scouts.'[24] A telegram which de la Rey sent Louis Botha in Natal read: 'They are swarming over like locusts. I can not shoot them back.'

On Saturday, 5 May, the Irish brigade was up early and set off to find de la Rey. When they found the Lion of the West and his men, there was general relief and rejoicing. The general was friendly to the Irish but when the fighting began that day, they were ordered to stay in reserve. Their punishment, however, did not last long and soon they were ordered to cross open ground under fire to defend the drift. Blake claimed that they were opposite an Irish regiment, which was possible. He also repeated a claim he had made about the battle of the Tugela Heights, that the English had turned guns on the Irish troops to push them forward. This was wishful thinking. The Inniskilling Dragoons would dearly have liked to catch up with the 'Flying Fenians'.

At sundown de la Rey ordered the Irish brigade to retreat, but they stayed on for a while and for a second time found themselves alone against the British army. This time, however, their retreat was less eventful.

It was about this time that de la Rey and Blake came to an agreement. A section of the Irish brigade would serve as a 'dynamite squad', who would destroy railway communications as the Boer army retreated. Whether this idea was Blake's, as he claimed, is not known. Certainly the Boers were then uneasy about the very concept of destroying property and the proposal was long debated at a *krijgsraad*, or council of war, before the okay was given.

Members of the dynamite squad, or the Wreckers Corps as it popularly became known, seem to have included among others the following:

> Lieutenant Gaynor
> Sergeant Major Frank O'Reilly
> Dick Barry
> Mike Halley from Waterford
> Tom Herlihy
> Jim O'Keefe from Co. Kilkenny
> Tom Tierney
> Joe Wade

In the early days of the war a group of Irish brigaders, 'all well-known dynamitards on the Rand', had carried out similar tasks. This early unit contained Malcolm McCallum, Jim O' Keefe, Pat Fahey, Joe Tully, Jo

Wade and Tom Balfour. By May 1900 Fahey was dead. O'Keefe and Wade were certainly still blowing up bridges, as no doubt were the other three members of the original unit.

It would be wrong to imagine that the Wreckers Corps was an independent unit. The rest of the brigade often helped in lifting rails with iron bars or drilling holes where dynamite was placed. The fact that most of the squad had been miners and were used to handling explosive helped.[25]

The squad blew up railway bridges, culverts, tracks and, some said, railway stations. It worked closely with the Boer artillery who often kept back the cavalry until the charges were laid. One of the problems, though, was that the Boer commanders often waited until the last minute before giving the order to blow. Occasionally the squad just went ahead on their own without orders.

One secret weapon the squad had was a cartoonist, one of the new Irish-American arrivals. It had been usual for this brigader to chalk or paint up a 'polite message' for the English after they had blown a bridge. This annoyance was now refined by:

> a capital caricaturist, and he amuses us and riled the enemy by drawing cartoons of John Bull, with appropriate inscriptions and verses underneath, which he fixed up for their benefit along the railway.[26]

On Sunday, 6 May, a twenty-one-year-old German-American arrived on the banks of the Sand River. His name was Ernest William Luther and on 28 February, thirteen days after O'Connor and his men had left the city, he had set out by himself from New York to join the Irish brigade. Teddy Luther, who had been in the 201st volunteer infantry regiment of the New York, had arrived in Lourenço Marques on 30 April on the *Herzog*, the same ship which had brought Arthur Lynch earlier in the year. Luther is interesting because a journal of his African adventure has survived: it is an account which lacks the hyperbole of those written by Blake, Lynch and MacBride.

Luther had very little money and spent his first night in the Transvaal Republic sleeping in the railway waiting room at Waterval Onder. In Pretoria he fell in with Harding Davis, Irish-American Lieutenant Reilly and a man named McQueen. Things went well for him now and he was put up in the Grand Hotel and fully equipped. On 5 May he set off by train, with his new horse, 'Shorty Kelly', on board, waited most of the next day in Kroonstad and finally arrived at the Sand River about 9 p.m.

The day after Teddy Luther reached the Sand River he crossed over to the far bank and was greatly excited to find the Irish brigade. They were camped beside the Pretoria police unit. It was an important day, for the long and high railway bridge was to be blown by the squad. They were excited, perhaps over-excited. When de la Rey 'bounced' on Mike Halley for showing too much glee at his work of destruction, the little Irishman spat back, 'What in hell do you know about it anyway?' Apologies were later given with the limp excuse that Halley did not know to whom he was talking.

Under fire, the Irish prepared to blow the great bridge. A report in Dutch in the *Diggers' News* read:

> I was told this morning that Col. Blake had been shot at from inside a shop near Sand River Bridge when he loaded the railway bridge with dynamite. Both assassins were, I've been told, tackled and immediately shot dead.[27]

Luther was beside himself with excitement when the bridge blew:

> Five heavy detonations followed, and a flame shot into the air 100 feet high, stones were flying in all directions. A piece of rail came crashing through the air with astonishing sound, dropped 400 yards away.[28]

Then they retreated at speed. Luther dropped and lost his revolver. After five hours in the saddle, the Irish brigade encamped beside the Volksstem commando.

According to Deneys Reitz, the Irish lost a man that day preparing to blow the bridge. This is likely. Accounts of Irish fatalities are rarely mentioned in reports. It is possible two of the Irish-Americans were lost. Those Irish brigaders wounded in the Orange Free State seem to have included John Dunn, John Riley, Paddy Maloney and possibly Sid Tennant. Several brigaders may also have been captured. One contemporary account talks of an 'Irish-American renegade' captured near Brandfort: 'He called us (quâ Englishmen) every foul name that he could lay his tongue to; he declared that he preferred death to capture by such a race.'[29] Lieutenant Thomas Enright was rounded up by the British near Bloemfontein as early as 23 March; perhaps he had been in the area visiting Dr Walsh.[30] One much-lamented casualty of the Sand River fight was one of the brigade's favourite horses, 'Irish Willie'. Michael Davitt put a photograph of the animal in his book.[31]

On Thursday, 10 May, the brigade was back in action again and twice that day hasty retreats were made – 'bags fell off the saddles but few stopped to pick them up'. In the middle of all the excitement, Luther records:

> Colonel Blake commandeers two horses from a storekeeper, and I two cans; commandeering covering all kinds of thefts, and we give receipts signed 'Imperial Horse'.

That evening the brigade halted at the Valsch river outside the Boers' new Orange Free State capital of Kroonstad.

The next morning Luther walked into town and was rewarded for his efforts by having his photograph taken by 'Mr Maylond of the N.Y. Herald and Mr Knight'. The fighting began at 2 p.m.

There was controversy at the time about the role of the Irish brigade in the evacuation of Kroonstad that Friday afternoon. Louis Botha had arrived from Natal and was now in command. He ordered the destruction of the railway bridge over the Valsch, which was duly done by the Irish brigade. What happened then is not clear. On Sunday, 13 May, Jannie Smuts, the Transvaal's able attorney-general, told Michael Davitt in Pretoria that the previous day the Irish brigade had been badly cut up when caught by the English in Kroonstad. He said, 'laughing', that they had been 'engaged at the time in emptying bottles at some hotel or drink store. This Brigade's weakness.' Davitt added, 'If story true it will be great disgrace to Irish name.' The *Natal Mercury* were quick to tell its readers that the Irish 'were all intoxicated'.[32] Later MacBride would hotly deny that refreshments were taken in the Grand Hotel. Perhaps he was not there, for MacBride was wrong when he said the brigade passed through Kroonstad without stopping. Some of the Irish did stop, and with spectacular consequences.

Mick Ryan (whether it was 'Mick the Liar' or 'Big Mick' is not clear) decided to burn down the great provisions depot in the town. He started several fires against the building, but these were put out by one of the English in the town and only when Ryan's rifle butt laid this enemy flat did the fire take.

It appears that Blake and about thirty brigaders remained in the town while Major MacBride, Captain McCallum and the rest of the corps moved out taking the wagons with them. Perhaps it was now that Blake and the lads adjourned to the Grand Hotel for refreshments. General Botha was convinced they had been captured and even cabled Pretoria with the news. But Blake had fought Geronimo and the Apache and knew when it was time to slip away from an advancing enemy. That night both armies watched the great glow in the sky as the Kroonstad depot burnt to the ground.

MacBride and McCallum – the two were soon to be working frequently as a team – got the men out of danger and headed along the railway line as fast as they could for the Rhenoster river where General Botha was preparing to make a stand. Great clouds of dust swept over the brigade and they could hardly breathe. Everyone was tired and grimy. The men looked 'like baboons who have not washed for a month'. Tempers were beginning to fray.

The river was reached and MacBride's men set to guarding the drift. The banks were steep and deep. The river bed was sandy with a skim of water on the surface. It was a good position to hold.

Meanwhile Blake had been prevented from following the railway out of Kroonstad by news that the British were moving round to the west of the town. He therefore took the road to Heilbron and camped after a five-kilometre ride. The next day the sight of 400 British cavalry put Blake and his men in their saddles and a chase ensued, with the Irish just making the safety of the town before the cavalry troop veered back.

In Heilbron Blake met President Steyn and General Hertzog and discussed the possibility of initiating a guerrilla campaign in the Orange Free State. The Irish then saddled up and rode along the banks of the Rhenoster until they hit the railway line and met up with the rest of the brigade, having had no contact with the main body of the corps for four days.

It was about now that the skeletal figure of Jim French appeared in the Irish camp. He had been ill in hospital in Johannesburg and heard of the destruction of his brigade at Kroonstad. Despite the protests from the medics, this lad from Connaught Place in Cork made his way down to the Free State. He was greatly pleased to see the lads as indeed they were to see him. French stayed on and recovered.

It is also likely that it was now that Charles Mallon and a friend from Belfast turned up – the last of the men sent out by Féis Ceoil. So while the brigade was losing men through various causes, there was a trickle of new blood arriving to carry on the fight.

One departure about now was Brigader Duff, despatched to Pretoria to give State Secretary Reitz the brigade's flag for safekeeping. On Thursday, 17 May, the day Mafeking was relieved, Luther records in his diary, 'moved camp two miles further south to rear a large pond. Digging out snakes. Eating all day. The Free State Artillery arrives.'

Next day things were not going well in the Irish camp:

> A bag of Lee-Metford ammunition, my property, caught fire and bullets went whistling through the air in all directions. Dissension and jealousies in the Irish Brigade. The few Dutchmen in our commando, who act as commissary scouts, are made scapegoats for losing 26 mules at the retreat to Kroonstad.[33]

The Boer units waited for the British but none appeared. That Sunday, mass was said in Major MacBride's tent, which seems to have been the practice throughout the war. Finally on Tuesday, 22 May, the Boers retreated. As usual the Irish disobeyed orders and waited for the English but when none appeared they too left, only to find three shells fired after them. They galloped away, stopping occasionally to blow up railway bridges. Luther stole a can of jam off a wagon. And, as in Natal, the retreat was covered by fierce grass fires which stretched for kilometres. As Tom Byrne said, 'It was a marvellous sight to see the whole country burning up'.

And so the Irish Transvaal Brigade retreated across the flat plains of the Free State, on one occasion setting off fifteen detonations on the railway track. On Wednesday, 23 May, the brigade crossed the Vaal at Viljoen's Drift. For Luther, ever mindful of his stomach, it was a red-letter day. A German doctor he had met on the boat ran into him at Vereeniging and gave him two pieces of meat. He bought six eggs (one shilling) and a loaf of bread, 'and I now cooked a meal'.

The next day the brigade was ordered by General Botha to stop dynamiting. 'What a puerile display of military knowledge!' was Colonel Blake's comment. Blake's proposal that he and the brigade should move to the Rand and destroy the mines was also firmly rejected. That was seen by the Boer high command as wanton destruction of property. The Irish brigade was ordered to retreat to Johannesburg. It was Friday, 25 May, and the Irish brigade had been in the Orange Free State for less than a month. It seemed a lot longer.

A footnote needs to be added: who should turn up on the Vaal at this juncture but Colonel Arthur Lynch and a handful of men. Perhaps it is fortunate that they did not run into Blake's commando. Lynch later boasted that his men were the last to cross the Vaal. Even if true, it was a meaningless claim as the Boers did not vacate the Free State. Indeed, a few days after Blake set off north in the direction of the Klip river, a battalion of Imperial Yeomanry, strong both in Irish and in 'blue blood', were ambushed and after stout resistance forced to surrender outside Lindley in the eastern Orange Free State. Over 500 troops were captured including Lieutenant James Craig, the future premier of Northern Ireland. Craig, tearing off his officer's insignia, joined his men in the long march to the prisoner-of-war camp at Nooitgedacht in the eastern Transvaal.[34]

Arthur Lynch does not seem to have done much to hold back Lord Roberts' army. A hapless American sightseer, G.A. Gregg, who had bicycled out with a party to Vereeniging to see the action, had been arrested. Lynch acted as an interpreter during the interrogation. Although he later denied it, Lynch was reported as saying, 'I want to show you these men are British spies and ought to be shot.'

In his autobiography, Lynch tells us he met Botha here. The Boer general was alone, sitting on a wooden gin case beside his high Cape cart and eating some Irish stew. The two men chattered. Botha produced two bottles of whisky, his last two. He gave one to Lynch as a present, which the colonel accepted. Of course, Arthur Lynch did not drink whisky.[35]

# CHAPTER NINE

# A hot time in the old Transvaal

## LATE MAY TO SEPTEMBER 1900

### THE FALL OF MAMMON

The Irish brigade 'ceased to exist as a corps' in May 1900, claimed brigader James Laracy of Kilkenny in a letter to the *Freeman's Journal* in 1907. Laracy was a bitter enemy of MacBride and as such his comments need to be treated with caution. Moreover he was soon to be captured by the British so he had no direct knowledge of the brigade's activities in the closing months of its existence. None the less he is correct in so much as the old united brigade of 150 to 200 did fracture in June 1900. The reasons for this were not so much the divisions within the unit but rather the circumstances of war: for the Irish brigade, like the Boer army, was now in retreat and defeat stared them in the face.

The day Lord Roberts crossed the Vaal river into the Transvaal Republic, Teddy Luther made a cryptic entry in his diary:

> Everything is Ireland in our Brigade, eg Pat O'Grady, when he told the prisoners [*sic*]. The ambulance corps and their supplies taken by Lynch, of the Second Irish Brigade. [Sat, 26 May 1900][1]

The concept of rapid retreat was not popular with the Irish lads and there was much grumbling, swearing and time-wasting when they were ordered back to the Klip river defences on Sunday, 27 May. Here, on 28 and 29 May, some of the brigade took part in the last-ditch attempt to hold the British back from entering Johannesburg. Here also were Lynch and the rump of his commando. But not all Blake's men were present.

The story was that MacBride and a dozen or so men had got lost on the night of Monday, 28 May. They included brigaders Harold, Hutchinson, Luther and Ryan. Running into Captain Theron and his famous scouts, they joined that unit for the retreat into Johannesburg – 'two splendid days' sniping'.

But many of the Irish were not prepared to accept even the most basic rules of military discipline and even this small group split up as they crossed the Bonanza mine dumps and entered Johannesburg from the south. There was another factor, too, which led now to desertions, both among MacBride's men and among Blake's at Baragwanath. There was the pull of relatives in Johannesburg as well as the desire to hide their 'little valuables and possessions'. With the distinctive 'dum-dum-dum' noise of the Maxim-Nordenfelt gun in their ears, many of the Irish Transvaal Brigade quietly slipped into the sidestreets of the Fordsburg suburb. Others drifted aimlessly around the empty town which had once been their home.

Tom Byrne, Mickey Dalton, James Harold, Pat Quinn and a few others went to see the nuns at the convent in Jeppestown. They were invited in for tea, but rifle fire not far distant made them move on, except for Dalton. He was chatting away with the sisters when the British army arrived. It is said the sisters got him away, but he seems to have been picked up not long afterwards.

And Dalton was not alone on the trains which would soon steam through the highveld packed with Boer prisoners of war. Some of the Irish lads were arrested by the British immediately they occupied the town. Others were tracked down over the following weeks by Military Intelligence. We do not know the names all of those interned at this time, but of the thirty-seven Irish brigaders who are known to have been rounded up by the British, twenty-seven were captured in the Johannesburg-Heidelberg-Pretoria area between late May and early June 1900. Of these twenty-seven Irish men, one was released, one, Bob McGibbon, was sent to St Helena and nineteen were transported to Ceylon; we do not know where the remaining six were sent.

The one brigader who was released was the diminutive Father van Hecke. On his release he jumped on a bicycle and set off to cycle the eighty kilometres to Pretoria to catch up with the brigade.[2] The names of the Irish brigaders captured at this time included:

| | |
|---|---|
| James Bain | James Laracy |
| Frank Connolly | Frank Lary |
| Mickey Dalton | Benedict Leeus |
| 'Prof' Duffy | Paddy Lennon |
| Frank Dunlop | John Lovely |
| Michael Dunville | Frank McDermott |
| — Gaynor | James P. McElroy (Lynch's commando) |
| James Harold | Jacobus McFighe |
| Arthur Kingsman | Bob McGibbon |

Albertus Meintjes (Lynch's commando)   — Thompson
Pierce Murphy                            Joe Tully
William O'Connor             Father Alphonse van Hecke
Frank O'Reilly                   Butch Wilson
Edward Slater

When Blake had crossed the Vaal he had been given direct and firm orders by Botha not to destroy property, be it mine installations, telegraph wires or railways.[3] This undoubtedly annoyed Blake greatly and he seems to have passed rapidly through Johannesburg and set up camp near Irene, south of Pretoria, where he fell in with Captain Carl Reichmann, the United States military attaché. In May and June 1900 Colonel Blake never seems to have been far away from various military attachés and one gets the distinct impression that he rather liked the company of such cognoscenti.[4]

Not all the Irish, however, wanted to listen to their Boer general. Some of the Irish brigade were also members of Judge Kock's band who were determined to destroy the Robinson mine and who were prevented from doing so only after a scuffle between Kock and Commandant Krause.

Some 'commandeering' was undertaken in Johannesburg and a group of Irish were in that 'band of desperate men' who were determined to 'leave no Johannesburg remaining for Lord Roberts to enter'. So despite the local armistice arranged to allow the Boers to vacate the town for Roberts, street fighting did take place. Ironically, the Irish, including probably Arthur Lynch, found themselves up against hardened Australian troops in the Barnato Park part of the town.[5] In the now-classic work, *With the flag to Pretoria*, H.W. Wilson firmly blamed the Irish as the chief obstacle in Roberts 'twenty-four–hour delay in entering the city of gold'.[6]

The town was nearly encircled by British troops when a Boer horseman appeared in a cloud of dust and shouted at the Irish to clear out quickly through the only escape corridor open. So it was that they shot their way out of Johannesburg through Orange Grove – 'I left by one end of the street as the British troops came in at the other.' Both brigades, of course, later claimed to have been the last to vacate the town.

On the road to Pretoria MacBride and Lynch met. Both were battle weary, MacBride leading Fenian Boy. They exchanged a greeting and parted for ever.

For Lynch the war was all but over. He was already ill with an attack of 'quinsy' – as he recalled later, 'every bone in my body creaking as we entered the capital'. Here he was visited by Dr Leach, who had served with

Lynch's commando the previous month. He was put to bed and fed on oranges, a rare enough thing to find in Pretoria with the British on the doorstep. Lynch claims that he recovered quickly but, having consulted 'with what was left of my troop', gave them some money and set off for the border with Mozambique.[7]

As with most of Lynch's actions in South Africa, there was even controversy about this retreat. A statement made after the war, probably by Andy Higgins of Blake's commando, claimed that Lynch had deserted and was caught by Higgins in the bushveld of the far eastern Transvaal. Higgins claimed Lynch told him he was going on a mission to Europe for the Boer government. Higgins cabled State Secretary Reitz, who denied this but instructed Higgins to let Lynch go.

The problem with this story is that it was meant to have happened when the Boer headquarters was at Waterval Boven, which would put the date as early September 1900. That being the case where had Lynch been since Pretoria fell three months earlier? What is more credible is Higgins' statement that Lynch wired Reitz from Lourenço Marques asking for his fare home. Reitz did not reply but was reported as saying, 'We are not beaten yet. Why should he want to run away?'

Lynch was not the only person connected with Ireland returning home at that time. When some of the Irish militia forces arrived back in Dublin in June 1900, the magazine *Irish Society* published an 'Ode of welcome' which is thought to have been written by St John Gogarty.[8] Soon Dublin was abuzz with the 'Ode', for it proved to be an acrostic, the first letter of every line making up the phrase, 'The whores will be busy':

> The Gallant Irish yeoman
>     Home from the war has come,
> Each victory gained o'er foeman,
>     Why should our bards be dumb?
>
> How shall we sing their praises
>     Or glory in their deeds,
> Renowned their worth amazes,
>     Empire their prowess needs.
>
> So to Old Ireland's hearts and homes
>     We welcome now our own brave boys
> In cot and hall; 'neath lordly domes
> Love's heroes share once more our joys.

Love is the Lord of all just now,
    Be he the husband, lover, son,
Each dauntless soul recalls the vow
    By which not fame, but love was won.

United now in fond embrace
    Salute with joy each well-loved face.
Yeoman, in women's hearts you hold the place.

Knocklong      J.R.S.

## THE FALL OF JERUSALEM

The activities of the Irish brigade in and around Pretoria are only slightly less confusing than its exploits in Johannesburg. MacBride and his men met up with Blake's men. Blake himself at first flitted about between Eerste Fabrieke, Irene and Pretoria.

The brigade's wagons seem to have been left at Eerste Fabrieke, to the east of the capital. It was here also on 31 May that Blake took his men to some kopjes where he was convinced the British would soon break through. Luther comments:

> We were foolish enough to follow his [Blake's] advice and we were led another of those famous wild goose chases of his. Camped on a farm. The Colonel had a bottle of whisky and that made it all right with the men.

From there the brigade moved south of Pretoria in a desultory manner around Irene station and along the Six Mile Spruit. It was here that Teddy Luther was amazed to see fifty vultures ('assvogels') feasting on the carcass of a dead horse. He shot into the boiling mass of birds.

For a number of days the brigade was divided. MacBride teamed up with Commandant Blignaut and he and three others broke into a hotel which had closed down and slept there. Luther spent a comfortable night in a house attended by an African groom and an Indian servant who cooked his dinner and waited at table.

MacBride was worried about the safety of the brigade's flag as Reitz had left town when the government had moved east on 2 June. At gunpoint he and some of the lads ordered the English-speaking telegraphist to track down Reitz and find out about the flag. After a few hours, the reply came: 'Tell Major MacBride make his mind easy. I have his flag safe.'

Some commandeering, especially of wagons, was done. In fact, this was not strictly legal: the permission given to the Irish brigade to commandeer by Special Commandant Schutte was an informal arrangement and had no legal foundation.[9] However, with the Boer government entrained for Machadodorp and the British only a few kilometres away, no one was going to argue with gun-toting Irishmen.

Someone not engaged in commandeering was Colonel Blake. He led a rather surreal existence in the Grand Hotel in central Pretoria between Friday, 1, and Monday, 4 June. He was already well known there, as were many of the Irish troops. But now things were different. The management was worried about who would pay the bills. And liquor, usually freely available at the Grand, was becoming difficult to get. Unless, of course, you were a foreign journalist. And Blake was very friendly with foreign journalists.

With his cravat, black coat, breeches, long boots and sjambok held in his right hand (his injured arm), the tall, long-haired, blue-eyed American was an impressive figure. Fred Unger of the Philadelphia *Press* had heard the colonel was in town and, approaching an Irishman outside the Grand Hotel, asked where he was. 'Insoid gettin' his grub,' came the reply. And inside there the colonel was, entertaining two wild-looking members of his commando. As always, Blake was charming and the two men hit it off. Unger remarked on how the Boers idolized Blake and what a great memory for names and faces he had. He continued:

> His manners were those of a thorough man of the world, equally at home in all societies, but he affects a carelessness of dress and rather boisterous manner which makes him very popular.

Blake's jokes could be rough enough. Concern for the situation of a woman in the hotel after the British arrived was discussed, Blake ventured the opinion: 'They [the British] may be brutes, but her face is sufficient protection.'

The earl of Rosslyn (*Daily Mail* and *Sphere*) also befriended Blake in the hotel and was pleased with the good copy he received. Rosslyn and another aristocratic journalistic, Lord Cecil Manners, were technically prisoners of war but were treated as their status dictated, an honour not bestowed on the Hon. Winston Churchill. Blake claimed it was the Irish brigade which had captured Rosslyn and Manners at Elandsfontein near Johannesburg. Blake also said the two were 'not prejudiced and thick-headed, as you generally find Englishmen of their class'.

Blake did Rosslyn and a fellow journalist a considerable service. With the Boer government gone, the journalists could not receive the necessary accreditation to allow them to travel east with the retreating army. Blake spoke to some friends, possibly including Gillingham as he was still in town. The accreditation came through, though Unger was greatly surprised and amused to find that on his document he had been made a member of the 'Irsche Corps'.[10]

So the journalists and Blake chatted and looked out over Pretoria from the balcony of the Grand Hotel, where British officers would stand a week later. It was not just of the war that they spoke. Blake told Rosslyn of his love of Carlyle and his dislike of the novel. These were probably some of the most contented days in the life of the American southerner. On the morning of Monday, 4 June, he came to say goodbye to Rosslyn. He gave the British peer a bottle of whisky. Blake had no doubt got it from Unger, who was generous with drink, but the thought was there. Colonel Blake had hardly left Rosslyn's room in the hotel 'when the sound of distant cannon was distinctly audible.'

Unger's farewell with Blake was equally poignant. Mounting his fine hunter, Blake waved to the journalist:

> and his white handkerchief about his neck showed up brightly in the sun as he turned a distant corner, and I had my last look at that gallant officer and soldier of fortune, Colonel Blake, formerly of West Point and the United States army.

## MAC BRIDE'S BRIGADE

There is no evidence to substantiate the claim that Irishmen fell into the hands of the British in Pretoria because they were drunk after having helped loot the government stores.[11] In fact, few of the brigade seem to have been captured in Pretoria. Their departure was, however, somewhat chaotic, with small groups of men setting off on various trains bound for Middelburg or even further to Machadodorp.

Blake had put the numbers of brigaders in the city at 140. MacBride said there were 110, sixty of whom were dismounted. Even MacBride's figures may be a slight exaggeration. It is, however, known that by now a majority of the brigade had lost their mounts. MacBride was critical of the Irish-Americans for not looking after their horses properly and this is probably true. Country boys would have more of an affinity with horses than would city lads. It is said that some of the Irish-Americans left their horses at Pretoria railway station, an indication perhaps that they had had enough and thought it was time to go home. Some horses and wagons, however, were entrained and proved of great value in the months to come.

The last Boer train out of Pretoria carried the journalist Fred Unger as well as Major MacBride and fifteen of his men. As they steamed south of the pretty suburb of Sunnyside and then out east, MacBride was in no mood to run away. Indeed, at Van der Merwe station, not far beyond Eerste Fabrieke, he suddenly announced that the men would get off the train. Not surprisingly, they had other ideas and a nasty scene ensued, with MacBride getting off the train by himself 'in disgust'. Off the train steamed and the fifteen men were punished by spending a very cold night in a railway siding in Bronkhorstspruit. Although one source claims it was at Machadadorp, it was probably here at Bronkhorstspruit on that early morning in June 1900 that the famous gold-train, containing the 'Kruger millions', pulled up. The Irish lads had made a great bonfire of railway sleepers. They gave the grim Boer officials on the train some coffee and rusks. The train then steamed off and the gold vanished. Given the impecuniosity of the brigaders in later life, it is reasonable to conclude that the Irish were not responsible for South Africa's greatest mystery – the disappearance of the 'Kruger millons'.

Next morning, 6 June, the Irish caught a different train to Middelburg, where a search was made for Captain McCallum who had gone missing. He turned up some time, but when is not known. Then from Middelburg it was a long journey by train on to Machadodorp. Many of the men arrived drunk. However, it was here that the brigade seems to have regrouped somewhat. This was undoubtedly due to MacBride appearing on the scene. Colonel Blake was nowhere to be found, so on Thursday, 7 June 1900, Major John MacBride took command of the Irish Transvaal Brigade, a position he would hold for nearly four months.[12]

We now know that Colonel Blake had given up on the Irish brigade and ridden out of Pretoria and joined his old friends in the Transvaal state artillery. In particular, Blake was friendly with Major Pretorius. Blake seems to have been allocated one of the Long Tom cannons and Pretorius the other. Certainly, at the battle of Bergendal Farm on 27 August this was how the two guns were divided. And it was during this battle that the two men and their cannon were separated. It was not until 1 October 1900 that

Blake finally caught up with Pretorius and his twenty-four artillery men on the Olifants river. However, when Blake was still in the eastern Transvaal 'our late Colonel' would occasionally run into his old unit. They saw him east of Balmoral on 23 June and again with Commandant Trichardt on 14 July near Silver Mines in the direction of Springs.

In his memoirs Blake skates over his leaving the commando and indeed asserts that he later discussed its future with President Kruger. This has to be taken with a pinch of salt. There is no other evidence that Blake had either any interest in or interfered with the running of the brigade after 7 June. It is not improbable that Blake regarded MacBride as being limited and conventional. The two men were very different. In his 411-page memoir Blake mentions MacBride only once and then in passing. This, of course, does not imply that there was a rift between the two men or indeed that MacBride disliked Blake and the two men seem to have had no problems in sharing a tent when in Natal. We do know that Blake had his supporters in the brigade. The Irish-Americans must have been drawn to their fellow-countryman and of the original brigaders Tom Byrne had no doubts that Colonel Blake had 'a most loveable character'.[13]

Blake always said that he would not be captured alive and that he would fight to the end. Perhaps by June 1900 he recognized that the Irish brigade would soon have to leave the country and that it would be best for himself to be attached to another unit.

## BACK FROM WHENCE THEY CAME

For a while Major MacBride restored morale in what was left of the Irish brigade. It seems as if with Blake gone, the officers could work more closely with each other. Captain O'Connor and Lieutenant Ryan were in charge of the men without horses – the footsloggers as the brigaders called them. MacBride and Captain McCallum had the more exciting task of leading the mounted troop. McCallum was not very popular but this is probably because he tried to enforce discipline. MacBride obviously thought highly of him. On 6 July a man named Molloy was elected the second major of the Irish brigade, but nothing is known either of him or of the reason for this election. Another mystery is the appearance of Captain Oates on Bronkhorstspruit station with 'a hundred' of the Irish brigade some time in June or July. It is possible that he fled Johannesburg ahead of the British army and with what remained of Lynch's brigade 'rejoined' Blake's outfit. Certainly Oates would have been a good man to have back in the corps.[14]

[126]

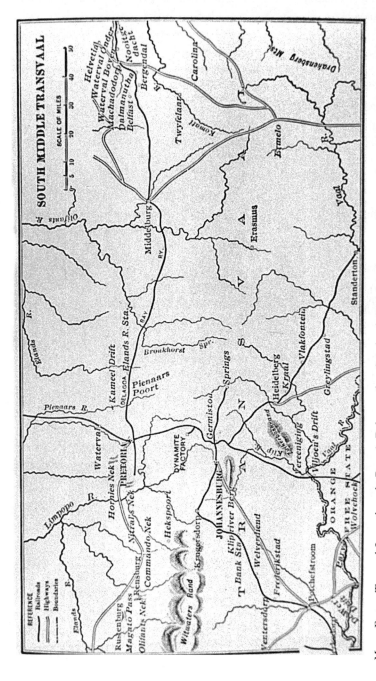

Map 4: Eastern Transvaal. It was along the Pretoria-Delagoa railway line that the Irish brigade retreated between June and September 1900: through Bronkhorstspruit, Middelburg and Belfast, and then over the escarpment and down to the lowveld and across the wild country to the Mozambique border. Great hardships were endured, men were killed, morale was low and discipline weak. Here also in the eastern Transvaal later fought the Irish bitterenders who stayed on when the Irish brigade disbanded. (Davitt, *The Boer fight for freedom*.)

Once at Machadodorp, MacBride seems to have divided his force. Those without horses were left in the area. It looks as if at least some of them were seconded for guard duty at the famous prisoner-of-war camp at Nooitgedacht which was not far off. George Moody from Ballarena, captured at Lindley along with Lieutenant Craig and other Imperial Yeomanry men, records in his diary for 8 August 1900: 'Most of the Johannesburg police who guarded us have been sent to the front and replaced by a rabble guard chiefly Irish American who only want a chance to shoot into us'.[15] Moody also records the day that James Craig, 'the best officer we have', was put over the border into Mozambique by the Boers. Craig had an injured ear.

MacBride and the mounted brigaders travelled back along the railway towards Pretoria. And far back they went, even to Eerste Fabrieke just outside the capital. Near here, just south of the railway, the brigade fought in the inconclusive battle of Diamond Hill on 11 and 12 June.

From then until early July the Irish brigade moved around in a bewildering fashion from place to place, but usually in the Elandsrivier-Bronkhorstspruit area. At one time or another they were with the Fordsburg, Krugersdorp or Johannesburg police (ZARPs) commandos. There was some skirmishing with British patrols and brandwacht or pickets were sent out. Perhaps the greatest worry was that of obtaining food, which was short. On 16 June Luther admitted the 'main concern now food'.

The brigade had a strange diet. This included crackers and jelly or figs, chicken, eggs, mealies and mealie pap, rice, a box of biscuits looted from a 'Hebrew store', cans of herring or meat, freshly slaughtered oxen, occasionally sugar and 'horrible coffee' (perhaps mixed with chicory). The chickens were usually stolen from farms, once from a destitute woman. It is said that one brigader gave his horse away for a feed. One feast was described as follows:

> our mess of ten men received nine tins of milk, five tins of butter, and 3 of syrup ... baked bread and plastered on butter and syrupped bread, and milk and coffee so that no one was able to partake of the five chickens we had captured this day.

Unger claimed the brigade on one occasion stole chickens from a wooden building and then used the wood of the building to cook the fowls.[16] Attempts to shoot passing springbok were unsuccessful.

A fourteen-year-old Boer girl recorded in her diary what her father had told her of the Irish brigade passing through Bronkhorstspruit. The account is no doubt exaggerated but it merits repetition:

1. John MacBride and Arthur Griffith in South Africa before the war. This is the only known photograph of Sinn Fein's founder, Arthur Griffith, in South Africa. John MacBride is leaning against the post. The photograph was probably taken in the Johannesburg area in early 1898.

2. Solomon Gillingham (face turned from camera) in front of Benburb House, Pretoria, May 1900. The wealthy friend of Paul Kruger, Gillingham was the shadowy figure behind the Irish Transvaal Brigade. In August 1900 he was arrested by the British and transported to Ceylon as a prisoner of war.

3. Irish uitlanders march in Johannesburg to join the new Irish commando. On the flag is written, 'Remember Michelstown', a reference to the 1887 attack on a police barracks in Ireland. This sketch appeared in *The Graphic* and *Leslie's Weekly*. *The Graphic* caption began, 'Traitors: The Irish Brigade serving with the Boers'. It went on to speak of the brigaders as 'the worst sweepings of Johannesburg' and as 'all loafers', a statement somewhat belied by the illustration.

4. Colonel John Blake, commander of the 'Irish Corps'. This colourful American had seen action in the 'Indian wars' as a US cavalry officer. Looking like Buffalo Bill, he was described as being, 'half wild, yet gentle ... the type of adventurer one reads of in a novel, yet never expects to meet'.

5. The officer corps of Blake's commando. Despite its small muster (*c.*150) Blake's commando had a large number of officers (28 known names). Here eleven officers pose, Blake centre in white jacket and MacBride on the right with revolver and rifle. The situation is probably behind Pepworth Hill outside Ladysmith in Natal.

6. The first Irish Transvaal Brigade behind Pepworth Hill. This brigade photograph was taken when the American writer Webster Davis visited Blake's commando in Natal. Davis is central in dark waistcoat. The commando saw action in three war zones – Natal, the Orange Free State and finally in the retreat across the Transvaal.

7. Colonel Blake (left) and Major MacBride on horseback with two African grooms standing to attention. The plight of the black population was not an issue for the Irish brigaders; they were fighting for the Boers against their common enemy.

# Le Petit Journal

Le Petit Journal
CHAQUE JOUR 5 CENTIMES

SUPPLÉMENT ILLUSTRÉ

Le Supplément Illustré
CHAQUE SEMAINE 5 CENTIMES

Huit pages : CINQ centimes

ABONNEMENTS

Dixième année          DIMANCHE 31 DÉCEMBRE 1899          Numéro 476

## EN IRLANDE
### Manifestation contre M. Chamberlain

8. Irish pro-Boer riot outside Trinity College, Dublin. Nationalist Ireland became fervently pro-Boer during the South African war. Here a French periodical (*Le Petit Journal* of 31 December 1899) portrays a Dublin crowd, complete with Boer flag, protesting on 18 December 1899 over the awarding of an honorary degree to Joseph Chamberlain, the British colonial secretary widely believed in Ireland to have engineered the conflict. The riot was precipitated by James Connolly, Maud Gonne, Arthur Griffith and John O'Leary appearing in an open wagon. 'Up the Boers, up the Republic', shouted Connolly.

9. Michael Davitt on the highveld. Michael Davitt left the House of Commons ostensibly in protest over British hostility to the Boers. He travelled to the Transvaal, where he reported for the *Freeman's Journal* and collected material for his now-classic book, *The Boer fight for freedom*. He also kept in correspondence with the Irish parliamentarian John Dillon, who strongly advocated the Boer cause at Westminster.

10. The flag of the first Irish Transvaal Brigade. This flag was sent to Blake's commando by the Irish Transvaal Committee, thanks mainly to the efforts of Maud Gonne. It was one of several the commando had, but was considered to be the main brigade emblem. It served with the commando until they were forced into rapid retreat, when MacBride sent it to State Secretary Reitz for safe keeping. After the war it was returned to MacBride who treasured it greatly. Before he was executed in 1916 MacBride instructed, 'Mind the flag.' Today the flag is on display in the National Museum of Ireland.

11. Long Tom on the retreat north through Natal. For over four months the Irish commando successfully protected one of the great French 'Long Tom' siege guns. They guarded it and other artillery pieces on Pepworth Hill, and risked life and limb by supplying the gunners with shells. 'To get my guns, the English will first have to kill my Irish troops,' said Commandant Trichardt.

12. Captain Oates (on horseback) and Colonel Lynch. Lynch was something of a maverick commando leader. This bookish colonial was strongly disliked by MacBride and many of his associates who saw him as a Johnny-come-lately. Yet such were the tensions in Blake's commando that some of its members, including the able captains Oates and Mitchell, joined Lynch's outfit.

13. The second Irish Transvaal Brigade. This second Irish commando was formed in 1900 by the Irish-Australian Arthur Lynch. It saw action in the mountains of the Biggarsberg in May 1900, but disintegrated in June after an existence of about three months. There was bitter rivalry between the two Irish commandos.

14. The Irish-American Ambulance Corps. In April 1900 some forty-seven Irish-Americans, mostly from Chicago, arrived in the Transvaal and were met by fellow-American John Blake (marked in the photo with a cross). All but a handful removed their Red Cross armbands, took up rifles and joined Blake's commando.

15. Irish-Americans meet President Kruger. The newly arrived Irish-American 'Ambulance' Corps is introduced to Kruger in front of the president's house in Pretoria.

16. Bridge blowing in the Orange Free State. Not all the railway bridges in the Orange Free State were blown up by the Irish brigade, but many of them were. The Irish men in the corps assigned to this duty were called the 'Wreckers Corps'. Having worked on the gold mines, many of the Irish were expert in handling explosives.

17. Field guns of the Transvaal State Artillery in the Orange Free State. To read some of the war accounts, one would imagine that the Irish guarded only one of the Long Toms. In fact, a number of lesser Transvaal State Artillery field guns were spread out across Pepworth Hill outside Ladysmith. In May 1900 it was only these light artillery pieces which were with the Irish on their retreat across the Orange Free State.

18. Irish brigaders making Irish stew. As the Irish commando retreated across the eastern Transvaal, increasingly the men suffered from shortages – horses, clothes and even food. Here a pot of Irish stew is cooked.

19. Bitter retreat: the eastern Transvaal. By July 1900 many of the Irish brigaders were 'footsloggers'. Here a group of the men had hitched a ride on the top of a Boer train retreating east along the line towards Lourenço Marques.

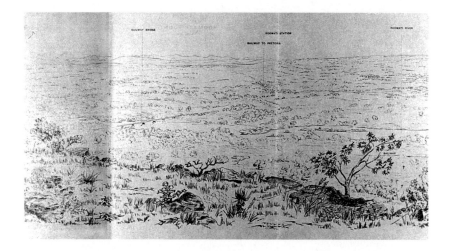

20. Komatipoort: the end of the retreat. At this beautiful spot in the lowveld the Irish Transvaal Brigade disbanded. Some brigaders stayed on as bitterenders to fight in the guerrilla war, but Major MacBride and most brigaders destroyed their stores and equipment and on 23 September 1900 boarded a train which steamed across this bridge (centre left) into Mozambique and Portuguese territory. The next day the British cavalry was in Komatipoort.

21. Boer (1916) rifles. These rifles were captured by the British army in Dublin after the failed 1916 insurrection. On their butts are carved Boer slogans and portraits. How they got to Dublin remains a mystery.

They [the Irish] had weathered the fortunes of war since its outbreak and were tired, worn-out, half-starved and discouraged. After months of roving about, their clothes were torn, shabby and dirty ... The first thing that the Irishmen did after their arrival ... was to rush into our kitchen and steal all the edibles obtainable. Father was cooking a chicken and one of these hungry fellows ran to the stove and seeing the pot containing the fowl and not knowing that it was boiling, plunged his hand into it and gave a yell ... Then they broke open the kitchen cupboards and stole forks, knives, plates, spoons etc. They went to the dining-room where one poor man licked the sugar basin although there was not a particle of sugar in it.[17]

A warehouse was robbed in the town and the Irish suspected, but no proof was found against them.

There were other problems and distresses. On Wednesday, 11 July, near Donkerhoek Teddy Luther recorded a dramatic skirmish with the British:

We dismounted and another shrapnel exploded not twenty feet away. My hat falls off my head and 'Shorty Kelly' [his horse] trembles like a leaf. The commandant then orders us to get behind a steep rock. I mount my horse shouting to Major MacBride, who had been behind and was only then coming up, 'We are going to put the horses behind the rock.' Riding down we had to cross some marshy ground, and I noticed how my horse shivered violently and breathed hard, and I thought it the effect of fright from bursting shells, which were being continually sent over and around us by the Khakis. Our guns had gone out of action as the English had got the range and were firing splendidly. Behind the hill I dismounted and still 'Shorty Kelly' trembled. He had never acted in that way under fire before, and on calling attention to his condition, I was told he was sick from mealies and that I had better take him out of fire. The English were now sending shrapnel over the part of the kopje behind which we were. I slowly walked the horse out of range towards the camp, and meeting an ambulance on the road I questioned a surgeon what I could do for the horse. He advised salt. At a winkel [shop] I secured a bottle of salt, and in camp I forced it down 'Shorty's' mouth. When I took the blanket off I discovered that a shrapnel ball had passed through the blanket and had entered 'Shorty's' side where, when mounted, my leg would be. There was no blood running out but he must have been bleeding internally, for soon after he stretched himself and suffered considerably, so I got a comrade to put a ball through his brain to stop the agony.[18]

By late July 1900 the British advance was at last under way and again the Irish brigade were in the rearguard, first to Balmoral and then back across the highveld to Middelburg.[19] Here in Arthur Griffith's 'world-forgotten dorp' his newspaper was no longer printed. In the pitch dark and with the rain beating down, MacBride and Luther set out from the empty house that the brigade had occupied in search of food for themselves and their horses. All the shops were closed and, drenched to the skin, the two brigaders entered the Masonic Hotel where all to be had were two tins of herrings.

The retreat was soon on again and under fire, losing one brigader, the Irish made it to Wonderfontein and then to Belfast, where a quarrel broke out over who should get some overcoats and other clothing found. Tempers were easily frayed now. One morning a German in the Irish brigade went for Luther with a rifle. The men disarmed him but the two then had a scrap 'for a minute'. A week later 'McQuiggan' [McGuigan?] was foolish enough to have a fight with the brigade's African cook. And there was trouble also back with the brigaders near Machadodorp. An undated letter from Commandant Blignaut to MacBride from Dalmanutha contained the following:

> I am very sorry to inform you that considering certain men left the positions without your or my orders and when I arrived asked the Captain to tell the men to go out this morning and they point blank refused. So I would be glad if you would make some arrangement to put a stop to such things in future.[20]

MacBride did his best to maintain discipline and indeed to supply his men. A requisition of his dated 2 August 1900 has survived. It included thirty-three pairs of boots, twenty suits, twenty-four hats, one dozen overcoats, two dozen suit underclothes and two dozen pairs of socks. It is doubtful if any of these were forthcoming to the Irish brigade given the desperate state the Boers were in by now.

The same day that McQuiggan attacked the cook, Luther's new horse ran off. That Monday he also saw a train of Boer women and children refugees pass through on the railway. MacBride comments on these refugees, too, and says the Irish made them tea and jollied them up, which is no doubt true.

Tension in the Irish ranks also surfaced three days later when McCallum came under criticism. Luther noted, 'Dissension in the command, and Major MacBride is always willing to sacrifice himself for the name and appearance of the Irish Brigade.'

The good name of the brigade was, however, soon to be confirmed when on 24 August they were surprised at Belfast railway station by a large force of British troops entering the town. Talk of their being surprised because they were drunk is unlikely. What is, however, certain is that the brigade was nearly captured and only after a heated firefight of several hours were the brigaders able to extricate themselves. They did, however, manage to get a wire through to General Viljoen warning of the renewed British advance. Yet again the Irish were the last to vacate a Boer town.[21]

That same Friday Solomon Gillingham was arrested in Pretoria. Within a fortnight he was on board a prison ship en route for the POW camp of Diyatalawa in Ceylon.

Rumours about Gillingham had been current all of August. It was believed he had been arrested and, with a man named Tossel, was to be shot for being implicated in an attempt to blow up the arsenal outside Pretoria. Captain O'Connor of the Irish brigade had suggested to State Secretary Reitz that, if the execution took place, the Boers should give the Irish ten British troops to shoot in reprisal. While President Kruger had vetoed this foolish proposal, it was said that General Botha had warned Lord Roberts of possible reprisals if the men were shot.

It is not unlikely that Gillingham and possibly some of the Irish who had remained in Johannesburg and Pretoria had been involved in the various subversive plots being hatched at the time, the most famous being the Cordua Plot to kidnap Lord Roberts. These schemes led to a general round-up of 'disaffected foreigners' and British subjects who had served on commando. Some 364 people were made prisoners of war and a further 475 were deported. That Gillingham, a burgher in the Commissariat Department in Pretoria, should be sent to Ceylon is significant.[22]

### THE LAST BATTLE

It was a pleasant summer in Ireland in 1900. The sun shone and Irish pro-Boer fever continued unabated.[23] Far away in Africa, however, it was winter and the final chapter of the formal war was about to be concluded. The

British now steadily moved east towards the great escarpment beyond Machadodorp, which divides the rolling grasslands of the highveld from the lush lowveld or bushveld. And with the British army went the men of Military Intelligence, gathering up the discarded and captured papers of the retreating Boer army. When Middelburg was occupied on 20 August, commando lists were discovered. Among these were the names and addresses of eighty-four Irish brigaders (numbers 3301 to 3384). It was not complete but it gave enough material for the military police or the RIC to make a few house calls.[24]

Though the remaining members of the Irish brigade must have realized that the end was close, there was still a fighting spirit in them. In the week before the final great battle, members of the Irish corps were regularly out on brandwacht. On one such patrol east of Belfast, Teddy 'Tottie' Hayes and Teddy Luther came on a British outpost and

> cowered down against a rock shivering like wet dogs and waiting for the time to pass. We could hear the English sentries conversing. Two were to the right and two to the front of us, not more than 300 yards away, but we could not see them without the moon. We could hear the Khakis in the stillness of the night enjoying themselves swearing and singing songs about the Transvaal butchers.[25]

The battle of Bergendal Farm or Dalmanutha took place on 27 August 1900. It was Buller's revenge on Botha. It was also another Irish against Irish fight. The First Inniskilling Fusiliers and the Second Rifle Brigade assaulted a strong position held mainly by the Johannesburg police and the Krugersdorp commando. Blake with a Long Tom was on the Boer side and MacBride and some of his men near the centre of the Boer line. As in Colenso, MacBride had a horse shot from under him and survived. And this time so did his horse, who may well still have been Fenian Boy. A bullet wound made the animal lame and he had to be led off the field of battle. Also taken off the battle field was a brigader with shell shock, from which he died that night in a veld hospital.

The brigade lost two members that day or the next. One was the Irish-American Edward M. Egan and the other was the draper's assistant from Lower O'Connell Street, the 'gallant Jack Mullins'. These losses, however, were nothing compared to the police commando. The ZARPs were said to have lost eighty per cent of their men trying to hold back the British. Given the numbers of the British and the state of the Boer army, a republican defeat was inevitable and many of the Irish lads had to take to their heels, making their way in twos and threes exhausted into Machadodorp that night.

There was little time for rest and the next day, 28 August, the British were in the small town and the Boer government had fled down the escarpment to the village of Nelspruit. As for the Irish, their retreat was slower. This was partly because they were once again going to be with the rearguard and partly because some brigaders stole 'a box of Greek cognac' from an ambulance and became 'beastly drunk'.

On Tuesday, 30 August, the Irish were present when the rankings in the POW camp at Nooitgedacht were released and sent to the British lines. A claim by MacBride is substantiated by Luther. An Irish POW from the Sixth Regiment begged to be allowed to join the Irish brigade and was accepted. Given the precarious state of the Boer cause, this was rather a surprising request but, unlike similar claims made outside Dundee and Ladysmith, this does seem to have happened.[26]

As most of the Boer guns were taken north towards Lydenburg, the Irish brigade was placed under the general command of General Viljoen. There was still skirmishing. On that Tuesday when the POWs were released, a joint Irish-Boer patrol was surprised by British troops between Nooitgedacht and Waterval Onder. When challenged, Mick O'Hara from Limerick shouted, 'Hands up, be damned! Run, corporal, run and warn the boys.' He was immediately shot down but his warning served its purpose and the patrol escaped, though it lost all its horses.[27]

Along the Elandsrivier valley, the Irish brigade retreated. O'Connor and the 'footsloggers' made a hasty retreat, probably by train, down to Nelspruit. O'Connor had a lot of trouble with some of those lads now. As for MacBride and the mounted brigaders, they camped about a kilometre from the Ngodwana river, which runs into the Elandsrivier. Perhaps too late, the Boers began to impose some discipline on their organization. The men were told they would be paid six shillings a day. This was to help those with families to support, but the Irish did not 'like the idea of pay'. Perhaps more relevant, it was also announced that in future looters would be shot.

On Saturday, 1 September, Lord Roberts announced the annexation of the Transvaal. The Irish were back on British soil and were rebels. No doubt this caused some wry comments. The war, of course, was not over and on the Monday an Irish patrol moved back up the Elandsrivier valley to do a bit of sniping near Waterval Onder. Their old friends in the Italian commando were not far off. Indeed, during those final days of the formal war there were upwards of 500 foreigners in the far eastern Transvaal with the Boer forces.

As one section of the British pursued the retreating Boers along the railway line, another under Buller veered north and soon captured Lydenburg, though the ensuing pursuit over the Long Tom Pass was another nightmare for the general. For the Irish, now attached to the Carolina commando, fighting was now on lower, hotter ground in bushveld territory, where wild game was more plentiful. A few miles south of the wood-and-iron railway village of Nelspruit in the beautiful Weltevreden area, another engagement took place on Sunday, 9 September, which is mentioned in *The Times history* of the war:

> Hutton cleared away the last obstacle to Pole-Carew's advance along the railway by taking Kaapsche Hoop, thereby also opening another road to Barberton. Starting from Machadodorp on the eighth [September], he found the Carolina commando, reinforced by some Irish-Americans under Lutter [Luther], strongly positioned at Weltevreden on Pole-Carew's right flank. A vigorous attack by Henry's force, in which 'J' Battery distinguished themselves by their dash and accurate shooting, soon drove back the Boer centre; flank attacks by Brabant's Horse and some Australian Mounted Rifles completed the rout.[28]

Teddy Luther was seriously wounded in this encounter and fell into the hands of the British, who took him back over the escarpment to the military hospital in Machadodorp.

The next day, Monday, Captain O'Connor in Nelspruit wrote to Major MacBride, who was still in the bush with his mounted men. His letter ran as follows:

> I intended going to see [you] but find it impossible.
> When we left you at Waterfall Onder we meant to go back a few stations in hopes to get some articles of clothing as we lost everything. We were told we couldn't get nothing 'till we got to Nelspruit.
> On arriving at Nelspruit we were immediately met by the chief of Police who asked us, or I should say ordered us, to proceed to Komatiepoort as men were urgently needed there.

We are still waiting for the clothing.

About 200 wounded men came also. There is some talk of an expedition but whether they intend taking us along or not I cannot say. We are camped about two miles from the station but the same gang who stayed about the station at Machadodorp are doing the same thing at Komatiepoort. I asked some of them if they would go on guard, they were not satisfied with refusing but insulted me every way they could. The General asked several embarrassing questions about them but for the sake of the Brigade I was loth to say anything against them. I came up here yesterday on business in connection with the boys we left in Pretoria, they are now at Cape Town. Things look very gloomy here at present, the President went away today where we do not know. The rest of the Government is preparing to move.

Capt. Reichman – the American Military Attaché – is going home tomorrow. I think they will soon give up the line so some of our boys are strongly in favour of going home. If the Brigade could be brought together we might be of some use but as we are now I am entirely discouraged if the line is cut we will be without horses, clothing or anything else. Under such circumstances I do not see what use we could be. If you would suggest anything I would be pleased to hear from you as soon as possible.

You will please inform any of the American boys with you the condition of affairs so that they may govern themselves accordingly.

Hoping that affairs are not as bad as they appear to be.[29]

Things were as bad as they seemed. The following day, 11 September, Paul Kruger left the Transvaal and Teddy Luther died in the Machadodorp military hospital. Either in his saddlebag or on his person were two note-books, one completely filled as a diary and the second only partially. The first volume ran from the day he left New York, 28 February 1900, to his fighting retreat in the eastern Transvaal on 13 August. The second volume runs from 15 August until 6 September 1900, three days before his capture.

The history of Luther's diaries is unknown, but one can surmise that its interest as an everyday account within the enemy camp, complete with admissions of thieving and drunkenness, was immediately recognized by British Military Intelligence, who saw to its prompt publication in a single volume. We do know that the finished printed version was in the Intelligence Division of the War Office in London on 19 November 1900, a mere sixty days after Luther's death and even before Paul Kruger arrived in France.[30]

O'Connor appears to have left for Lourenço Marques on Saturday, 15 September, with the intention of preparing for the arrival of the brigade. He may have then returned to the Transvaal to help with the evacuation.

On the Sunday MacBride was at the remote railway halt of Hectorspruit about thirty kilometres from the frontier. Here the major was given several testimonials from Boer leaders. One, in Dutch, from State Secretary Reitz simply ran:

> In the name of the Government of the South African Republic, I hereby express my hearty thanks to Major MacBride and the Irish Brigade for the valuable service rendered to our country during the war.

It should be noted that it is MacBride and not Blake mentioned in the document, a confirmation that, despite what Blake implied later, by this stage he had broken his links with the Irish corps. It is also clear that if Reitz had the brigade flag with him, MacBride asked him to keep it for the time being. However, it is unlikely that the state secretary was carrying the Irish emblem around the veld with him.

The second testimonial, also in Dutch, was from the head of the Boer army, Commandant-General Louis Botha and the Irish brigade's commanding officer, General Ben Viljoen. This document, also addressed to MacBride, reads:

> Hereby we have much pleasure in expressing our deepest gratitude towards you and the Irish Brigade for all the military service rendered to us during the past twelve months, in which we were engaged in a war against Great Britain.
> We appreciate very highly the assistance which you have so sincerely rendered to us during this war. We wish you and your men a hearty farewell on your return voyage.

A list of Irish brigaders was also drawn up, probably for the Boer authorities at the frontier. Sadly, this list does not seem to have survived.

The next day, Monday, 17 September, General Viljoen scribbled a note of introduction for MacBride to General Coetzee at Komatipoort. When the Irish brigade, or what was left of them, arrived at the frontier is not certain. Conan Doyle states that from that Monday trains crammed with 'homeless burghers and with the mercenaries of many nations' arrived and passed over into Portuguese East Africa.[31] Pole-Carew and his troops were in Hectorspruit on the Saturday. At Komatipoort thoughts of a last stand were voiced, but it was obviously pointless; besides the Portuguese had indicated that they did not want fighting up against their border.

The railway siding of Komatipoort was near where the Crocodile River and the Komati river met. Just beyond the confluence of these two rivers on the Komati was the great iron railway bridge. The fever-ridden country around was wild and beautiful. The crossing of this bridge by John MacBride and perhaps as few as twenty comrades on Sunday, 23 September 1900, marked the end of the Irish Transvaal Brigade. The Irish corps had existed for 375 days.

Behind the Komati bridge, not many kilometres away, was the British cavalry, and at the railway siding a gigantic blaze sent smoke pluming into the bushveld sky as hundreds of railway trucks and provisions were destroyed.

Also behind MacBride's railway coach as it steamed over the metal bridge were the six remaining brigade horses, the remnants of an original complement of possibly 300. One of the six surviving horses was MacBride's. Let us hope it was Fenian Boy.

# CHAPTER TEN

# Bitterend

## OCTOBER 1900 – MAY 1902

Major MacBride and the Irish brigaders arrived in Lourenço Marques to find that they were to be interned by the Portuguese authorities. A large camp had been established a little way out of town where the commandos were to be sent and guarded.[1] From there some of the men, including the Irish, were transferred to an old ship lying in Delagoa Bay. Tom Byrne recalled what happened:

> After a few weeks' semi-starvation on board the vessel, we were given the option of remaining prisoners or of going to Europe or any country we wished, until the war would be over. We elected to sail for Europe and America.[2]

It was Byrne's belief that it was the British who were behind the transfer of the Irish onto the prison hulk. This may well be so.

In the end it was the Boer representative in Lourenço Marques who, prompted by General Botha, came to the rescue. The men were each given a small sum of money and their passage overseas was paid for them.[3] They left Africa on the SS *Styri* bound for Trieste. From there most of the brigaders made their way to Hamburg, where they boarded the *Furst Bismarck* for the United States of America.

## THE IRISH BITTERENDERS

Michael Davitt's comment that some Irish did not join the Irish brigade 'but have the good sense to remain with their Boer Officers' was fortunately made in private.[4] How many of these less ethnic-conscious Irish there were is not known; Davitt's estimate of 1,200 is too high. We know that the Barberton, Fordsburg, Heidelberg, Lydenburg, Kroonstad and Pretoria commandos all had Irishmen in their ranks. And although Colonel

Blake was refused permission to join General Smuts' famous expedition into the Cape, as mentioned in a previous chapter, two Irishmen named Lang and Gallagher were on that adventure.[5] Theron's scouts had a few Irish members, including an Irish-American quartermaster called O'Brien.

With the main bulk of the Irish brigade now out of the country and the guerrilla phase of the war begun, some ex-Irish brigade members remained behind as bitterenders. We do not know how many, perhaps no more than twenty or twenty-five. Another Irishman who stayed behind was Dr Walsh. At the end of October 1900 he was at Ottoshoop near Lichtenburg in the western Transvaal. He was still attached to an ambulance. Writing to 'My dear Pat', he says:

> Tell Kathleen Mavourneen I have several curios and relics to send her when the war is over – one a Catholic Prayer Book called 'Catholic Picking' I am sure she will value as it has a history to it. I wrote her name in it the other day whilst we were being bombarded and the shells were falling within a few hundred yards of the ambulance and I was watching for wounded to be brought to me ... I shall be glad if you will kindly send my mother forty pounds (£40) of the money you owe me as I have absolutely no chance of remitting to her. I will make everything right with you when postal communication is re-established.[6]

The bulk of the Irish brigaders who remained behind in the Transvaal joined the Johannesburg commando of General Ben Viljoen, where already a number of Irish and Irish-Americans had found a home. The newcomers included the following:

| | |
|---|---|
| Lieutenant Charles Coetzee | Captain Malcolm McCallum |
| Jim French | John McGlew |
| Mike Halley | Lieutenant Malan |
| Mike Hannifin | Jerry O'Leary |
| Dick Hunt | Mike Ryan |
| Joe Kennedy | Sergeant Joe Wade |

Colonel John Blake could be added to this list, but the truth is Blake flitted around from unit to unit and was most at home with Major J.L. Pretorius and the state artillery, or what was left of it. When Pretorius was captured by the British in December 1901, Blake was devastated: 'Now that he had been captured, I felt very lonely, and took but little pleasure in every-day life.'[7]

The activities of these Irish bitterenders centred mainly around the eastern Transvaal, the Pretoria-to-Komatipoort railway line and occasional sorties up to the northern Transvaal. Blake had retreated north from the railway line in late August 1900. The report that he had set off on horseback for German South West Africa [Namibia] was false, though the claim that he had a large price on his head at the time was one he himself asserted even after the war had concluded.[8]

Blake caught up with Major Pretorius and the state artillery near what he terms the Devil's Pulpit on the Olifants river. From there they moved north into the lowveld to the tiny and remote settlement of Leydsdorp and then moved west to Pietersburg, where they arrived on Sunday, 7 October 1900. By the end of November, Blake had come full circle and was back with the Irish and Johannesburg commando at Renosterkop, some twenty-five kilometres north of Balmoral and the railway line. It was here on 29 November that an advance by Major-General Paget was driven back.

A month later, on the night of 28/29 December, the Irish fought with Viljoen's men when the fort at Helvetia, north of Machadodorp on the Lydenberg road, was captured.[9] Just over a week later, on the night of 6/7 January 1901, the Irish were involved in two simultaneous attacks in the Belfast area. The more significant was a Boer assault on the British position on Monument Hill, to the north-east of the railway settlement. The centre of the Boer attack was defended by Captain Fosbery and eighty-three men of the Royal Irish Regiment. Fosbery was killed as was a Private J. Barry. When surrounded by Boers (and possibly Irish), Barry smashed at a UK Maxim gun with a pickaxe to prevent it falling into enemy hands. He was shot dead. Easons, the Dublin newsagents, produced a postcard portraying the event, albeit inaccurately.[10]

In the assault on Monument Hill, a Boer victory, there was one known Irish casualty. Dick Hunt, an old friend of Hugh Carberry, was shot three times, once in the lung. He survived but his health was seriously impaired.[11]

The attack on the colliery just to the north-west of Belfast also produced a casualty from the old Irish brigade. Lieutenant Coetzee – if not formally a brigade member, he had been very closely connected with Blake's outfit – was wounded in the fighting that night at the colliery. Blake later claimed Coetzee was killed by an armed African sentry. Certainly the British did use black guards along the Delagoa railway line. These men were a new threat to the Boer forces, as were the heavily armoured trains mounted with cannon and fitted with powerful searchlights.[12]

In his memoir of the war, John Blake makes much of an epic, though as it turned out rather fruitless, trip that he, Pretorius and Gustave Preller made to the western Transvaal to deliver despatches to de la Rey. From 29 April until about 9 June 1900, the three crossed enemy-occupied territory and returned safely to the eastern Transvaal after an 800-kilometre trip.

One skirmish known to have involved the Irish bitterenders was the surprise attack launched on the night of Wednesday, 12 June, when the Irish were with 'Fighting Bill' Muller. Three hundred and fifty Australians were routed and two cannon and 300 horses taken. This incident led the exasperated (British) leader of the force, General Beatson, to tell the colonials that they were 'a lot of wasters, and white-livered curs'. They mutinied and three were court-martialled and sentenced to death. They were eventually pardoned.[13] This affair would have given great amusement to the Irish lads had they known the trouble they had caused the colonials from Victoria.

## CASUALTIES

It is possible that a golden-haired, twenty-six-year-old Irish-American called Walter Wilson, who died on 16 July 1901, was the last Irish brigader to be killed. We are not, however, certain that Wilson was a member of the Irish corps. The last confirmed Irish brigade death was 'the brave and reckless' little Mike Hanafin. According to one account, Hanafin precipitated the Australian surrender in the June skirmish when he 'threw his rifle into the [Australian] bugler's face and told him to sound "Cease fire".'[14]

In the later encounter General Viljoen was attacking two blockhouses along the railway line near Balmoral with the aim of clearing the track so he could cross with cannon and wagons. From 'a hole in the ground under the blockhouse', a soldier shot Hanafin at pointblank range. Dick Hunt, Joe Wade and Joe Kennedy dragged the body back a little and then rushed the blockhouse, killing all its occupants. Hunt had been slightly wounded in the face retrieving the body.[15]

Mike Hanafin had been a popular member of the brigade and clearly was a courageous fighter. As with so many of the men, we know little of him. That he had tenacity is certain. On landing at the port of Beira in Portuguese East Africa, Hanafin had walked the 800 kilometres south through wild enough country to Lourenço Marques, from where he worked his way on the railway up to the Transvaal.

Statements by contemporaries about the number of casualties suffered by the Irish brigades tend to be on the low side. Michael Davitt spoke of about ten brigaders killed and a small number taken prisoner. In 1900 John MacBride claimed that seventeen brigaders were killed and total casualties were about eighty men. In America the following year he was speaking of fifty per cent casualties. His enemy, Captain James Laracy, writing in 1907, bluntly said most of the brigade were captured and only MacBride and a few others got through to Delagoa Bay.[16]

We know the names of 238 brigaders, both in Blake's corps (including the Chicago Irish) and in Lynch's outfit. Of these, the following were known casualties:

*Table 5: Known Irish brigade casualties and losses*

| | |
|---|---|
| Killed, died of wounds or died of disease (all Blake's corps) | 31 |
| Wounded | 23 |
| Prisoners of war (of whom 34 belonged to Blake's corp and 3 to Lynch's) | 37 |
| Place of internment: Ceylon (59 per cent) | 22 |
| Unknown | 8 |
| St Helena | 4 |
| India | 2 |
| Released | 1 |
| GRAND TOTAL | 91 |

This grand total of ninety-one must be reduced to eighty-seven as two POWs were wounded or captured, one wounded brigader was later killed and we are uncertain whether another brigader was just wounded or killed.

If one takes Blake's corps, including the Irish-Americans, then of the known 238 members the casualties were: 31 (thirteen per cent) died; 23 (ten per cent) wounded; and 34 (fourteen per cent) captured. Known casualties and losses were about thirty-seven per cent. It is likely that other brigaders, even those whose names we know, were also casualties. These figures must be treated as conservative.

These figures are tiny in comparison to the losses in the Irish regiments.[17] And as many Irishmen were in other regiments and militia, such as the Royal Artillery and the Imperial Yeomanry, Irish casualties were even higher than it would seem. The following is the official casualty toll in the eleven Irish regiments which fought in the war:

*Table 6: Casualties and losses in Irish regiments*

|  | Killed or died of wounds | Died of disease | Wounded or POW | Missing | TOTAL |
|---|---|---|---|---|---|
| Officers | 47 | 15 | 124 | 31 | 217 |
| NCOs & men | 532 | 527 | 1,679 | 1,497 | 4,235 |
|  | 579 | 542 | 1,803 | 1,528 | 4,452 |

The regiments with the highest casualties were the Irish Fusiliers (1,121), Royal Irish Regiment (805) and the Dublin Fusiliers (674). In the first two regiments men captured accounted for nearly three-quarters of all losses. The Dublin Fusiliers' casualties included two generals and six colonels.

Reports circulated in 1900 of Irishmen with the Boers being captured and shot. The *Birmingham Daily Post* recorded a British tommy as saying in January:

> ... at Modder River seven Boers who had fired on the doctors and two Irishmen who had been captured at Belmont were placed in a row with their heads tied to stakes and a company of the Cornwalls gave them their last Beecham – as our fellows call the bullet. They made the other Boers see them shot and dig their holes.[18]

On 30 January 1900 a meeting of the Irish Transvaal Committee in Dublin unanimously adopted a resolution of the Wexford Men's Association which had 'expressed abhorrence at the murder of Irish prisoners of war and non-combatants by General Lord Methuen and Colonel Baden-Powell'.[19] Be this as it may, those who were known to be brigaders and who were captured were sent off into exile, most to the bleak POW camp at Diyatalawa, where some 4,700 burghers were incarcerated. Some of the Irish may have been moved on to a camp at Ragama.[20] Gillingham, however, remained at the main camp. Like many of the POWs he passed the time with wood carving. He sent a 'beautifully carved paper knife' to Mark Ryan in London. It bore the inscription, 'Prisoners of war, Diyatalawa, Ceylon 1900–1901. To Dr Mark Ryan London, with Sol Gillingham's complts'.[21]

The surprising thing about the Irish POWs overseas is that they were forgotten in Ireland. No campaign was organized for their release, neither by the parliamentary party nor the advanced nationalists – nor, indeed, by MacBride or any of the brigaders who made it to Europe or America. One has a certain sympathy with Captain Laracy when he later lashed out at John MacBride for going on a lecture tour of America:

> while his comrades-in-arms who had no counsel to protect their interests were suffering privations and tortures the world has not yet heard of, and the Major never took the trouble to inquire as to their welfare.[22]

The Irish-Americans fared little better. The US State Department believed that though they would not lose their citizenship by fighting for another power, brigaders could 'claim no immunities on account of their nationality'.[23]

Only one Irish POW is known to have escaped. That was Thomas Enright. In November 1902 the forty-seven-year-old former brigade lieutenant caused a stir in the Colonial Office in Downing Street when he escaped from St Helena on the steamer *Galician*. The RIC was not very helpful pursuing the matter.[24]

## SYMPATHY IN IRELAND

The closing phase of the war was a very difficult one for those bitterenders who held out. The farmhouse burnings, confiscation of livestock and destruction of crops gradually dried up supplies. In Ireland these methods of war caused revulsion, conjuring up events in Ireland's own history. Reports of a plot to assassinate General Kitchener by Irish nationalists living in Paris were taken seriously by Dublin Castle. Assistant Commissioner John Mallon noted: 'I have no doubt this is true as the thing is in the wind and I would say Maud Gonne would be in it'. On the other hand, talk in September 1901 of Fredrick Labelle of Holyoke in the United States raising a Franco-American brigade to fight alongside the Boers raised only the dry comment from Commissioner Gosselin of the DMP, 'I hope the news is true.'[25]

One poster confiscated by the Dublin Metropolitan Police proclaimed:

> Honours for Field Marshal Lord Roberts for Burning the Farms of the Boers. Honours. Honours for Driving the Boer Women and Children Homeless and Starving Out on the Wintry Hillsides ... The

methods of English War have not varied since the days of Carew and Mountjoy. Cecil Lord Salisbury under Queen Victoria follows Cecil Lord Salisbury under Queen Elizabeth.

Another such seized by the DMP quoted Father Kavanagh denouncing Irish recruitment and advising the militia not to volunteer to fight in Africa or China. On this leaflet a rounded hand had written in pencil 'Cheers for Krgruger [sic].' And Kruger himself appeared – wearing a green sash – in a poster published by the *Freeman's Journal* on 23 February 1901. By now many GAA clubs bore the names of Boer generals and as already mentioned a 'Major MacBride Club' at 18 High Street, Dublin, served as a 'youth league' for the Irish Transvaal Committee. In June 1901 Maud Gonne took some children as a treat to see Wolfe Tone's grave at Bowdenstown. She gave them little Irish and Boer flags and encouraged them to boo and hiss whenever they passed British soldier on the way.

The khaki general election had come and gone largely without excitement in Ireland. Home rule was for the moment on the back burner with the Liberals and no longer an article of faith for the party. As Sir Edward Grey wrote to Herbert Gladstone, 'Things must advance towards Home Rule but I think it must be step by step'.[26]

Lord Rosebery, seeing home rule now as a millstone, went further: because of the Irish attitude to the war, he wanted a 'clean slate' approach in Liberal policy towards Ireland. The idea was now being firmly established that Ireland was the norm by which 'trouble' was judged in Britain, and at that time South Africa was 'another Ireland seven thousand miles away'.[27] In Ireland itself a few 'little Irelanders', such as William O'Brien, D.P. Moran and the Revd J. Fénélon tried to argue that it was pointless carrying on support for the Boers.[28] They remained a minority. If anything, Irish support for the Boers in the House of Commons increased. John Redmond, but more often than not John Dillon, denounced the concentration camps for Boer women and children and the policy which had reduced the Boer republics to a 'howling wilderness'. On one occasion Dillon denounced Chamberlain as a liar and was named by the speaker.[29] One contemporary, an English radical, wrote of Dillon:

> But there are Irishmen and Irishmen. In the grey light of yesterday morning the Dublin Fusiliers helped to break the arrogant power of the Boers. Just after dinner, under the cosy gaslight of the House of

Commons, Mr Kruger's patron, after a pointless squabble with the authority of the chair, got himself suspended.[30]

A proposal to put forward Kruger's name for the 1901 by-election in Galway against the liberal unionist Sir Horace Plunkett came to nothing. In the event Arthur Lynch was nominated and elected. As will be seen, this had dramatic consequences. It did not go unnoticed that Lynch did not mention South Africa in his manifesto. That Lynch should have been elected to an Irish constituency and not MacBride must have seemed grossly unfair to Foxy Jack.

As the war had progressed, Irish MPs had not been slow to criticize the British establishment for using Irish regiments as front-line troops. When the peace of Vereeniging was signed and a vote of thanks to the British army proposed in the House of Commons, John Redmond led the only opposition:

> It is not necessary for us, nor is it our desire, to make any attack upon the Army or upon the soldiers who carried out this campaign in South Africa, but they are being thanked in this Resolution for carrying out a work, as it was their duty to carry it out, which we have regarded from the first with absolute abhorrence, a work against which we have protested at every stage, and for the furtherance of which we have refused to vote a single shilling.[31]

### THE WAR ENDS

The last months of 1901 saw the Irish brigaders range as far afield as the northern Pietersburg railway line, Dullstroom, north of Belfast, and Witkrans, thirty kilometres north of Ermelo. A serious loss must have been Captain McCallum, who was captured at Toneldoos north of Belfast on 27 August. The forty-eight-year-old was sent to a POW camp in India. Mick Ryan was captured after this period so there must have been some contact with the enemy in the closing months of 1901.[32]

In January 1902 we find John Blake with Commandant Joachim Prinsloo at Klip-Koppies, ten kilometres from Bronkhorstspruit. The home range remained the hinterland to the Delagoa railway line. But when peace came on 31 May, Blake was somewhat north of that area, on the beautiful Sabie river not far from Lydenburg with the Johannesburg commando.

The Irish lads surrendered with the Johannesburg commando at Potloodspruit, thirty kilometres to the east of the Sabie river. The local

British officers wanted to put the Irish over the Mozambique border but they refused to go and were allowed to stay in the Transvaal Colony, at least for a while. In usual style, Blake seems to have left his former comrades and with Pienaar, Young, Blignaut and Malan set off on horseback for Pretoria. They camped at Klip river and were pleasantly surprised at how civil the British tommies were to them. By 20 June Blake was back in his old stamping ground, though probably not in the Grand Hotel. The sight of the union jack over the city must have annoyed him; the first such flag raised by Lord Roberts had had a small shamrock embroidered on it by Lady Roberts. Blake was not slow to denounce the peace settlement and with his pals openly flaunted the Boer colours on 26 June, the day of Edward VII's coronation.[33]

One suspects that Blake found himself in the same position as Alfred Aylward had been after the first Anglo-Boer war in 1881. Truth to tell, things could be made hot for someone like John Blake, who would not be inclined to be discreet when in the company of South Africa's new rulers. The problem for him and the other Irish and Irish-Americans was how to raise the funds to get out. This was solved about August 1902 when Clan na Gael cabled $3,000 to Blake so that he and those of the men who remained and wanted to leave could buy their passage home.[34]

According to article seven of the peace terms relating to prisoners of war, 'Foreigners will not be allowed to return to South Africa'. So it was that by the African spring of 1902 very few members of the former Irish commandos or former Irish members of Boer commandos remained in South Africa. The great Irish African adventure was over.

# CHAPTER ELEVEN

# Last post

## MAY 1902 TO EASTER 1916

### A GAS-FILLED ROOM

Most of the Irish brigade who escaped with MacBride in September 1900 made for America. Tom Byrne concludes their story:

> On our arrival in New York, we were received by the Irish societies and John Devoy came on board. I suppose there were about fifty or sixty of us, including an odd few Irish-Americans. We were received by the Clan na Gael and were given the option of going to any of the mining camps. They would send on word to the Irish societies in those places to receive us. The majority of us went to mining camps in the West. We worked in Montana, Nevada, Colorado, California and other places for eleven or twelve years. Most of them died there … I had no actual contact with the movement in Ireland until I returned there late in 1913.[1]

In March 1901 we find Jack Donnelly living at 20 Woodland Avenue, Dawtucket, Rhode Island, and writing to the *Irish News* letting 'the boys in the Falls Road' know he was alive and well.[2]

The Clan na Gael erected a memorial to killed brigaders Egan and O'Hare in Chicago's Mount Carmel cemetery – 'topped with a statue of a soldier who looks curiously British'.[3]

Like Alfred Aylward, John Blake also made for America. He worked quickly on his history of the war and continued to involve himself in Irish affairs, being a vice-president of the Cornell branch of the United Irish League. He ended up in a rented room at 275 West 22nd Street, New York, off Broadway and near Columbia University. Here, on Thursday, 24 January 1907, he was found dead in his gas-filled room. He was fifty-one years old. Earlier in the week his landlady's father had died and on the Wednesday night he had sat up late with the landlady, Irene Cunningham, and her mother. Suicide was denied. As with Alfred Aylward, it was a sad end for a man of adventure.[4]

Blake's number two also met an unnatural death, but not for another nine years. Quite who was at the Gare de Lyons to meet John MacBride when he arrived in Paris in early 1900 is uncertain. MacBride himself says it was his mother, his brother, Dr Ryan, 'etc.' According to Maud Gonne, who names none of these people, MacBride was met by herself, Arthur Griffith (who is said to have jokingly called MacBride 'Rooinek'), Stephen McKenna and some members of the Paris Young Ireland Society. As Griffith telegraphed MacBride greetings on 3 November, the likelihood is the Young Ireland welcome came second, though MacBride may have meant Maud Gonne *et al.* in his 'etc.'[5]

Whatever the true circumstances of MacBride's arrival in Paris, it was soon determined by Maud Gonne and Arthur Griffith that he should make a lecture tour of America talking about his war experiences. Just before MacBride set off on this lecture tour, Paul Kruger arrived in Paris. He had landed at Marseilles on 22 November 1900 and had been greeted by Dr Leyds and Michael Davitt, Davitt presenting the old man with an address of support. Later he would write to the Boer patriarch, 'England's is but a brigand's triumph, transcient and insecure.' It was soon being reported to Dublin Castle that on this occasion Kruger had given Davitt at least £12,000 which was passed on to the IRB. What truth there is in these stories is unknown.[6]

In Paris Maud Gonne was beside herself with excitement at the arrival of Kruger. With MacBride, John O'Leary and members of the Paris Young Ireland Society, she presented the old man with an address in Irish, Dutch, French and English from the society:

> He put his hand on my shoulder, as he took the scroll on which the address was written, and kept me near him awhile though the rooms were crowded with delegations waiting to present addresses. He said: 'The Irish have proved their sympathy by fighting for us. The Irish Commando has done fine work.'

Other addresses were presented by the Irish clubs of London, the Michael Dwyer National Club of 47 York Street, Dublin, the Major MacBride National Athletic Club and the Independent Nationalists of Dunleary.[7]

Dr Leyds' Irish informant had warned the Boer emissary of Maud Gonne's planned presentation, though obviously to no avail:

[149]

Avertissement!!! You are warned that the ridiculous Maud Gonne with one of her amoureux, the third-rate poet Yeats, is getting up a pretended Deputation to meet President Kruger. As she is universally laughed at, she must be kept to one side.[8]

Soon poor MacBride was sent off across the Atlantic with an introduction to John Devoy. Things did not go terribly well, even after Maud Gonne joined him in February 1901. MacBride suffered agonies as a public speaker and Maud Gonne alienated several prominent Irish leaders in the States. She later claimed that it was on this coast-to-coast tour that John MacBride proposed to her. If that was so, MacBride was no doubt flattered and dragooned into it.

The death in May 1901 of Griffith's close friend William Rooney led Maud Gonne to leave MacBride in America and return to Europe. Though a member of the Irish Transvaal Committee, Rooney was no great enthusiast for the Boers. One suspects that it had been largely Rooney's pressure which had originally brought his close friend Griffith back from Africa. Now he was dead and Griffith so devastated that he had to be admitted to hospital for a short period.[9]

## AN EXILE IN PARIS

MacBride finished his tour and returned to Paris. While Maud Gonne's apartment was at number 7 in the fashionable avenue d'Eylau (with its view of the Eiffel Tower), and later nearby at 13 rue de Passy, MacBride's attic room across the river was at 40 rue Gay de Lussac up near the Jardin du Luxembourg in the Latin quarter. Life was not easy for the former officer in the Boer army. He had little cash and half-hearted attempts at journalism proved nearly as taxing as public speaking. But there were some distractions for the exile, such as when he received an illuminated address and a sword of honour in November 1901, and when former State Secretary Reitz came to town.

When the war ended in 1902, a number of the Boer generals arrived in Europe. On 18 August MacBride received a message from Reitz: he would be in Paris in five or six days and would bring the brigade's flag with him. On 25 August he delivered MacBride's much-treasured trophy. On a piece of card attached to the parcel was written:

Though many a sigh and tear it cost
For those who rose at *Freedom's call*
'Tis better to have fought and lost (?)
Than never to have fought at all.

F.W. Reitz[10]

Other presentations came MacBride's way from Ireland, including a revolver.

MacBride saw many of the Boer visitors, but it was Michael Davitt who seems to have been the main link between the celebrity generals and Irish politicians. Davitt himself travelled to Europe in 1902 to meet many of them. On 24 August he wrote to John Redmond from the Hague:

> You will feel some little human envy, I am sure, when I tell you I spent most of last evening with De Wet and Delarey 'who fought their battles o'er again' amidst clouds of tobacco smoke. It was one of the most delightful evenings I have ever had. I saw Botha in Brussels on my way here. Steyn will recover. I had tea with his wife yesterday evening.

A report in the *Evening Standard* concerning Reitz and a British officer in a Boer farmhouse elicited a letter from Reitz to MacBride. A picture of Gladstone hung on the wall. The British soldier on seeing this shook his fist at the picture and shouted, 'You old fool, it's your fault that we are having all this trouble.' Reitz confided the home was his.

The marriage of John MacBride to Maud Gonne on 21 February 1903 at the church of Saint-Honoré d'Eylau in Place Victor Hugo impinges slightly on the tale of the Irish brigades. It was the war which had created MacBride as a military hero in Maud Gonne's mind. She believed, not unreasonably, that the Irish brigade 'had done more for Ireland's honour than all of us at home, for it is action that counts'. Later she would confide in John O'Leary that she thought that by marrying this national hero, she was marrying Ireland.[11] Many people advised against the match: Arthur Griffith, W.B. Yeats (naturally), MacBride's old mother and, according to Maud Gonne, even her own dead father who had sent her a message from beyond the grave.

It must have been reassuring for John MacBride to have the brigade's chaplain, Father van Hecke, conduct the ceremony in the bleak church. And there was also on display the flag which had flown in the camp behind Pepworth Hill in far-off Natal.

[151]

That flag was once again prominent when Jean Seágan MacBride was christened. It was the major's most precious possession – and the way the marriage was going, his only one. When the rift occurred, catholic Ireland reeled over the sensational separation. During the 1905 divorce proceedings a rather intriguing letter was produced signed by 'Louis Botha, J.J. Smuts and N.J. de Wet, Pretoria'. It stated that these persons 'do not know of any person called Fritz Joubert Duquesne, ZAR, who has made statements injurious to Major John MacBride'.[12]

Whether the French court heard of a child of MacBride's born in the Transvaal is uncertain. Given Maud Gonne's own history, this might seem irrelevant but it was not. Maud Gonne was of ascendancy stock and seemed half-French. She could get away with things that Edwardian puritan catholic Ireland would frown on from one of their own. Then again the tales from South Africa might have been about something else. There was, after all, no shortage of shocking stories circulating about MacBride much nearer home. But at the end of the day MacBride was still a national hero. That he must remain so was important in 1905. After 1916 it was vital. As Barry O'Brien insisted in 1906, 'For the sake of the country … the MacBride legend must keep its lustre.'[13] Whatever the truth, John MacBride must have wished he was back on the highveld with his men and Fenian Boy.

## IRELAND MOURNS

By the time the war in South Africa ended, the Boer farmers had become folk heroes in Ireland, especially in the rural areas. Pride at Boer victories had given way to pity. The parliamentary party firmly unified, except for Tim Healy, went on its way, but the advanced nationalists pondered the war, what had been achieved and what might be achieved the next time round. As Skin-the-Goat in *Ulysses* said, 'The Germans and the Japs were going to have their look in, he affirmed. The Boers were the beginning of the end.'[14]

In the early 1920s former Irish Transvaal Committee member George Lyons picturesquely summed up his feelings about the war for Ireland:

> The war did not conclude without its lessons upon the Irish people. It had come upon them whilst they slept; it wakened them with its thundering voice; but alas! it had passed off before they had finished rubbing their eyes.[15]

The Irish Transvaal Committee was still in existence in November 1901, but in reality Arthur Griffith had already decided it was time to 'nationalize' his little group. So on 30 September he had founded Cumann na Gaedheal largely out of the Irish Transvaal Committee's membership.[16] This in turn metamorphosed into Sinn Fein in 1905, thus creating a chain linking the South African agitation and the movement which was to take Ireland to independence. Though the Dublin advanced nationalists might be thinking more of home politics, Limerick, which had given Maud Gonne the freedom of the city in 1900, remained staunchly and actively pro-Boer right up to the end of the war.

None of the Cape Boer delegations which visited Britain in 1900 and 1901 dared venture across to Ireland.[17] This prejudice seems to have continued after peace was concluded, though former Boer officers Colonel Shiel and his adjutant, Captain Brockhoff, caused a mild sensation when they spent a day in Cork in July 1902 on their way from St Helena to Britain and Europe. This might have been because most Boers did not wish to travel through England, but it may also have been because they were cautious about alienating their new masters unnecessarily, especially as 'home rule' for the old republics was a possibility in the medium term. When de Wet sent a message of thanks via Davitt to John Dillon for all his pro-Boer speeches, he told Davitt to 'see that no one else is present but you and he' when the message was passed on. Of course, there were exceptions, especially among those who had fought alongside the Irish brigade. Commandant Stephanus Trichardt actually sent his son Luke to study at Trinity College, Dublin. In October 1902 the general probably closest to the Irish, at least in the closing phase of the war, Ben Viljoen, visited Ireland. On 28 October he delivered a lecture in Dublin's Shelbourne Hotel and the following day lectured in Belfast. The Shelbourne had been the venue of a hoax during the war which had put Dublin Castle officials in a spin. Reports had come through that Boers, including Dr Leyds, were dining there. On investigation, it was discovered that these were actors from the Gaiety Theatre hamming it up.[18]

Perhaps the last manifestation of Irish pro-Boerism occurred in the city of Armagh on 8 June 1902. That Sunday some 5,000 people gathered in the catholic cemetery for the unveiling of a memorial to the thirty-two-year-old Hugh Carberry who had died of a stroke in Pretoria three months after being shot in the head at the battle of Modderspruit on 30 October 1899 (the date on the memorial is incorrectly given as 23 October). Michael Davitt was the star of the occasion. The police reported that he:

delivered a characteristic speech defaming the British soldier and eulogizing the Boers. Sedition was freely indulged in, but as the Police note taker was ejected from the meeting, evidence of the language used was not available.[19]

After the ceremony there was a riot in the streets of Armagh.

The three-metre-high memorial is impressive and worthy of a visit. One side of the column has reliefs of a round tower and a profile of Carberry. The obverse has a statue of Erin, a hound at her knee, set against it. The whole is topped by a celtic cross. The inscription at the base reads:

> Erected by a few Irish patriots to the memory of Hugh Carberry of Armagh, who fell in the battle of Modderspruit, 23 October 1899, aged thirty-two years, bravely fighting for the Boers and their independence, and against the unjust aggression of England. RIP[20]

Reports later circulated that Carberry was in fact still alive and living in Pretoria. These were dismissed as Orange propaganda. This it may have been, but the belief that a dead hero still lived was not unknown in Ireland. During the Boer war there were those who believed de Wet to be none other than Charles Stewart Parnell.

## THE MEMOIRS

Of the few accounts of the brigades' activities written contemporaneously, Teddy Luther's diaries are the most reliable. However, they cover only the period from May to early September 1900. It is also the account of a new arrival and a trooper rather than one of the leaders who had close contact with the Boer generals. Though Tom Byrne's account covers the whole campaign, it is only fourteen typed pages long and was dictated more than fifty years after Byrne left South Africa.

In 1903 John Blake's book, *A West Pointer with the Boers*, dedicated to the memory of the 22,000 Boer women and children who were 'murdered' in the British concentration camps, was published by Angel Guardian Press in Boston. It has been denounced as a polemic and as being 'so egotistical and so virulently anti-British as to be almost valueless as history'.[21] In fact, the book is very useful for the historian of the Irish brigade. The polemical passages are clearly identifiable and can easily be passed over by the reader. It is of more value and more honest than the eight Boer war chapters (which totalled only forty-eight pages) in Arthur Lynch's autobiography, *My life story*, published by J. Long of London in 1924. Lynch's article in *The Gael* in December 1900 is of some interest. One source mentions that Lynch wrote a piece entitled *En campagne avec les Boers: Notes critiques* which was published in Brussels.

Michael Davitt's *The Boer fight for freedom*, the *raison d'être* for his visit to the highveld, is one of the classics of contemporary Boer war literature. Published in New York by Funk and Wagnalls Company, it was subtitled *From the beginning of hostilities to the peace of Pretoria*, dedicated to the memory of General Philip Botha and went into three editions, all dated 1902. A first section, dealing with the causes of the war and events up to June 1900, includes a chapter entitled 'Blake's Irish Brigade'. The second part of the book is a diary of events from June 1900 to March 1902; in the third edition this continues up to May 1902. This second part is heavily reliant on Irish press reports. The first edition of the book ran to 603 pages and the third to 607 pages with forty-one chapters, 111 illustrations and seven maps. It is biased and paternalistic towards the Boers, and with the prejudices of the age. None the less, it is an impressive book which no historian of the war can ignore. What is disappointing is how personally detached it is. Very little is said about Davitt's visit to the war zone, what he did, what he saw and what he really thought.

Davitt had hoped to make a little money out of the book, but in August 1902 he was writing to John Dillon:

> Alas for my poor book! De Wet's book is already in the hands of a London publisher and Botha and De La Rey have another in preparation.

Two days later Davitt gloomily reported that Mrs de la Rey was also writing a book, and that de Wet had been offered £100,000 for his volume.[22]

As for MacBride, he had written an article on the brigade while in Paris in 1900, which was published in the *United Irishman* on 22 December. He began with the words, 'Some time, perhaps, when there is no better work for me to do I shall sit down and write a full history of the Transvaal Irish Brigade.' In November 1904 he confided to John Devoy, 'I started my account of the Irish Brigade a short time back, but with one thing and another I never got very far on with it.'[23]

At long last MacBride made the effort and began to write a series of articles on the brigade for the *Freeman's Journal*. The cash was very useful just then but he grumbled to Devoy about being censored by the paper, 'I received word from the Freeman that I must avoid politics and moderate my language. They cut several good things out of my first'. Pity.

In all, thirteen articles were published, starting on Saturday, 13 October 1906, and appearing weekly for seven weeks until 1 December. Dublin must have looked forward to this Saturday morning read. Then came MacBride's libel case with the *Irish Independent* over his separation from Maud Gonne. A four-week gap left the reader wondering what had happened after the battle of Colenso. Finally, on Saturday, 5 January 1907, the series was started again and continued in an irregular fashion until 2 April. Seventeen weeks later, on 29 July, the final episode appeared. What should have taken thirteen weeks to complete stretched out for forty. One can only guess at what the editor had to say about this.

The articles evoked correspondence in the paper's columns from P. O'Fionn (20 October 1906), James Laracy – hostile (29 December 1906 and 12 January 1907), John MacBride's reply to Laracy (5 January 1907), Fred Allan (5 January 1907) and John Whelan (12 January 1907). Eleven of the thirteen articles concern the organisation of the brigade and its activities in Natal. It is clear that by February 1907 MacBride had lost interest in the project. The fact that the brigade's retreat was not without its problems would also have hastened the writer to conclude the series.[24]

Six years later, in 1913, Sir Roger Casement met and described MacBride as 'another Antrim glens Protestant and congenial character'. Forgetting his earlier censure of the Irish Transvaal Brigade, Casement enthused to Alice Stopford Green that MacBride had done 'splendid work' in South Africa, 'I begged him to write the story – to have on record the fight that little band of Irishmen (three hundred strong) made for Boer freedom. It was a fine fight and should be told.'[25] But MacBride was done with writing. Perhaps if Casement had had a manual from Foxy Jack, though, he might have made a better job of putting together his own Irish brigade from Irish POWs interned in the kaiser's Germany.

Ironically, three weeks after MacBride's concluding article appeared in the *Freeman's Journal* in 1907, the duke of Connaught unveiled a handsome triumphal arch on Stephen's Green at the top of Grafton Street. Modelled on the arch of Titus in Rome, it was a memorial to the members of the Royal Dublin Fusiliers who had fallen in South Africa. While the *Irish Times* was deeply moved by the unveiling, the *Freeman's Journal* was moved only to fury. Part of the Latin inscription read, 'Dublin dedicates it to her brave soldiers'. The *Freeman's* response to this was:

Dublin has nothing to do with the erection or dedication of it. As the promoters well know, it would have been impossible to have even obtained a site for the monument from the representatives of the citizens of Dublin. They had to appeal to the Castle-controlled Board of Works. From first to last Dublin believed, and believes, the war in which those men were engaged to be unjust and disgraceful.[26]

It was soon dubbed 'the traitors' gate'. In fact, it is one of eleven regimental memorials in Ireland to Irish soldiers who fought in the second Anglo-Boer war.[27] No memorial to the Irish Transvaal Brigade was ever erected in Ireland.


## THE HOUNDING OF ARTHUR LYNCH

When Arthur Lynch got out of the Transvaal, he made for the United States. He claimed, probably falsely, that the Boers had ordered him there to 'place the situation' before the American public.[28] From there he returned to Paris, no doubt carefully avoiding his former associate Maud Gonne. One detractor claimed in Paris that Lynch basked 'in the sunshine of the Boulevards in his slouch hat and Boer uniform, moryah! The envy of men, the hero, and the delight of the ladies.'[29]

He pestered the leaders of the Irish parliamentary party for nomination for an Irish constituency for the khaki election of 1900. He was out of luck, but not for long. In 1901 the Hon. M.H.F. Morris succeeded as Lord Killanin and a by-election was held for his old seat at Westminster. Edmund Leamy had contested the seat twice before but was now so ill that he had to withdraw from the race. Arthur Lynch was the second choice. Proposed by the local United Irish League convention, Lynch was in a direct fight with the eminent liberal unionist Horace Plunkett. It was not the first time Lynch had contested this seat. Back in 1892 he had been defeated by fifty-one votes.

Plunkett might have been liberal but he had supported the British in the Boer war. To what extent Lynch's record featured in the contest is unclear. He was absent in Paris and the fight seems to have been more anti-Plunkett than pro a Boer war hero: in fact, Lynch's election manifesto did not even mention the Boer war. Be that as it may, Lynch won by 1,247 votes to 472.[30] The problem was that there was now a warrant out for Lynch's arrest for his treasonous activities in South Africa. Though no one else on the Boer side had been tried since the war concluded, when Lynch arrived in England to take up his seat in parliament on 11 June 1902, he was promptly arrested by Scotland Yard detectives. The charge was high treason, the first man so tried since Smith O'Brien in 1848.

Two weeks later it was reported in the *Irish Independent* that the flag of Lynch's commando had been presented to the mayor of Kingston-on-Thames by a British soldier. It was in the Transvaal colours, had the name of the brigade on it, as well as the words 'For Liberty, and Remember '98'. Pinned to the flag was the flyleaf from a bible, on which was written 'in blood' 'Send this flag to Dublin, and pray for the soul of Patrick Mooney. Goodbye.' The *Surrey Comet* makes no mention of such a presentation and the Kingston Museum has neither possession nor record of such a flag, so what became of it is uncertain.[31]

The trial of Arthur Lynch took place from 21 to 23 January 1903, not in the Old Bailey but in the Court of the Lord Chief Justice in front of three judges and a jury. Among those appearing for the crown was the attorney-general, Sir Edward Carson. The barristers for the defence were Messrs Shee KC, Biron and Dwyer and Lynch's solicitor was the Charles Russell who had exposed the Piggott forgeries. There were three charges, all pertaining to Lynch taking up arms and fighting against Britain.

Lynch did not dispute that he had taken up arms and fought against British forces but pleaded not guilty on the grounds that he had been a citizen of the Transvaal. Lynch's problem was that he had sworn allegiance to the South African Republic on 18 January 1900 – after the war had commenced. Blake, MacBride and the lads had become Transvaal citizens before the outbreak of hostilities and thus were in a different category of disaffection. The crown argued that for a British citizen to become naturalized in an enemy state in time of war was in itself committing an act of treason. It was argued against Lynch that if each soldier in an army accepted letters of naturalization from an enemy and then deserted 'in the hour of battle' then they would most certaininly be liable to the penalties of treason.[32]

Lynch later claimed that the government throughout the case 'displayed a spiteful spirit'. No doubt he also felt that his fellow former brigaders George Kidmey and E. Viljoen, who had been brought to London to testify against him, also showed a spiteful spirit by agreeing to do so.[33] He also said that subsequently General Botha told him that he would not have signed the peace treaty had he not been assured by Roberts and Kitchener that no prosecutions for high treason would be brought against any of his followers.

Arthur Lynch was found guilty by the jury after a twenty-six-minute consideration of their verdict. But he was not sentenced to be hanged, drawn and quartered as is often stated and was popularly believed at the time; he was simply sentenced to be hanged. Of course, as always, Lynch was lucky and he escaped the hangman's noose. It has been claimed that President Theodore Roosevelt's intervention saved Lynch. This is unlikely given the push for post-war reconciliation in South Africa. Even the Conservatives would pause before sending Lynch through the trapdoor. This is confirmed by the fact that having served only one year of a life sentence, Lynch was released on a ticket-of-leave. He wisely set off for Paris.[34]

As a convicted felon, Lynch lost his Galway seat and a new by-election was held on 9 March 1903. In July 1907, following the Liberal landslide of the previous year, Lynch received a full pardon. The death in 1909 of James Halpin, member for West Clare, gave Lynch a new opportunity. He was elected to the seat once held by Cecil Rhodes' associate Rockfort Maguire but despite this, Lynch spent most of his time in London. Perhaps this was just as well for there were those, Irish nationalists and former Irish Transvaal brigaders, who would not have been sorry to see Colonel Lynch hanged, drawn and quartered after all. Lynch had broken the rules. He had gone it alone and formed a rival Irish commando in the Boer war. Then he had dropped Dr Ryan and the advanced men when he had got into parliament. He was foreign, bookish and thought a lot of himself. Too clever by half. He was not one of them.

In 1909 Lynch felt compelled to defend his war record to the Irish-American leader, Judge Daniel F. Cohalan. He had heard that John Devoy had been told unfavourable things about his record by 'the Boer Secretary'. The New York *Daily News* had also recently questioned Lynch's right to the title of colonel. Lynch's letter in response was a good one, though pointless if he imagined it would silence his enemies. He wrote, 'I was sentenced to death in London, for having been on the spot, and for having fought at several places in my rank as Colonel.'

In May 1914 an unpleasant, sneering letter appeared in the *Gaelic American* from James Harold, one of MacBride's men. Tom Clark, who had spent several years of his childhood in South Africa and had been a fervent pro-Boer, though outside Maud Gonne's circle, also hated Lynch. In June 1914 Clark wrote to John Devoy:

> We have Lynch nearly flattened out as it is. Tom Hayes, Ben Parsons and others here in Dublin have been going for his scalp, and

Maguire, Editor of the Clare Champion, is after him. So between us we will do for the S— of a B——.

The Devoy papers in the National Library of Ireland contain several unsigned sheets of paper denouncing Lynch for horse stealing, looting the town of Dundee, general theft and desertion. These were probably written by Devoy and by Andy Higgins of Blake's commando. Near the comment that the stolen loot was stored in the Johannesburg home of Captain Oates is written, 'Don't mention name of Oates.' It was Lynch they were gunning for. They had no quarrel with the decent Oates.

When the first world war broke out in August, Arthur Lynch actively recruited for the British army. Ironically enough, he ended up with the British army rank of colonel – but then Jannie Smuts became a British army field-marshal. As Lynch said himself, he was denounced as 'a wretched poltroon and bad lot altogether'.[35] He did not stand against Sinn Fein's Brian O'Higgins in 1918. What was the point?

Lynch was lucky as always and settled into the pleasant life of a London gentleman doctor at Haverstock, near Hampstead Heath, writing his esoteric books. He died on 25 March 1934, the longest-surviving and the only one of the three senior officers of the Irish commandos to die naturally in his bed.

# 1916

There is no evidence that the Dublin authorities took any action against any of the brigaders who returned to Ireland or indeed that they were intimidated in any way by the police. Looking at police reports one gets the impression that the policy was one of 'let sleeping dogs lie'. In many respects the retirement in December 1901 of Assistant Commissioner John Mallon, after forty-three years' service in the DMP, symbolically closes the Boer war chapter in Irish history. Whatever foundations were being laid for the future, Mallon and his men had held Ireland in a difficult period and it would be some time yet before warning bells would ring in Dublin Castle. Indeed in March 1905 a secret police report spoke of there being 'no political activity in Ireland for the last two and a half years'.[36]

John MacBride's life when he returned to Dublin in 1906 was somewhat sad. Hero he might have been, but a somewhat neglected one, though on 9 May 1910 he was loudly cheered when he addressed a gathering in Cork city hall. He could not even get a permanent job until 1911 when a corporation post as water bailiff came his way. It was an incongruous job for the soldier of the veld, but it brought in a bit of money. Not that his methodist landlord Fred Allan, a fellow IRB man, would have turned him out.

MacBride was not in the inner circle of revolutionary plotters. Perhaps it was the drink and perhaps it was other things. He was not excluded from IRB activities, though. Nor was he forgotten by former comrades. At Christmas 1912 we find Solomon Gillingham sending MacBride an elaborate card – complete with real silver-tree leaves and the following greeting:

> Erin's Sons Ne'er Forget old Friends
> > Though distance may divide us,
> > Upon this Christmas day,
> > Heart to heart sends greeting,
> > More than words can say.
>
> > > > Pretoria, Dec 1912
> > > > S. Gillingham[37]

After his death in 1916 the card was among MacBride's meagre possessions.

Nineteen twelve also brought MacBride a formal typed invitation from Padraig Pearse to address the 'young Gaels' of St Enda's College at Rathfarnham. At the bottom of the letter, a handwritten postscript read 'P.S. – what the boys would really like is an account of your experiences in the South African war'. This letter, too, was kept.

Nineteen hundred was a dry run for the Irish revolution but if James Connolly had had his way it would have been the real thing. In November 1899 his socialist paper, the *Workers' Republic*, made it clear what action was necessary:

> England's difficulty is Ireland's opportunity. Opportunity to do what?
> To shout, to cheer, to curse, to hold meetings and a host of other things which have no more effect upon England than the pattering of raindrops upon an ironclad.[38]

Griffith restrained Connolly then. He would not do so again. Besides there were others equally determined, like Pearse and Captain James White, founder of the Citizens' Army and son of Field-Marshal Sir George White, the defender of Ladysmith. It was just as well the old man was dead.

The 1916 Easter Rising came as a suprise to MacBride. The field general court martial papers contain a statement made by MacBride:

On the morning of Easter Monday I left my home at Glengeary with the intention of going to meet my brother who was coming to Dublin to get married. In waiting round town I went up as far as Stephens Green, & there I saw a band of Irish Volunteers. I knew some of the members personally & the commander told me that an Irish republic was virtually proclaimed. As he knew my rather advanced opinions & although I had no previous connection with the Irish Volunteers I considered it my duty to join them. I knew there was no chance of success and I never advised nor influenced any other person to join. I did not even know the position they were about to take up. I marched with them to Jacobs Factory. After being a few hours there I was appointed second in command & I felt it my duty to accept that position. I could have escaped from Jacobs Factory before the surrender had I so desired but I considered it a dishonorable thing to do. I do not say this with the idea of mitigating any penalty they might impose, but in order [to] make clear my position in the matter.[39]

What is significant is that Thomas MacDonagh had enough confidence in John MacBride, a very different type of man from himself, to make him his senior officer. Once again, MacBride was number two.

Nineteen sixteen was less exciting for MacBride than the Boer war. The fighting at Jacobs' factory was confined to sniping and sorties, some of which MacBride led, no doubt ably. But the fight was short, there were no victories to cheer the heart and there was no Fenian Boy.

Giving evidence to the royal commission of inquiry into the insurrection, Royal Navy Commander W.V. Harrel, formerly assistant commissioner of the DMP, remarked that some of 'the persons who were prominently connected with the recent outbreak were also connected with the societies that were formed during the South African War'. Apart from MacBride in the Jacobs' factory, there were others in Dublin that extraordinary week who had been members of the old Irish Transvaal Brigade and who now struck a second 'blow for Ireland'. We cannot doubt that their experience in the field – probably the only body of battle-hardened troops on the side of the 1916 insurgents – proved valuable to the revolutionaries. Tom Byrne was among these former burghers.

Echoes of the Boer war were the dashing Boer-style hats worn by the insurgents which, as Dr Lowry points out, were known as 'De Wet caps'.[40] The rifles with Boer carvings on their butts used by the insurgents and captured by the British army remain a mystery. It might seem reasonable to think that they were brought to Ireland by former Irish Transvaal brigaders but if this was so, how was it done? The Portuguese disarmed any Boer troops who crossed the Komati bridge. It is possible the rifles had nothing directly to do with MacBride's brigade. They could, for example, have been transported to Germany after the Boer war, or near its conclusion. These old rifles were then later dumped by the Germans on the Irish revolutionaries. Hopefully time will tell which thesis is correct.

By all accounts Major John MacBride fought as bravely in 1916 as he had seventeen years before. His behaviour on capture and at his field general court martial brought out the best of this sad figure. This, of course, did not prevent a host of conspiracy theories from emerging to blur accounts of the court martial and his execution.

Central to the conspiracy theories is the notion that the British wanted vengeance on MacBride for his activities in South Africa. To this end, it is pointed out that General Maxwell and Colonel Blackadder had served in South Africa. This is so, but there was not a senior British officer who had served his time who had not been in the Boer war. Maxwell was not the most pleasant of men and one suspects he would have executed many more insurgents if he had been free of political masters. The 1916 executions were the classical military solution – 'Throw the leaders off the Tarpeian Rock and flog the ranks.' What is interesting is that MacBride was considered a leader and dangerous. Fifteen men were executed in May 1916: seven were signatories to the proclamation of the provisional government of the Irish republic; MacBride was one of the remaining eight.

Colonel Blackadder, who presided at the court martial in Richmond Barracks, had South African service but, if Tim Healy is to be believed, Blackadder with 'his fellow officers was anxious to save the lives of several prisoners, especially Major MacBride, but the accused wished to die'. Turning the tables on the conspiracy theorists, it can be argued that Healy was right: that Blackadder, who shortly afterwards resigned his commission, recognized that in MacBride he had found a genuine soldier, who had fought in campaigns and who at the court martial behaved like a soldier – as Blackadder himself would have behaved had he fallen into the hands of the kaiser in the war Britain was then fighting with Germany. At the end of the day, it is likely that Maxwell confirmed the sentence on the grounds of MacBride's past reputation as a revolutionary. Whether that constitutes revenge is a matter for debate.

Another theory current even today is that MacBride died because of the intervention of Winston Churchill. The theory goes that Churchill bribed MacBride to escape from the Pretoria Model School in December 1899. Then in 1916 – seventeen years later – Churchill wanted MacBride dead to shut him up. Well, maybe. Churchill escaped on Tuesday, 12 December. On Thursday, 14 December, MacBride is known to have been on the Tugela Heights. Anyone who has ever travelled on a South African steam train through the passes of the Drakensberg will marvel at the energy of the stokers in transporting MacBride from Pretoria to Johannesburg and down to Ladysmith in such a time. This is without accounting for the night ride of some twenty kilometres from Ladysmith to the Tugela river. This, of course, does not preclude the possibility that Churchill did, in fact, bribe his way out – the very fact that he mentioned such speculation is of interest: '... the truth is that the bribery market in the Transvaal has been spoiled by millionaires. I could not afford with my slender resources to insult them heavily enough.'[41]

The crown prosecutor at MacBride's court martial gave Tim Healy an account of what the major had said at the hearing. This is confirmed largely from the court martial papers, but it contains the following addition which may or may not be accurate:

> I thank the officers of the Court for the fair trial I have had, and the Crown counsel for the way he met every application I made. I have looked down the muzzles of too many guns in the South African War to fear death, and now please carry out your sentence.[42]

MacBride died as a soldier, shot by firing squad at 3.47 a.m. on 5 May 1916. It is said that prior to the execution, he asked Fred Allan's wife to 'Mind the flag.' This is a significant comment. There can be little doubt that this was the flag of the Irish Transvaal Brigade, still MacBride's most precious possession. In 1906 he had refused to hand it over to the lord mayor of Dublin when demanded to do so by James Laracy. In July 1907 MacBride concluded his series of articles on the brigade for the *Freeman's Journal* with the words:

> I pray that we may meet once more under the flag of ours in a struggle even nearer and dearer to our hearts.[43]

Yet MacBride did not have the Irish Transvaal brigade flag with him in Jacobs' factory. This would seem to confirm the belief that MacBride did not come into the centre of Dublin with the intention of joining a revolution.

A week before MacBride was executed, General Louis Botha sent a message of sympathy and support to John Redmond, who was opposed to the insurrection. A similar message was sent from the South African premier in 1918 when Sinn Fein was driving the Irish parliamentary party into extinction. It is as well MacBride did not know of his former commander's attitude. John Blake, however, would not have been surprised. He had always been suspicious of Louis Botha.[44]


## DISTANT ECHOES

There is a danger of reading too much into the long-term impact of MacBride's brigade. There have been distant echoes and references to it in the century since it was operational, but these echoes are bewilderingly different: from the opening by Mrs Betsie Verwoerd on 1 November 1975 of a brigade memorial, the future of which is now in doubt, to the references to John MacBride in the 1989 trial of MK commander Robert McBride, and again in 1998 when Robert McBride was arrested in Mozambique. The truth is that the importance of the brigade in the second Anglo-Boer war was that it galvanized nationalist Ireland, dragging it out of its lethargy. It reunited the Irish parliamentary party and it gave new hope and enthusiasm to the advanced nationalists. But the dramatic events of the second decade of the century leading to the establishment of the Irish Free State eclipsed for many, and especially many later historians, the memory of the brigade and the Irish pro-Boer fever it had engendered.

The interference in Irish politics from 1917 of General Smuts – 'nursery rhymes set to African lullabies for Irish ears'[45] – was not a direct consequence of nationalist Ireland's record during the Boer war. Indeed Sinn Fein had little time for Smuts and his naive peacemaking efforts. The statesman's reference to de Valera, Griffith, MacEoin and Childers as 'small men' was a comment both as false as it was indiscreet. But the alliance of William Cosgrave with General Hertzog, Vincent Massey's "fellowship of disaffection", was given a firm foundation by the old war-time alliance. For a decade the Irish and South African governments hunted as a pack to undermine the unity of the British empire and to press for 'equal sovereignty'.

One last chapter in the saga of militant Irish nationalist activity in South Africa still had to be played out. In the African spring of 1920, there emerged the Irish Republican Association of South Africa.[47] It was overtly republican and bitter, a pastiche of a zealous and fervent expatriate political movement. The association eventually had twenty-five branches, including nine on the Rand and one in Rhodesia. Its fortnightly periodical, *The Republic*, ran from 20 November 1920 to 3 June 1922. It was edited by one of the association's two intellectuals, the classicist Benjamin Farrington from Cork. The other great figure of the association was Alfred Ernest O'Flaherty, the former newspaper editor now back on side again. Other prominent members included Ella Nicholson, Advocate G.A. Mulligan, James McLoughlin, R.I.C. Scott-Hayward and Eamon Brugha, brother of Cathal Brugha.

As well as public meetings and social events, highlights of the IRA(SA)'s existence were two Irish national conventions in Bloemfontein and the sending of Ben Farrington to the Irish International in Paris in January 1922.[48] The arrival in South Africa of a special envoy from the revolutionary Dail in 1921 caused considerable excitement. Patrick J. Little toured the country addressing well-attended Irish gatherings.

On 5 May 1921, five years to the day after John MacBride was executed, Little addressed a packed town hall in Pretoria. It was reported that:

> The bullet-pierced flag of the Irish Brigade was hung on the platform, and among those on the platform were men such as Mr Gillingham, who had fought under that flag.[49]

This was one of the several flags the brigade had used. It appears that it had been given to Michael Cassidy of the IRA(SA) by a former brigader called Stephen Cavanagh. In 1952 Cassidy sent it to the Military History Bureau in Ireland from where the taoiseach instructed it to be deposited in the National Museum of Ireland.[50]

The IRA(SA) was killed by the Anglo-Irish treaty. Ben Farrington destroyed what little hope there was of unity in South African-Irish nationalist ranks by attacking de Valera in *The Republic*: 'Mr De Valera is the victim of his personality and of the Irish instinct for hero-worship.'[51]

The bitterness and in-fighting which followed well mirrored that back in Ireland. One IRA(SA) man, Scott Hayward, went to the extreme of rushing to Ireland to join de Valera and the irregulars. For his efforts, he was locked up in Kilmainham.

Scott Hayward was not the only IRA(SA) member to take up arms that fateful year. South Africa, too, had its troubles. When the Rand Revolt of white workers – the white soviet – erupted against the Smuts government,

Fordsburg, the old working-class suburb of Johannesburg, became a focus of discontent and of armed insurrection. Since the 1890s Fordsburg had been an area of Irish settlement and it had been there that some of the Irish Transvaal Brigade had gone when the British army entered the town on 31 May 1900, only to be rounded up by troops and shipped off to Ceylon. Now hostile troops were again entering Fordsburg and a new 'Irish brigade' fought as of old. Once again Fordsburg fell and when the Durban Light Infantry charged and overran the trenches of the revolutionaries, they captured a large green Irish republican flag.[52]

APPENDIX

# Roll call of known members of Irish commandos and of other Irishmen who fought for the Boers in the second Anglo-Boer war

'The roll was called punctually at 5.30 every morning; and in this conection I may say that it is a matter of sincere regret to me that I have not a complete list of the names now, as I think they should one and all be known and remembered in Ireland' (John MacBride, *Freeman's Journal*, 3 November 1906).

## ABBREVIATIONS

| | |
|---|---|
| * | known to be a founding member of Blake's commando |
| + | medical doctor |
| bitterender | commando member who probably stayed on fighting after September 1900 |
| Jhb | Johannesburg |
| list no. ... | reference number of Irish brigaders on list captured by British at Middelburg, August 1900. List is incomplete. |
| LM | Lourenço Marques |
| OFS | Republic of the Orange Free State |
| PO | post office |
| POW no. ... | prisoner of war number for those brigaders captured by the British |
| SA | South Africa |
| Tvl | Republic of the Transvaal (South African Republic) |

N.B. No complete list of brigaders has been traced. Given the turnover of personnel in the commandos it is unlikely that a full list of men ever existed. The following lists were compiled from sources in South Africa, London and Ireland which are included in the bibliography.

## I. FIRST IRISH TRANSVAAL BRIGADE
### (Blake's commando/Irish corps/MacBride's brigade)

Anderson, F.K.: Bergen, Norway; list no. 3309

Bain, James Thompson: Scottish labour organizer & journalist; Box 867, Jhb (box rented by Paterson & Co., produce merchant, Harrison St West); Tvl secret service; helped organize Irish corps; captured Heidelburg pre-August 1900

Balfour, Tom: 'dynamitard'

*Barnes, —: wounded at Modderspruit

Barrett, Michel: Modderfontein, G.M.C., Boksburg; list no. 3374

Barrett, P.: Meath

Barry, Dick: dynamite squad

Baudry, Father Alexandre: 1846–1910; PO Box 430, Jhb (box rented by Revd Father Du Puys, Fox St); list no. 3367; first catholic chaplain of the brigade – till early 1900 when 'infirmities rendered him unfit for an active campagne' [sic]

Bedford, Tom Alexander: Longford; list no. 3359

Bianes, Giovanni: Italian?; PO Box 936, Pretoria (box rented by Jahon Perino); list no. 3356

*Blake, John Y. Fillmore: colonel and brigade commander; Irish-American; wounded at Modderspruit; bitterender

*Blake, Sidney

Boetts, P.: Meath

Boers, A.G.: wounded at Modderspruit, 30 October 1899

Bouwer (Snr), Ben D.: Skinner St, Pretoria, entry in *Longland's Pretoria Directory*; list no. 3364

Bouwer, Pieter William: Skinner St, Pretoria; list no. 3370

Boyle, Johnny P.: Meenavalley House, Ardara PO, Co. Donegal; list no. 3347; said to have ridden up to three British tommies and shot them dead; later in USA

*Brennan, Mat: killed at Vaalkrantz, 5 February 1900

Burns, M.E.: 84 Parliament St, The Hill, Port Elizabeth; list no. 3317

Burns, William: Queen's Co; list no. 3357

*Byrne, Thomas (Tom) Francis: 14 St Vincent St, North Dublin; born Carrickmacross, 1877; to Jhb, 1896; list no. 3314

*Carberry, Hugh: English St, Armagh; son of cattle dealer Patrick Carberrry; played for Armagh against Cork in 1890 gaelic football semi-finals; shot in head at Modderspruit; died of stroke in Pretoria three months later (aged 32); 7–metre-high memorial in Armagh dedicated 8 June 1902

Cavanagh, Stephen: had possession of one of the commando's flags after the war

Cluggan, —

Cockburn, John: 16 Harrington St, Dublin; list no. 3362

Coetzee, Charles François: captain intendant/lieutenant(?); in charge of commissariat; list no. 3383; Gerechtsbode, Pretoria; bitterender; wounded & later killed; closely associated Irish brigade

Connolly, Frank: Drummiller, Scarva PO, Co. Down & Fordsburg, Jhb; pre-war member of Jhb Irish Amnesty Association; list no. 3327; captured Jhb, 1 July 1900 (aged 28); sent to Ceylon, POW no. 3252

Connolly, Tom: Co. Antrim; pre-war member of Jhb Irish Amnesty Association
*Conolly, J.
Cooke, Darcy Augustin: c/o his uncle, John Jex Chapman, Pietermaritzburg; aged
    c.26; was in SA by 1893; list no. 3306
*Cox, Dominic: colonial Irish (?); killed at Modderspruit, 30 October 1899, buried
    Pepworth Hill outside Ladysmith
Crosby, James: Kildangan, Co. Kildare; list no. 3318
*Dalton, Mickey: defended Transvaal flag during pro-Boer demonstration in
    Dublin, 17 December 1899; arrived from Ireland early 1900; captured in Jhb
    area, May 1900
Daly, Jack: sent out by Féis Ceoil, Belfast, arrived northern Natal c.April 1900
Daly, Thomas: Ballycroy, Co. Donegal; formerly in US army
D'Arcy, Martin MacDonnell: arrived in Natal from Ireland early 1900; killed by an
    electric tram, San Francisco, c.1904
Darragh, Pat: corporal; 'Amtremore Clontoe Richardson Cough Moneymore, Co.
    Tyrone' – another source says from Derry; list no. 3321
*Davey, —: killed at Nicholson's Nek
Davila, J.J.: Livingstone House, 20 Kildare Terrace, Bayswater, London, W; list no.
    3337
Donnelly, Jack: sent out by Féis Ceoil, Belfast, arrived northern Natal c.April 1900;
    brought MacBride a letter & shamrock from Ethna Carberry; by February
    1901 in Dawtuchet, R.I., USA
Duffy, 'Prof': took the brigade flag to State Secretary Reitz for safekeeping;
    captured Jhb area, June 1900; sent to Ceylon
Duggan, —: Co Down; captured, sent to Ceylon
Dunlop, Frank Arthur: Balbriggan, Co. Dublin & c/o Miss Lewington, 21 Highgate
    Hill, London N; was said to have edited a Jhb weekly paper before the war;
    captured Heidelburg, sent to Ceylon; had a wooden stump having lost a leg in
    an engagement in south America; list no. 3336
Dunn (Dunne?), John G.: Irish-American; received flesh wound in OFS when
    accidentally wounded by a fellow brigader; POW in India; on release
    returned to Dublin
Dunne, James F. (MacBride claimed that two brigaders called Dunne were killed)
Dunville, Michael James: lieutenant; 53 Bramah Rd, North Brixton, London SW
    & Fordsburg, Jhb; 'best commisariat officer on the Brigade's staff'; list no.
    3324; captured Jhb, 1 July 1900 (aged 39); sent to Ceylon, POW no. 3261
Edge, D.W.: list no. 3346; Plasllangaffe Cottage, Dundrum, Dublin
Enright, Thomas: lieutenant; Monaco Hotel, Jhb; possibly later in a commando led
    by Mitchell; list no. 3377; captured Bloemfontein, 23 March 1900 (aged 45);
    sent to St Helena, POW no. 3783, from which he escaped on the *Galician* on
    22 Nov. 1902
Evans, G.M.: stand 631, Burgersdorp Station Rd, Jhb; list no. 3338
Fahey, Pat C.: born Clare (MacBride says from Louth); list no. 3304; 'dynamitard';
    killed at Vaalkrantz, 5 February 1900; Davitt calls him Michael Fahey;
    remains now interred at Caesar's Camp overlooking Ladysmith
Fitzgibbon, Thomas: Balbriggan, Co. Dublin & Queen St, Port Elizabeth; list no.
    3378

Fleming, James: PO Box 1018, Jhb (box rented by T. Rundle, builder, Commissioner St); list no. 3373

Flynn, Michael: Newton Forbes, Co. Longford; list no. 3331; son of national schoolmaster; to SA with John Thompson, *c*.1897; brother, James Flynn of Inniskilling Fusiliers, killed in British advance on Ladysmith

Focks, John Louis: PO Box 378, Pretoria (box rented by auditor-general); list no. 3371

Focks, John Pieter: PO Box 329, Pretoria (box rented by Solomon Gillingham); list no. 3369

French, Jim: Connaught Place, Cork; (Dublin carriage builder) & 106 Pritchard St, Jhb; 'a plucky lad'; ill in military hospital (Jhb area), May 1900; returned to brigade; bitterender; list no. 3382

(Ten Frenchmen, names unknown)

Gatzki, Robert: PO Box 131, Pretoria (box rented by A.C.Vlotman); list no. 3365

*Gaynor, —: lieutenant; Longford; wounded with two bullets in the arm at Modderspruit, October 1899; captured Jhb, June 1900

*Gerraghty, J.: Pretoria; treasurer of John Daly branch of Irish National Foresters; bricklayer(?)

Gillingham, Solomon William: JP; baker & confectioner; Church St West, PO Box 329, Pretoria, entry in *Longland's Pretoria Directory*; unlikely if actually fought, but helped to organize first Irish Transvaal Brigade and later Lynch's commando; was in the Commissariat Dept, Pretoria; captured Pretoria, 24 August 1900 (aged 41); sent to Diyatalawa, Ceylon on 3 September 1900, POW no. 11253; active member of the Irish Republican Association of SA, 1920/22; died 1927

Glancy, —: died

Gorman, John: Nenagh, Co. Tipperary; list no. 3342

Guigan, J.

*Halley, 'little Mike': Waterford and San Francisco, California; small in height; with MacBride at Colenso; dynamite squad; bitterender; list no. 3333

*Hanafin/Hannifin, Mike: walked 800 kilometres from Beira to Lourenço Marques to catch train to Tvl to join Irish corps; killed at Balmoral in 1901

*Haney, Tom

Harold, James: Castle St, Dalkey, Co. Dublin; possibly came out with Dr Walsh; Natal early 1900; captured in Pretoria, *c.* 5 June 1900; 1914 wrote a vitriolic attack on Lynch & his commando

Hawney, Thomas: Ballybunnion, Co. Kerry; list no. 3305

Hayes, Teddy: known as 'Tottie'; Wexford & Mafeking

*Herlihy (Herlily?), Tom: dynamite squad

*Higgins, Andy: sergeant; Co. Down; knee shattered at Modderspruit; returned to duty Christmas 1899; fought at Pieter's Hill; apparently asked by Boers to investigate Lynch's commando

Hindon, Oliver John (Jack): Scot; does not seem to have been formally in Blake's commando but was closely associated the brigade; later captain of his own commando

Hinton, J.

Hughes, E.: Aberdeen St, 23 Woodstock, Cape Town; list no. 3328

Hunt, C.D.: c/o A.L.Murphy, Garrison Lewis Co. Kentucky, USA; list no. 3310

Hunt, Dick: (possibly the same as C.D. Hunt); New York state; friend of Hugh Carberry; shot three times at Balmoral on 7 Jan. 1901, survived; bitterender with Jhb commando

Hutchinson, —: for a period in OFS he & Luther with Theron's Scouts

Joyce, Maurice: Ballyryan, Westmonard, Co. Tipperary (Clare?); list no. 3322

Kavanagh, Danny: Galway; arm smashed at Modderspruit

*Kennedy, Joe: Balbriggan, Co. Dublin; bitterender

*Kepner, —: wounded at Modderspruit

Kidd, J.Baird: 17 Ibrox Terrace, Ibrox, Glasgow; list no. 3345

King, J.N.: Madaline King, Phillipsburg Centre Co, Box 95, PA, USA; list no. 3315

Kingsman, Arthur William: Fordsburg, Jhb; captured Fordsburg, 21 June 1900 (aged 28); sent to Ceylon, POW no. 3249

Lalor, P.: Ballmahalla, Cordal PO, Co. Kerry; list no. 3320

*Langtrey, —

*Laracy, James J.: captain; Walker St, Kilkenny; list no. 3360; captured, sent to Ceylon where remained for two years; later enemy of MacBride; 1907 thirty-four verses ('The captive soldier of the veldt') by Annie M. Laracy appeared in the *Kilkenny People*

Larissey, — : Dublin; wanted by Dublin Castle(?); possibly the same person as Laracy

Lary, Frank: Malmesbury, Cape; list no. 3350; captured Heidelburg

*Lasso, Jim: killed at Vaalkrantz, 5 February 1900

Leeus, Benedict: Jhb; captured Jhb, 3 July 1900 (aged 23); sent to Ceylon, POW no. 3074

Lennon, Paddy: 'big sturdy fighter'; Co. Down; with MacBride at Colenso; captured Jhb, c.1 June 1900, sent to Ceylon

Lethiec, Lewis: PO Box 895, Jhb; same address as Charles O'Connell; list no. 3351

Lovely, John R.: lieutenant; c/o Mrs G. Lovely, 64 Haman St, Jeppestown, Jhb; list no. 3339, captured, sent to Ceylon

Luther, Ernest (Teddy) William: b. Halberstadt, Germany 1879; fought in Greek army; 1898 joined 201st New York volunteer regiment; left New York, 28 February 1900; LM, 29 April 1900; joined Blake in OFS, 7 May 1900; with Theron's Scouts for period before rejoining the brigade; died Machadorp hospital 11 September 1900 of wounds received in action near Weltevreden on Sunday, 9 Sept 1900; two manuscript war diaries published posthumously in one volume – very rare

Lynch, —: died

McArdle, Jack: arrived Natal from Ireland, early April 1900

*MacBride, John: Westport, Co. Mayo, & Jhb; assayer, Langlaagte block B mine; main influence behind pre-war Jhb Irish Amnesty Association; he & Gillingham key figures in est. of brigade; special JP of Tvl Republic; major and brigade second in command; brigade commander, 7 June–23 September 1900; list no. 3335; court-martialled and executed, 1916

*McCallum, Malcolm: lieutenant & later captain; American who had never been to Ireland; protestant; Jhb though possibly Pretoria stonemason; fought well at Colenso; prominent in brigade during retreat in Tvl; unpopularity in brigade probably due to attempts to impose discipline but a close comrade of

MacBride; bitterender; captured Tonteldoos, 27 August 1901 (aged 48); sent to Shahjahanpur, India, POW no. 22986

McCarthy, Michael John: killed on Natal front, aged about 26

*McCormack, Jim: Longford

McDermott, Frank: Listowel, Co. Kerry; captured Jhb, sent to Ceylon

*McDonagh, Dick: corporal; Listowel, Co. Kerry & 13 Crown Rd, Fordsburg, Jhb; one of the original organizers; list no. 3302; later lieutenant, Irish Volunteers, New York

McDonnell, —: killed or died

*McDonough, Mick

McElroy, James P (see entry on p. 179 below)

McGee, —: killed or died

McGibbon, Bob: Co. Down; captured Jhb area, sent to St Helena

McGlade, —*: Belfast; aged 33; 1.93m (6ft 4in) tall; (Long Jack ?); went missing from brigade camp at Pepworth Hill, rumoured to have been shot by British as an 'Irish rebel'

*McGlew, Jack: Rowans, Balbriggan, Co. Dublin; wounded at Balmoral; bitterender; list no. 3332

MacGoey, Brian: settled in New York after war

McGuigan, J.: sent out by Féis Ceoil, Belfast; northern Natal c. April 1900; possibly the McQuiggan who had a fight with the brigade's African cook on 21 August 1900

McKibbin, Bob: Kildeel, Co. Down & Jhb; flagbearer after death of Tommy Oates; list no. 3340; captured Jumpers Deep (aged 27); sent to St Helena, POW no. 12169

McLade, —: Belfast; captured at Ladysmith

Magee, Thomas: 83 Albert St, Belfast; list no. 3375

*Malan, —: lieutenant

Mallon, Charles: sent out by Féis Ceoil, Belfast, April 1900

*Malone, Pat: 'fiery old Pat'; sergeant; Louth & 13 Crown Rd, Fordsburg, Jhb; veteran of the Irish 1867 insurrection; probably the Paddy Maloney who received a light wound on the arm at Thaba Nchu in 1900; list no. 3301

Martin, G.: 266 City Rd, London; list no. 3316

Matthews, —: arrived from Ireland in early 1900

Maximitiz, Oscar: killed at Spioen Kop, 24 January 1900

Menton, Thomas: (originally Madden); Galway; major; list no. 3081; pre-war, governor Jhb prison – Revd Forsyth, Roslin Villa, Observatory, claimed Menton was a brigade member

Mitchell, John Joseph: captain; former Invincible(?); list no. 3303; Galway & 106 Pritchard St, Jhb, where he ran a clothes cleaning shop; later joined Lynch's commando and possibly afterwards returned to Blake's commando or led his own commando

Molloy, —: elected major 6 July 1900

Mulder, Jan: uncle of Denys Reitz; member of the Irish corps for short period in 1900

*Mullins, Jack: c/o Miss D. Mullen, 27 Lower O'Connell St, Dublin; draper's assistant; list no. 3307; killed at Bergendal, 27 August 1900

Murphy, James: Patrick St, Kilkenny: list no. 3361; 'a bright young fellow'; died of fever outside Ladysmith, February 1900

Murphy, Pierce: possibly pre-war member of Jhb Irish Amnesty Association; captured, sent to Ceylon

Murray, John: c/o Mrs D. Davidson, 822 Rutherglen Rd, Glasgow, NB

Nolan, John: Ballyseedy, Tralee, Co. Kerry; list no. 3325

Nolan, John: Holywell Row, Mildenhall, Suffolk; list no. 3381

Norris, Dave

Oates, P.J.: captain; Killarney, Kerry; father of Tom Oates; later joined Lynch's commando; Davitt had tea with Mr & Mrs Oates in Jhb in April 1900; was with a group of Irish in the retreat along the Delagoa Bay railway line in the E. Tvl; in Brooklyn after the war

Oates, Tom: Killarney(?); flag bearer; killed by a shell at Modderspruit, 30 October 1899 (aged 19); buried on Pepworth Hill

O'Byrne, T.

O'Connell, Charles: Flesichack's Court, PO Box 895, Jhb; same address as Lewis Lethiec; list no. 3353

O'Connell, 'Long' Jack: Chapel Gane, Skibbern, Co.. Cork; list no. 3323; wounded(?)

O'Connell, John: same Jhb address as Charles O'Connell; list no. 3352

O'Donnelly, J.

O'Grady, Pat

*O'Hare, Dan: major(?); Belfast

*O'Hare, P.

O'Haughey, James: Derrynoose, Co. Armagh; list no. 3344; friend of Anna Johnston

*O'Keefe, Jim: sergeant; Co. Kilkenny; dynamite squad; list no. 3358; died in USA, c.1903

O'Kelly, Owen: assistant at Egan's, Talbot St, Dublin; arrived Natal from Ireland in early 1900

*O'Leary, Jerry: wounded at Balmoral; bitterender

O'Neil, Arthur: PO Box 617, Pretoria (box rented by Durrant & Co.); single; captured at Pieters Hill, POW no. 70 (An Irishman named O'Neill deserted to the British at Ladysmith. MacBride claimed a brigader called O'Neill died in SA.)

*O'Reilly, Frank: sergeant-major; colonial Irish; saved MacBride's life at Colenso; captured Jhb June 1900, sent to Ceylon

O'Shea, Michel John: PO Box 510, Pretoria (box rented by W.W. Brooke Howard); list no. 3380; this may be the O'Shea who came with the Chicago Irish

*Olsen, —: 'a sturdy Norwegian, who had joined the Brigade pending the raising of a Scandinavian Corps'; wounded in the breast at Modderspruit; left the brigade; killed at Magersfontein

Papillon, —: sergeant; injured outside Ladysmith in vehicle accident

Pearson, G.A.: Mrs Pearson, c/o R. Calderwood, Kimberley, Adv. Office, Kimberley

*Pearson, S.

*Plunkett, —: protestant

Pollard, —: captain

Power, Bill: Knockawn, Co. Waterford; list no. 3376

Quinn, Pat: Ballyardle PO, Co. Down; list no. 3326

Raw, F.: sent out by Féis Ceoil, Belfast, April 1900

Richardson, Pat: Irish-Australian; Melbourne, Victoria & Westminster Club, Brunswick St, Fitzroy; killed at Vaalkrantz; list no. 3312

Riley, John: Holyoke, USA; possibly came out with ambulance corps in Feb 1900; wounded on highveld by shrapnel in thigh

Rowand, Clarence: 97 Nichol St, Newark, 'NZ', USA; list no. 3319

Russell, A.: 'Irish Red Cross, afterwards fought for the same Brigade'; LM, June/July 1900

Ryan, John Michel ('Mick the liar'): 23 Nelson St, Tralee, Co. Kerry; list no. 3354

Ryan, Mick ('Big Mick'): Bishopswood, Dundrum, Co. Tipperary. (At least one Mick Ryan was in the original intake and at least one appears to have been captured & sent to St Helena. MacBride claimed a brigader called Ryan died, but he may be the Irish-American who arrived in April 1900. It is said one Mike Ryan was the son of a US senator.)

Shea, —: captain (This may be Michel O'Shea listed above or John Shea who fought with the American Scouts.)

Shenton, Thomas: major

Sheppard, Reginald: PO Box 701, Pretoria (box rented by Mann & Co.); list no. 3368

Slater, Edward Thornhill: lieutenant; Jhb, journalist on *The Star* & then the *Standard & Diggers' News*; captured Jhb, 22 June 1900 (aged 36); sent to Ceylon, POW no. 3241

Smith, —: deserted from British army; wounded in one arm; LM, June/July 1900

Smith, Willie: Jhb, aged 13

Tennant, Sid: wounded right side at Damfontein; aged 21

Thompson, —: captured Jhb, June 1900

*Tierney, Tom: dynamite squad

*Tinen, —: wounded at Modderspruit

Tully, Joe: colonial Irish, Kimberley; 'dynamitard'; with MacBride at Colenso; list no. 3311; captured Jhb, June 1900, sent to Ceylon

Tully, Tim: died of wounds received at Spioen Kop or Vaalkrantz

Tynan, Dan: Higgins Town, John's Well, Co. Kilkenny; list no. 3355

Unger, Fred: American journalist who was with the Irish corps as it retreated from Pretoria eastward & who was officially a member of the brigade, though through no wish of his own

van Blommestein, William Osmond: PO Box 365, Pretoria (box rented by P.G.van der Byl); list no. 3384

*van Hecke OMI (van Eek), Father Alphonse: 1872–1928; chaplain from early 1900; Belgian; aged *c*.25; captured in Jhb, June 1900, but soon released; cycled to Pretoria to catch up with the brigade; later solemnized marriage of John MacBride and Maud Gonne in Paris in 1903

Wade, Joe: sergeant; Whiteheart, Balbriggan, Co. Dublin; friend of Hugh Carberry; dynamite squad; with MacBride at Colenso; wounded at Balmoral; bitterender; dressed in uniform of 19th Hussars; list no. 3330

*Waldeck, George

*Walsh, Dr M.S.: Swords, Co. Dublin; leader of the proposed Irish Ambulance Corps; arrived from Ireland *c*. March 1900; short visit to Lourenço Marques from Tvl, 28 June 1900

Watermeyer, Philip: Staats Prokureur Kantoor, Pretoria; list no. 3363

(Whelan, John R.: arrested and imprisoned in Mafeking while preparing to leave to
    join the brigade)
White, T.: c/o Miss White, PO Box 2435, Jhb (box rented by C.de G. Canisius, law
    agent, Loveday St); list no. 3308
Wieland, G.C.: Tadema, Rosemekal Dist., Middelburg; list no. 3341
William, W.: Mrs A. Clair, Rufane Vale, Port Elizabeth; list no. 3349
Willis, Robert William: Leeuwin St, Cape Town; list no. 3379
Wilson, Butch: probably member of Irish corps; Irish-American; captured Jhb, 10
    July 1900; sent to Ceylon, POW no. 3341 (see also p. 180 below)
Wilson, Harry: Mrs G. Herbert, 37 Ackers St, Oxford Rd, Manchester; list no.
    3348
Wilson, Walter: Irish-American; golden hair; uncertain if brigade member; killed
    16 July 1901, aged 26

*Known names of horses in Blake's commando*
Fenian Boy: (John MacBride); 'a beauty of a pony'; not MacBride's horse killed at
    Colenso; probably was the lame horse MacBride had to leave when he
    crossed into Mozambique in September 1900
Irish Willie: 'The mascot of the Irish-American Brigade, missing since the fight at
    Sand River, but sure to turn up'
Shorty Kelly: (Teddy Luther); died of wounds sustained in battle at Donkerhoek in
    E.Tvl on Wed. 11 July 1900
'5 DG [Dragoon Guards] B136 JH': brand on the Irish hunter captured at
    Ladysmith and ridden by Colonel Blake

### 2. CHICAGO IRISH-AMERICAN AMBULANCE CORPS

## (Amalgamated into First Irish Tvl Brigade on arrival in Jhb in April 1900)

+Alderholt, Dr A.D.
Cahill, Richard J.
Carroll, Patrick
Cashel, Thomas
Castello (Costello?), John
+Conroy, Dr A.F.
Costello, John
Coyne, James E.
Daley, Daniel
Davis, Richard Harding: author; accompanied by his wife, Davis was not a corps
    member but travelled with it from LM
Davy, Michael: Sligo
Duff, John

Dunn, J.G.: this may be one of the two brigaders called Dunne whom MacBride claimed died in SA
Dwyer, William
+Ederholt, Dr E.
Egan, Edward M.: killed, probably at battle of Bergendal, 27 August 1900
Enright, Mike: lieutenant
Foley, Daniel
Griffin, Patrick J.
Hawkins, Edward
Healy, Edward G.
Hill, James
(?) Hollis —
Hurley, William
Linchloter, R.
+Long, Dr Ross D.
+McCauley/McAuley, Dr Herbert H.: ill in hospital when British entered Pretoria, rejoined brigade in E. Tvl, 16 August 1900
McFighe, Jacobus Harold: Wood Park, Chicago; captured Pretoria 2 July 1900 (aged 20); sent to Ceylon 3 September 1900 on the same ship as Gillingham, POW no. 11337
MacHugh, Daniel
*McNamara, Dr James P.: corps' medical leader
MacTeigne, W.
(?) Mann, James R.
Morrissey, Joseph Richard
Murphy, John A.
Murray, Thomas
Naughton, Thomas: Ardare, Limerick; killed E. Tvl, c.August 1900
O'Connor, Patrick: captain & corps leader; MacBride claimed he was from Moylough, Co. Galway
O'Hare, Hubert: Mayo
O'Hara, Mike C.: born West Limerick; bad fever in E. Tvl, July 1900; killed between Nooitgedacht and Waterval Onder
O'Shea, — (see p. 175 above)
Quinn, John J.: lieutenant
Reilly, John: lieutenant; Transvaal Hotel, Pretoria; captured Tobakop, 1 May 1900 (aged 31); sent to Ceylon 6 August 1900, POW no. 3363
Rickard, Joseph
Rogers, John J.
Ryan, Hugh B.: lieutenant & later in joint command with O'Connor; Tipperary; Fred Unger, the journalist, used Ryan to carry his despatches to LM for cabling to America; MacBride claimed a brigader called Ryan died in South Africa
+Slattery, Dr James J.
Varslius, Frederick
Welsh, John

## 3. SECOND IRISH TRANSVAAL BRIGADE
### (Lynch's commando)

(Gillingham, Solomon: originator of the commando; see entry under p. 172 above)

Hayes, Joseph: may have joined MacBride later in the war

Heron, M.F.

Kidmey, George: gave evidence at Lynch's 1903 treason trail in London

⁺Leach, Dr: with commando *c.* April/May 1900

Lynch MA, Arthur Alfred: colonel and brigade commander; Australian-Irish; condemned to death for treason, 1903, but pardoned, 1907

McElroy, James P.: Monaghan and Jhb; formerly in Blake's commando(?); (list no. 3313); captured Jhb, 16 July 1900 (aged 37); sent to Ceylon, POW no. 3079

Meintjes, Albertus Jacobus: Braamfontein, Jhb; captured Pretoria, 10 July 1900 (aged 25), sent to Ceylon, POW no. 3080

Mitchell, John Joseph: major (see p. 174 above)

Mooney, Patrick

Oates, P.J.: captain; formerly in Blake's commando

O'Connor, William: Jhb; captured Jhb, 2 June 1900 (aged 30); sent to Ceylon, POW no. 3087

Terpend, —

Viljoen, E.: gave evidence at Lynch's 1903 treason trail in London

von Gotsch, —: one of a number of German members

Lynch's commando contained members of the following nationalities:

American (USA)
Austrian
Australian
Boer (Cape colony, Orange Free State, Transvaal)
Bulgarian (2)
Dutch
English (1)

French (several)
Greece
German (several)
Irish
Italian
Russian

## 4. IRISH OR IRISH AMERICANS IN OTHER COMMANDOS

General Cheere Emmet (colonial Irish)

*Barberton commando*
Murphy, Thomas F.

*Blignaut's commando*
Six former members of Blake's corps

*Bouwer's commando*
Gallagher, —
Lang, —

*General de Wet's staff*
O'Donnell, —: captain; Limerick

*Fordsburg commando*
Corbett, William: Stand 750, Jhb; captured Jhb, 7 August 1900 (aged 44); sent to St Helena, POW no. 12020

*Heidelberg commando*
(F.C. Lombard/Walter Mears: 'looting corps of scoundrels')
⁺Allport, Dr Percy: 1860–1932; graduate of Royal University of Ireland; to SA 1882
Flanaghan, F.C.: killed at battle of Spioen Kop, January 1900
O'Grady, W.: corporal (Irish?)
Wilson, Butch: Irish-American; Jhb; captured Jhb 10 July 1900 (aged 53), sent to Ceylon 7 August 1900, POW no. 3341; previously in Blake's corps ?

*Johannesburg commando*
Condon, Patrick: Jhb; captured Frederikstad, 16 June 1900 (aged 50), POW no. 12019, released 9 November 1901
Ramsland, Herman Adolfus: Irish-American; captured Jhb, 15 August 1900 (aged 40); sent to Ceylon, POW no. 14771
Wood, Harry McGaw: Irish-American; Jhb; captured Barberton, 13 September 1900 (aged 26), sent to Ceylon, POW no. 15023

The following formerly served in Blake's corps (see individual entries):

Blake, John Y.F.: colonel
Coetzee, Charles: lieutenant
French, Jim
Halley, Mike
Hannifin, Mike
Hunt, Dick
Kennedy, Joe

McCallum, Malcolm: captain
McGlew, John
Malan, —: lieutenant
O'Leary, Jerry
Ryan, Mike
Wade, Joe: sergeant

*Lydenburg commando*
O'Grady, —: Transvaal-Irish; family farmed near Dullstroom from 1870s; two generations in concentration camp at Balmoral, where two children died

*Kroonstad commando*
Whelan, William Thomas: 1849–1943; colonial-Irish, born Cape Town; worked on *Argus*, at diamond fields, C.M.R.(?); with his commando at Ladysmith; possibly POW near East London

*Theron's Scouts*
(closely connected with Blake's corps)
O'Brien, —: quartermaster; Irish-American Luther, Hutchinson, MacBride & a few other Irish brigaders were with the scouts for a short time, c.May/June 1900
O'Donnell,—: captain; bitterender; same man as on de Wet's staff?

*Pretoria commando*
Dally, Charles: Irish-American; 1035 North, Illinois, USA; captured Pretoria, 4
June 1900 (aged 24); sent to India, POW no. 17809

*In one of General Cronje's commandos*
Donnelly, Arthur: Irish-American; Pretoria detective force before war; captured,
POW on prisonship *Manila* (Table Bay), released because of (false) claim to
be Red Cross member

*Commando unknown*
Delaney, —: comdt
Kelly, Patrick Aloysius: Maryborough; captured *c.*January 1900, sent Ceylon as
POW; 1920s & 1930s owned & ran White House Hotel, Marine Parade,
Durban (demolished 1970s)


## 5. POSSIBLE BRIGADERS OR THOSE CLOSELY ASSOCIATED
WITH THE BRIGADES

Langtry, J.
Mooney, P.
Norris, D.
Stone, J.
Swanton, John George: born 21 February 1878, son of Timothy George Swanton
from Cork; died 9 August 1954
Thompson, John: from Newtown Forbes, Co. Longford
Tynan (no. 1), Patrick J.P.: Invincible
Whittall, Dr L.J.
Worthington, Dr

# Notes

### INTRODUCTION

1   Quoted in McCracken, 'The land the famine Irish forgot', Crawford (ed.), *The hungry stream*, p. 53.
2   General commentaries on the history of the Irish in South Africa include Akenson, *The Irish diaspora: a primer*, chapter 5; Akenson, *Occasional papers on the Irish in South Africa*; McCracken (ed.), *The Irish in southern Africa, 1795–1910*, as vol. 2 of *SAIS* (1992); and McCracken (ed), *Ireland and South Africa in modern times*, as vol. 3 of *SAIS* (1996).
3   Bull, 'Aided Irish immigration to the Cape, 1823–1900', *SAIS*, vol. 2 (1992), pp 269–77.
4   McCracken, 'Alfred Aylward, fenian editor of the *Natal Witness*', *Journal of Natal and Zulu History*, vol. 4 (1981), pp 49–61; and Smith, *Alfred Aylward, The tireless agitator*.
5   Bulpin, *Storm over the Transvaal*, pp 42–5; and Ronan, *Forty South African years*, pp 110–23.
6   See, for example, J.L. McCracken, *New light at the Cape of Good Hope: William Porter, the father of Cape Liberalism*; and Henderson, *An Ulsterman in Africa*.
7   McCracken, 'The Irish in South Africa: The police, a case study', *Familia: Journal of the Ulster Historical Guild*, pp 40–6.
8   Southey, 'Dogged entrepreneurs: some prominent Irish retailers', *SAIS*, vol. 2 (1992), pp 163–78.
9   McCracken, 'Irish settlement and identity in South Africa before 1910', *Irish Historical Studies*, vol. 110 (November 1992), p. 135.
10  Holt, *The Boer war*, p. 82.

### CHAPTER 1: STORM CLOUDS ON THE HIGHVELD

1   McCracken, 'The nature of the Irish settlement in southern Africa', *SAIS*, vol. 2 (1992), p. 11.
2   Mr M. Whelan to D.P. McCracken, 9 April 1997.
3   *Standard and Transvaal Mining Chronicle*, 12 & 19 March 1887.
4   Daniel, 'Irish networks in the Cape and Natal, 1871–1914', *SAIS*, vol. 2 (1992), pp 73–90.
5   McCracken, 'Irish settlement and identity in South Africa before 1910', *Irish Historical Studies*, vol. 28, no. 110 (November 1992), pp 146–7.
6   Banks, *Edward Blake*, p. 227 *et seq.*
7   McCracken, *Irish Pro-Boers*, pp 31–4.
8   *The Great Transvaal Irish conspiracy* (anonymous pamphlet, *c.*1899), p. 4.
9   Seton, 'Irishmen in South Africa', *The Gael* (January 1900), pp 19–21.
10  *Freeman's Journal*, 13 October 1906 and 12 January 1907; *Shan Van Vocht*, vol. 1, no.2, 7 February 1896; and *Weekly Star*, 4 January 1896. Some Irish-South Africans such as St John Carr and acting chief detective Andrew Timble were sympathetic towards the Jameson raid.
11  *Report of the director of census, 15 July 1896* (Johannesburg, 1896), pp 54–5.
12  National Archives of Ireland, State Paper Office, Crime Branch Special (DMP) 5/13020, 14 January 1897.
13  Jordan, *Major John MacBride*, p. 80.
14  Colum, *Arthur Griffith*, p. 32.
15  Ryan, *Fenian memoirs*, p. 187; and NAI, SPO, CBS, S/11534, 'Suspect John McBride', 26 March 1896.
16  *Proceedings of the Irish Race Convention* (Dublin, 1896), p. 8.

17 *Evening Telegraph* (Dublin), 5 and 31 October 1896; *Freeman's Journal*, 12 January 1907; and *Johannesburg Times*, 7 September 1896.

18 *The Nation*, 13 July 1897; and NAI, SPO, CBS, 5/13923.

19 P.A. McCracken, 'Arthur Griffith's South African sabbatical', *SAIS*, vol. 3 (1996), pp 227–62.

20 *The great Transvaal Irish conspiracy*, pp 4–5.

21 Brain (ed.), *The Cape diary of Bishop Patrick Raymond Griffith for the years 1837 to 1839*, p. 160.

22 *Sunday Press*, 15 January 1989.

23 *United Irishman*, 11 November 1899.

24 See Edwards, Evans, Rhys and MacDiarmid, *Celtic nationalism*, pp 127–8; *The Leader*, 23 December 1899; and *United Irishman*, 15 July and 23 September 1899, and 17 February 1900.

25 Ryan, *Fenian memoirs*, pp 186–8.

26 No copies of the *Middelburg Courant* have been traced. See P.A. McCracken, 'The quest for the *Middelburg Courant*', *SAIS*, vol. 3 (1996), pp 282–90; and National Library of Ireland, ms. 19934, Celtic Literary Society, 24 & 28 October 1898.

CHAPTER 2: THE IRISH TRANSVAAL
BRIGADE IS FOUNDED

1 A copy of this curious document is housed in the South African Library.

2 Pádraig O Cuanancháin to D.P. McCracken, 9 September 1996.

3 Ruda, 'The Irish Transvaal Brigades', *Irish Sword*, vol. 11, no. 45 (1974), p. 204.

4 Conroy, 'The "Loyal" Irish rebels', *Kommando* (December 1956), p. 23; Lupini, *Camillo Ricchiardi*, p. 40; Monick, *Shamrock and springbok*, pp 60–1; and *United Irishman*, 22 December 1900.

5 The saga of the Russian involvement in the second Anglo-Boer war appears in Davidson and Filatova, *The Russians and the Anglo-Boer war, 1899–1900*.

6 Macnab, *The French colonel* (Johannesburg, 1975); and Spaight, *War rights on land*, pp 494–5.

7 Hillegas, *With the Boer forces*, pp 255–6.

8 *Freeman's Journal*, 13 October 1906; and Jordan, *Major John MacBride*, pp 24–5.

9 *The Times history of the war in South Africa*, vol. 3, p. 76n.

10 Davitt, *The Boer fight for freedom*, p. 318.

11 Cammack, *The Rand at war, 1899–1900*, p. 54.

12 P.A. McCracken, 'Shaping the times: Irish journalists', *SAIS*, vol. 2 (1992), p. 152.

13 *The great Transvaal Irish conspiracy*, pp 9–11; and the *Standard and Diggers' News*, 28 September 1899.

14 McCracken, *The Irish pro-Boers*, pp 46–7; and *Freeman's Journal*, 2 October 1899.

15 *Irish News*, 9 March 1901; and *United Irishman*, 22 December 1900.

16 Blake, *West Pointer with the Boers*, p. 51.

17 Hillegas, *With the Boer forces*, p. 249.

18 Lynch, *My life story*, pp 165–6.

19 Byrne typescript, p. 4.

20 Aylward, *The Transvaal of today*, chapter 4; and Smith, *Alfred Aylward, the tireless agitator*, chapter 4.

21 Rossyln, *Twice captured*, pp 390–2.

22 McCracken, 'Alfred Aylward, Fenian editor of the *Natal Witness*', *Journal of Natal and Zulu history*, vol. 4 (1981), pp 49–61.

23 *Natal Witness*, 30 September and 9 December 1899.

24 Ms Judith A. Sibley, US Military Academy Archives, West Point to D.P. McCracken, 29 October 1996.

25 *Official register of the officers and cadets of the U.S. Military Academy, West Point, N.Y., 1877, 1878, 1879* and 1880; and *Biographical register of the officers and graduates … West Point*, vol. III (1891), p. 338.

26 *The Post*, 5 January 1900.

27 National Archives, Washington DC, USA, file 4635, ACP, 1889 (J.Y.F. Blake) (9W3/19/36/L/BOV 1212). See also *Thirty-Ninth annual reunion of the association of the graduates of … West Point, June 12th, 1908* (Saginaw, 1908), pp 72–4.

28 *The great Transvaal Irish conspiracy*, p. 12.

29 *United Irishmen*, 21 December 1901.

30 Hickey and Doherty, *A dictionary of Irish history since 1800*, p. 268.

31 Davitt, *The Boer fight for freedom*, p. 322; and Zimmermann, *Irish political*

street ballads, p. 293. See also *Daily
Express* (Dublin), 16 October 1899.
32 Byrne typescript, p. 5.
33 NAI, CBS, S/21831, 21 May 1900.
34 *Freeman's Journal*, 13 October 1906;
and *Irish News*, 9 March 1901.
35 Daniel, 'Irish networks in the Cape
and Natal, 1871–1914', *SAIS*, vol. 2
(1992), pp 82–3.
36 Davitt, *The Boer fight for freedom*,
p. 320.
37 Reitz, *Commando: a Boer journal of the
war*, pp 296 and 299.
38 Trinity College, Dublin, Library,
Davitt papers, Davitt to John Dillon, 4
April 1900.

CHAPTER 3: THE ROAD TO
LADYSMITH

1 *Freeman's Journal*, 20 October 1906.
2 Greenwall, *Artists and illustrations of the
Anglo-Boer war*, p. 123.
3 *The Graphic*, 18 December 1899.
4 *Irish Sword*, vol. V, no.21 (1962),
p. 266; and Hayes-McCoy, *A history of
Irish flags*, p. 184.
5 *Standard and Diggers' News*, 11
October 1899; and Cammack, *The
Rand at war*, p. 55.
6 *Standard and Diggers' News*, 11
October 1899.
7 Pakenham, *Boer war*, p. 106.
8 For reports of the Irish in the Boer
camp, see *Natal Witness*, 12 and 14
October 1899.
9 Maurice, *History of the war*, vol. 1, p. 49.
10 National Archives, Pretoria, PSY73,
Affidavits in connection with alleged
looting etc., affidavit by H.S.
Lombard, 19 June 1900. See also
Cammack, *The Rand at war*, pp 88–9.
11 *Contemporary Review* (December
1901), pp 867–8.
12 *Natal Witness*, 24 March 1900.
13 Reitz, *Commando*, p. 94.
14 Hillegas, *With the Boer forces*, p. 269;
and Macnab, *The French colonel,
Villebois-Mareuil and the Boers*, p. 116.
15 Trinity College, Dublin, Davitt
papers, Davitt to John Dillon, 4 April
1900. See also *Daily Express* (Dublin),
16 October 1899 and *Freeman's
Journal*, 29 July 1907.
16 *Natal Witness*, 27 November 1899.
17 Pakenham, *Boer War*, p. 132.
18 *Freeman's Journal*, 20 October 1906.
19 Blake, *A West Pointer with the Boers*,
p. 64; and Griffith, *Thank God we kept
the flag flying*, p. 38.
20 Inglis, *Roger Casement*, p. 53.
21 NAI, State Paper Office, Crime
Branch Special S/20225A, 20 October
1899.
22 McCracken, 'The Irish literary
movement, Irish doggerel and the
Boer War', *Études Irlandaises*, no.22
(1995), pp 112–13.
23 Gregory, *Poets and dreamers*, pp 75–6.
24 Griffith, *Thank God we kept the flag
flying*, p. 35.
25 Blake, *A West Pointer with the Boers*, p.
68; and *Freeman's Journal*, 20 October
1899.
26 Blake, *A West Pointer with the Boers*,
p. 59.

CHAPTER 4: LADYSMITH AND THE
TUGELA

1 Lady Gregory, *Poets and dreamers*, p. 73.
2 Blake, *A West Pointer with the Boers*,
p. 79; and *Freeman's Journal*, 3
November 1906.
3 *Natal Witness*, 3 February 1900.
4 Belfield, *The Boer war*, p. 24.
5 Blake, *A West Pointer with the Boers*,
p. 79.
6 Ibid., p. 81. Martin in his *The Boer
war*, p. 74, claims that Blake's men
manned Long Tom in this battle.
7 Conan Doyle, *The great Boer war*, p. 124.
8 See Blake, *A West Pointer with the Boers*,
p. 87; *Die Volksstem*, 4 November 1899;
*Freeman's Journal*, 3 November 1906;
and Jordan, *John MacBride*, p. 30.
9 Blake, *A West Pointer with the Boers*,
pp 84–5; Byrne typescript p. 5;
*Contemporary Review* (December
1901), pp 856–92; and *Natal Witness*,
17 November 1899.
10 *Times history of the war in South Africa*,
vol. 2, pp 224–5 and 230. See also
Hall, *Long Tom*, pp 47–57.
11 *Times history of the war in South Africa*,
vol. 3, p. 154; and Maurice, *History of
the war*, p. 539.
12 *Contemporary Review* (December
1901), pp 868–9.
13 *Die Volksstem*, 7 and 15 November
1899; Lynch, *My life story*, p. 158.

14   Davitt, *The Boer fight for freedom*,
     p. 290; and *Freeman's Journal*, 3
     November 1906.
11   Blake, *A West Pointer with the Boers*, p. 94.
16   *Natal Witness*, 18 November 1899.
17   *Cassell's history of the Boer war*, vol. I
     (London, 1903), p. 304; and Davitt,
     *The Boer fight for freedom*, p. 290.
18   *The Ladysmith Bombshell*, 26 November
     1899.
19   Breytenbach, *Die Geskiedenis van die
     Tweede Vryheidsoorlog in Suid-Afrika,
     1899–1902*, vol. 2, p. 451.
20   Haldane, *How we escaped from Pretoria*,
     p. 6.
21   Pearse, *Four months besieged*, pp 67–8.
22   NLI, Allan papers, ms. 26755, B.M.
     Gird to John MacBride, Paris, 11
     November 1910 (date uncertain); and
     *Freeman's Journal*, 10 November 1906.
23   *Standard and Diggers' News*, 1 March
     1900.
24   *Natal Witness*, 1 December 1899.
25   Haldane, *How we escaped from Pretoria*,
     pp 14 and 17; and Churchill, *London to
     Ladysmith*, p. 125.
26   *Natal Witness*, 1 December 1899.
27   Pearse, *Four months besieged*, p. 70.
28   Maurice, *History of the war*, pp 455–6,
     471–6 and 480.
29   *Freeman's Journal*, 17 November 1906.
30   Baring Pemberton, *Battles of the Boer
     war*, pp 131–3.
31   Griffith, *Thank God we kept the flag
     flying*, p. 183; and Pottinger, *The
     foreign volunteers*, p. 225.
32   Conan Doyle, *The Great Boer War*,
     p. 180.
33   Brown, *War with the Boers*, vol. 2, p. 159.
34   Griffith, *Thank God we kept the flag
     flying*, pp 186–8 and 201; and *Cassell's
     history of the Boer war*, vol. 1, p. 309.
35   *United Irishman*, 20 December 1899.
36   Blake, *A West Pointer with the Boers*,
     p. 103; and Davitt, *The Boer fight for
     freedom*, pp 283 and 319.
37   *Le Petit Journal*, 31 December 1899.
38   McCracken, *The Irish Pro-Boers*, pp 62–7.
39   Foster, *W.B. Yeats: a life*, vol. 1, pp 223
     and 239. See also *Standard and Diggers'
     News*, 8 February 1900.
40   *Natal Witness*, 6 June 1900; and
     *Standard and Diggers' News*, 8 February
     1900.
41   Hayes-McCoy, *A history of Irish flags*,
     p. 185.

42   Monick, *Shamrock and springbok*,
     pp 65–6. At least two other flags were
     associated with the Irish Transvaal
     Brigade.
43   Gonne MacBride, *Servant of the queen*,
     p. 310.
44   *Standard and Diggers' News*, 11 May
     1900.
45   Blake, *A West Pointer with the Boers*,
     p. 107.
46   Beaslai, *Songs, ballads and recitations by
     famous Irishmen: Arthur Griffith*, p. 5.

CHAPTER 5: THE NEW CENTURY

1    This old prophecy was quoted by Lady
     Gregory in her *Poets and dreamers*,
     p. 72.
2    Blake, *A West Pointer with the Boers*,
     pp 110–114 and *United Irishman*, 22
     December 1900.
3    See *Freeman's Journal*, 12 January 1907.
4    Ibid.
5    *Standard and Diggers' News*, 16
     February 1900.
6    Churchill, *From London to Ladysmith*,
     pp 331–2.
7    McCracken, *The Irish pro-Boers*, p. 69.
8    Blake, *A West Pointer with the Boers*,
     p. 118.
9    Davitt, *The Boer fight for freedom*,
     p. 368; and G.H. de Villebois-Mareuil,
     *War notes …*, p. 67.
10   *Standard and Diggers' News*, 16
     February 1900.
11   Ibid., 20 February 1900.
12   Blake, *A West Pointer with the Boers*,
     p. 128.
13   *Freeman's Journal*, 9 February 1900.
     One source gives the figure of 40
     brigades, not 70, being sent down to
     the Tugela Heights. See Wessels, 'The
     Irish Transvaal Brigades', *Christiaan
     De Wet-Annale* (1978), pp 176–84.
14   Byrne typescript, p. 7.
15   Coetzer, *The road to infamy*, p. 245;
     and T.P. Kilfeather, *The Connaught
     Rangers*, p. 77.
16   There is no evidence to support the
     claims of the Boer press, nor indeed
     those of Blake, that there were
     mutinous rumblings in the ranks of
     Irish regiments or that Irish regiments
     had to be forced into battle at cannon
     point: see *Standard and Diggers' News*,
     16 and 28 February 1900.

17 *Freeman's Journal*, 9 February 1907.
18 Blake barely mentions his unit's role in the battle of the Tugela Heights. See Blake, *A West Pointer with the Boers*, pp 125–7. Both Blake and Tom Byrne claimed the Long Tom was brought off Bulwana Hill and not nearby Lombard's Kop as stated by MacBride.
19 Hillegas, *With the Boer forces*, pp 270–1.
20 Coetzer, *The road to infamy*, p. 255.
21 Farwell, *The Great Boer War*, p. 231. The Irish brigade succeeded in retreating to the Biggarsberg without 'loss of a single man or an ounce of stores': *Standard and Diggers' News*, 9 March 1900.
22 Conan Doyle, *The Great Boer War*, p. 294. See also Churchill, *From London to Ladysmith*, p. 473; and Davis, *With both armies in South Africa*, p. 80.

CHAPTER 6: THE IRISH PRO-BOER MOVEMENT

1 P.A. McCracken, 'Arthur Griffith's South African sabbatical', *SAIS*, vol. 3 (1996), pp 227–62. Griffith left Ireland on 31 December 1896.
2 For a study of the Irish pro-Boer movement see McCracken, *The Irish pro-Boers*.
3 NLI, ms. Celtic Literary Society.
4 NAI, State Paper Office, Crime Branch Special, S/23178, 2 November 1900.
5 NAI, SPO, CBS, S/20142, 9 October 1899.
6 *Irish Figaro*, 14 April 1900.
7 For W.B. Yeats' involvement in the pro-Boer movement, see Foster, *W.B. Yeats*, chapters 8 and 9.
8 NLI, ms. 19933, Irish Transvaal Committee minute book, 14 October 1899.
9 Casey, *Pictures in the Hallway*, pp 287–92.
10 Ruda, 'Ireland and *The Boer fight for freedom*', p. 36.
11 Reported in the *Natal Mercury*, 7 November 1899.
12 *Annual report of the Inspector-General of Recruiting for the year 1902*, cmd.1417 (London, 1903); and Denman, 'Irish politics and the British army list: the

formation of the Irish Guards in 1900', *Irish Sword*, vol. 19, no.77 (1995), pp 171–86; and Denman, 'The red livery of shame: the campaign against army recruitment in Ireland, 1899–1914', *Irish Historical Studies*, vol. 29, no.114 (November 1994), pp 212–219. See also MacBride, White and Jeffares, *Always your friend*, pp 112–13.
13 NLI, ITC minute book, ms. 19933, 17 October 1899.
14 McCracken, 'The Irish literary movement, Irish doggerel and the Boer war', *Etudes Irlandaises*, no.22, n.s. (autumn 1995), pp 97–115.
15 Leeson, *Reminiscences of the Franco-Irish Ambulance*.
16 Foster, *Modern Ireland, 1600–1972*, p. 456; and NAI, CBS, S/20886, 19 December 1899.
17 McCracken, *Irish pro-Boers*, p. 93; and Smythe (ed.), *Seventy years, being the autobiography of Lady Gregory*, pp 374–5.
18 *Hansard*, House of Commons, 25 October 1899, cols. 614–22; and *Irish Figaro*, 11 November 1899.
19 McCracken, *Irish pro-Boers*, p. 106.
20 McCracken, *Irish pro-Boers*, pp 70–5; and NAI, CBS, S/21353. John O'Donnell remained an MP until 1910.
21 Lyons, *Some recollections of Griffith and his times*, pp 13–14.
22 Colles, *In castle and court house*, pp 51–3; and *United Irishman*, 12 May 1900.
23 NAI, SPO, CBS, S/27373; and O'Bróin, *Revolutionary underground*, p. 115.
24 Foster, *Yeats*, p. 222.
25 Student record for Arthur Lynch (student no. 18780026) supplied by the University of Melbourne, 22 November 1996.
26 Walker (ed.), *Parliamentary election results in Ireland*, p. 350.
27 Gonne MacBride, *Servant of the queen*, p. 182.
28 *Ibid.*, p. 289; and NAI, SPO, CBS, S/12250a, 13 August 1896.
29 See Davitt, *The Boer fight for freedom*, p. 322; Lynch, *My life story*, p. 154; and Transvaal Archives, Leyds archive, 320 Gezantschap, ZR, 3/99 n.d.
30 See O'Donnell, *The history of the Irish Parliamentary Party, 1870–1892*, vol. 1.
31 Gonne MacBride, *Servant of the queen*, chapter 22, 'Betrayed'.

32  Transvaal Archives, Leyds archive, Ierse Geheime Korrespondensie, vol. 191, n.d. Original in French.

33  NAI, SPO, CBS, S/20797 and S/23367. In a limp way of justifying these injections of cash O'Donnell was reduced to pointing out to Leyds that British army recruitment in Ireland must be down because of the many English and Scottish names of soldiers in war missing lists. See also PRO, HD/3/111, report on 'Irish disloyalists and anti-government parties in France', by Sir J.C. Ardagh, 17 January 1901 and NAI, SPO, CBS, S/23489 and S/23726. Later Maud Gonne would associate herself with 'Indian seditionists' in Paris.

34  *The Leader*, 7 June and 5 October 1902.

35  'Roomse gevaar' translates as the 'Roman peril'. See for example, *The Dublin Review*, July 1900, pp 24–5.

36  *United Irishman*, 6 October 1899.

37  O'Casey, *Pictures in the hallway*, p. 285–7.

38  D.P. McCracken, 'Royal visits to Ireland' (typescript).

39  Davitt, *The Boer fight for freedom*, p. 34; and *Die Volksstem*, 26 March 1900. See also *Hibernia*, vol. 4, no.6, 1 June 1900.

40  NLI, Anna Johnston to John MacBride, 10 April 1900. The Irish Guards saw little service in the Boer war. Some members did sail for South Africa in November 1901. See Verney, *The Micks*, p. 7.

41  Public Record Office, CO 904/159 and Henry, *The evolution of Sinn Fein*, pp 62–3.

42  See NAI, SPO, CBS, S/23367, October 1900, S/32578, November 1901 and S/25788, 12 November 1901.

43  NLI, Alice Stopford Green papers, ms. 15118.

44  *Weekly Freeman*, 30 March 1901.

45  Lyons, *Some recollections of Griffith and his times*, p. 27.

CHAPTER 7: REINFORCEMENTS AND RIVALRY

1  *Freeman's Journal*, 2 April 1907. There is no evidence to support the rumours which circulated in Johannesburg at the time that the Irish commando had suffered heavy losses in the retreat to the Biggarsberg.

2  *Standard and Diggers' News*, 19 and 20 March 1900.

3  *United Irishman*, 22 December 1900.

4  Byrne typescript, p. 6.

5  NLI, Irish Transvaal Committee minute book, ms. 19933

6  NLI, Walsh papers, mss. 18287, M.S. Walsh to Johnnie, Easter Sunday, 1900. For a £50 receipt of monies paid to Walsh, see NLI, ms. 21981, 23 June 1900.

7  Beaslai, *Songs, ballads and recitations: Arthur Griffith*, p. 5; and O'Bróin, *Revolutionary underground*, p. 109.

8  Sheehy-Skeffington, *Michael Davitt*, pp 167–9.

9  NLI, Allan papers, ms. 26755, Anna Johnston to John MacBride, 21 February 1900. See also *Irish News*, 9 March 1901.

10  NLI, Allan papers, ms. 26757, letter from Gillingham probably to Mark Ryan, Lourenço Marques, 27 March 1900.

11  *Standard and Diggers' News*, 27 March 1900; and Blake, *A West Pointer with the Boers*, p. 376. Hillegas, *With the Boer forces*, p. 271, says the Irish brigade was at Helpmekaar for six weeks.

12  See Trinity College, Dublin, Library, Davitt papers, mss. 9572, 9527 and 9573. See also NAI, CBS, S/21342, 19 February 1900.

13  *Ibid.*, Davitt to Dublin, Pretoria, 25 April 1900.

14  Batts, *Pretoria from within*, pp 136–41 and 230.

15  *Natal Mercury*, 16 May 1900.

16  *Freeman's Journal*, 12 January 1907.

17  See *Standard and Diggers' News*, 24 April 1900.

18  Lynch, *My life story*, pp 158–9.

19  TCD, Davitt papers, vol. 2, ms. 9527, 25 April 1900.

20  Davitt, *The Boer fight for freedom*, p. 322.

21  James Harold to Daniel F. Cohalan, 9 March 1909, quoted in *Devoy's Post Bag*, vol. 2, p. 443.

22  Public Record Office, London, War Office, 108/380, Secret South African Despatches, vol. 1, pp 368–9, cipher

message 223, Buller to Roberts, 19 March 1900; and *Die Volksstem*, 14 February 1900.

23 *Standard and Diggers' News*, 24 March 1900.

24 Lynch, *My life story*, pp 198–9; and Macnab, *The French Colonel*, p. 230.

25 *The Times history of the war*, vol. 3, pp 77–8.

26 NLI, Devoy papers, ms. 18138.

27 *Natal Mercury*, 31 March 1900.

28 *The Times history of the war*, vol. 4, p. 176; and Maurice, *History of the war*, vol. 3, p. 263.

29 Lynch, *My life story*, p. 191.

30 *The Times history of the war*, vol. 4, p. 176. At Lynch's trial it was claimed that he fired on British troops from 'the Sundays River bridge'. This must have been on either the Beith-Ladysmith or, more likely, the Glencoe-Ladysmith roads. When this occurred is not known.

31 Davitt, *The Boer fight for freedom*, p. 324; and Macnab, *The French colonel*, pp 200–1.

CHAPTER 8: 'PAYING AN INSTALMENT ON THE IRISH DEBT'

1 *Devoy's post-bag*, vol. 1, pp 392–3 and 408–11.

2 Unger, *With 'Bobs' and Kruger*, p. 314.

3 *Irish Sword*, vol. 5, no. 20 (summer 1962), p. 194.

4 Ferguson, *American diplomacy and the Boer war*, p. 65; and *Natal Mercury*, 15 January 1900.

5 Ibid., p. 60; Roosevelt to Spring-Rice, 21 January 1900.

6 Blake, *A West Pointer with the Boers*, p. 132.

7 *Evening Echo*, 30 May 1956.

8 *Chicago Daily News*, 15 February 1900.

9 Batts, *Pretoria from within*, p. 120.

10 *Natal Mercury*, 2 July 1900.

11 National Archives, Pretoria, MGP, 205, c/19, 12 August 1900; and Cammack, *The Rand at war*, p. 36n.

12 Spaight, *War rights on land*, p. 489. While not involved in the war as a belligerent, Portugal was not formally designated a neutral power. This suited the British as they could then still use Delagoa Bay as a coaling station.

13 Harding Davis, *With both armies*, pp 90–2.

14 Blake, *A West Pointer with the Boers*, pp 131–2.

15 *Die Volksstem*, 17 April 1900; Ferguson, *American diplomacy and the Boer war*, p. 67; and MacNab, *The French colonel*, p. 166. The US consul was meant to look after British interests during the war.

16 Batts, *Pretoria from within*, pp 121–4; Harding Davis, *With both armies*, pp 142–3; and Unger, *With 'Bobs' and Kruger*, p. 362.

17 Blake, *A West Pointer with the Boers*, pp 131 and 133.

18 Hillgas, *With the Boer forces*, p. 251.

19 NLI, Walsh papers, ms. 18287, Walsh to Johnnie, Easter Sunday 1900.

20 *Natal Mercury*, 19 March 1900.

21 Davitt, *The Boer fight for freedom*, p. 320.

22 Uys, *Heidelbergers of the Boer war*, p. 46; and *The Times history of the war in SA*, vol. 4, p. 103.

23 Blake, *A West Pointer with the Boers*, pp 166–9.

24 *Standard and Diggers' News*, 5 May 1900.

25 Byrne typescript, p. 10; and *Freeman's Journal*, 3 November 1906.

26 *United Irishman*, 22 December 1900.

27 *Standard and Diggers' News*, 14 May 1900. See also *Die Volkstem*, 11 May 1900.

28 *Diary of E.W. Luther*, p. 12.

29 (Rankin), *A subaltern's letters to his wife*, p. 41.

30 One of many mysteries surrounding the Irish in the war is a reference to Enright as belonging to Major Mitchell's commando. No such commando is known to have existed though Mitchell may for a while have led a breakaway faction of either Blake's or Lynch's units.

31 Davitt, *The Boer fight for freedom*, p. 318.

32 See Trinity College, Dublin, Davitt papers, vol. 3, ms. 9573, p. 23; and *Natal Mercury*, 16 May 1900.

33 *Diary of E.W. Luther*, p. 16.

34 Public Record Office of Northern Ireland, Craig papers, D1415/B.

35 Lynch, *My life story*, p. 193; and Marjoribanks, *The life of Lord Carson* vol. 1, pp 289–90.

## CHAPTER 9: A HOT TIME IN THE OLD TRANSVAAL

1   *Diary of E.W. Luther*, p. 18.
2   One source says Father van Hecke was not released but escaped from the British. See *Freeman's Journal*, 29 July 1907.
3   Blake, *A West Pointer with the Boers*, p. 184.
4   See *War Department (US) ... Reports on military operations in SA*, p. 219.
5   University of Stellenbosch Library, Lipp ms. p. 76; Lupini, *Camillo Ricchiardi*, p. 147; and Cammack, *The Rand at war*, p. 110.
6   Wilson, *With the flag to Pretoria*, vol. 2, p. 678.
7   NLI, Devoy papers, ms. 18138, Lynch to Dr Mark Ryan, 22 August 1900; *Devoy's post-bag*, vol. 2, p. 441; and Lynch, *My life story*, p. 195.
8   O'Connor, *Oliver St John Gogarty*, p. 24.
9   Cammack, *The Rand at war*, p. 88; and *Freeman's Journal*, 29 July 1907.
10  Rosslyn, *Twice captured*, pp 390–3; and Unger, *With 'Bobs' and Kruger*, p. 305.
11  Pottinger, *The foreign volunteers*, p. 313; and Wilson, *With the flag to Pretoria*, vol. 2, p. 678.
12  *Diary of E.W. Luther*, p. 2; and NLI, Allan papers, ms. 26755. For the episode of the Irish and the gold-train see Kruger, *Die Kruger miljoene*, p. 32.
13  Byrne typescript, p. 9.
14  May, *Music of the guns*, p. 91.
15  Public Record Office of Northern Ireland, Craig papers, D1454/1–3.
16  Unger, *With 'Bobs' and Kruger*, pp 374–5.
17  May, *Music of the guns*, p. 91–6.
18  *Diary of E.W. Luther*, p. 33–4.
19  P.A. McCracken, 'Arthur Griffith's South African sabbatical', *SAIS*, vol. 3 (1996), pp 227–62.
20  NLI, Allan papers, ms. 26755.
21  Ibid.; and *United Irishman*, 22 December 1900.
22  See *Natal Mercury*, 13 August 1900; *The Times history of the war*, vol. 3, p. 78, and vol. 6, pp 593–4; and University of Stellenbosch Library, Lipp ms. p. 240.
23  Lyons, *Some recollections of Arthur Griffith and his times*, p. 27.
24  National Archives, Pretoria, 50/POW, vol. 4, file PR527.
25  *Diary of E.W. Luther*, p. 46.
26  Ibid.; and *United Irishman*, 22 December 1900.
27  Davitt, *The Boer fight for freedom*, p. 325; *Freeman's Journal*, 29 July 1907; and NLI, Allen papers, ms. 26755.
28  *The Times history of the war*, vol. 4, p. 472.
29  NLI, Allan papers, ms. 26755, O'Connor to MacBride, 10 September 1900.
30  The author knows of only one surviving copy of Luther's diary. The text of the diary appears to be genuine and many details can be confirmed elsewhere, however there are gaps in the chronology and it is possible that British military intelligence edited out certain entries. The slim volume was probably for the general information of British officers in the field. Plans are underway to republish the diaries.
31  Conan Doyle, *The great Boer war*, p. 506.

## CHAPTER 10: BITTEREND

1   *Natal Mercury*, 26 September 1900.
2   Byrne typescript, p. 13.
3   *Freeman's Journal*, 29 July 1907.
4   Trinity College, Dublin, Library, Davitt papers, Davitt to Dillon, Pretoria, 4 April 1900.
5   Reitz, *On commando*, pp 296–9.
6   NLI, Walsh papers, ms. 18287, 30 October 1900.
7   Blake, *A West Pointer with the Boers*, p. 311.
8   Ibid., p. 291; and NLI, Allan papers, ms. 26755, 'Extract from letter Mr Lynch (Paris) wrote to Dr Ryan Aug 22nd 1900'.
9   Blake, *A West Pointer with the Boers*, p. 208; Kruger, *Good-bye Dolly Gray*, p. 396; and *The Times history of the war*, vol. 5, pp 121–2.
10  Conan Doyle, *The great Boer war*, pp 588–9. The postcard incorrectly shows Barry firing into the maxim with a rifle.
11  Blake, *A West Pointer with the Boers*, p. 220.
12  *The Times history of the war*, vol. 5, p. 123.
13  Kruger, *Good-bye Dolly Gray*, p. 435.
14  Blake, *A West Pointer with the Boers*, p. 281.
15  Ibid., p. 282.

16 Davitt, *The Boer fight for freedom*, p. 320;
*Freeman's Journal*, 12 January 1907; *Irish
News*, 9 March 1901; and the *United
Irishman*, 22 December 1900.

17 *The Times history of the war*, vol. 7,
pp 17–23.

18 *Birmingham Daily Post*, 8 January 1900.
See also Blake, *A West Pointer with the
Boers*, p. 300.

19 NLI, Irish Transvaal Committee minute
book, ms. 19933, 30 January 1900.

20 Brink, *Recollections of a Boer prisoner-of-
war at Ceylon*, p. 117.

21 Ryan, *Fenian memoirs*, p. 187.

22 *Freeman's Journal*, 29 December 1906.

23 Ferguson, *American diplomacy and the
Boer war*, pp 67–8.

24 NAI, SPO, CBS, S/28134, 26 January
1903.

25 PRO, CO 904/208/258 (11 December
1900); and NAI, SPO, CBS, S/25283,
5 September 1901.

26 British Library, Viscount Gladstone
papers, vol. 7, Add.ms. 45992,
ff.77–80, 11 October 1901. See also
Ibid., Add.ms. 41216, ff.171–2; and
Campbell-Bannerman papers, vol. 31,
Add.ms. 41236, f.166.

27 See Childers, *The framework of home
rule*, p. 139; and Russell, *Ireland and
the empire*, p. 258.

28 See, for example, Revd J. Fénélon,
'Ireland and the Boers', *New Ireland
Review*, vol. 12 (February 1900), p. 342.

29 See *Hansard*, vol. 105, 20 March 1902,
col.591–2; Lyons, *John Dillon*,
pp 217–8; and NLI, Redmond papers,
ms. 15182(3), 22 March 1902.

30 Lucy, *A diary of the Unionist parliament,
1895–1900*, p. 321.

31 *Hansard*, vol. 108, 5 June 1902, cols
1593–4.

32 Blake, *A West Pointer with the Boers*,
p. 300. •

33 Ibid., p. 364.

34 *United Irishman*, 4 October 1902.

CHAPTER 11: LAST POST

1 Byrne typescript, p. 14. See also
*Freeman's Journal*, 29 July 1907.

2 *Irish News*, 9 March 1901.

3 Young, 'Chicago's wild geese', *Military
Images*, vol. vii, no.6 (1986), p. 15.

4 One report incorrectly stated that
Blake was electrocuted by a space

heater. See Monick, *Shamrock and
springbok*, pp 78–80; and *New York
Times*, 25 January 1907.

5 *Freeman's Journal*, 29 July 1907; and
Maud Gonne MacBride, *A servant of
the queen*, pp 308–9.

6 PRO, CO 904/208/258 (MacBride)
and Rhodes University, Grahamstown,
Cory Library for Historical Research,
Gold Fields papers, ms. 16094, Davitt
to Kruger, 2 June 1902. Strangely,
Davitt does not mention in his book
his meeting with Kruger.

7 Jordan, *Major John MacBride*, p. 49;
*The Lantern*, vol. 33, no.4 (October
1984), pp 54–60; and Gonne
MacBride, *Servant of the queen*, p. 341.

8 South African Archives, Pretoria,
Leyds archive, vol. 191, Ierse Geheime
Korrespondent, n.d.

9 *Irish News*, 9 March 1901; *Irish World*,
18 February 1900; Maud Gonne
MacBride, *A servant of the queen*,
p. 235; and McCracken, *Irish pro-Boers*,
p. 89.

10 *Independent and Nation*, 18 November
1901; NLI, Allan papers, ms. 26757;
and *The Times*, 26 August 1902.

11 NLI, O'Leary papers, ms. 8001(34),
Maud Gonne to John O'Leary, n.d.; for
a report of Davitt going to Paris, see
NAI, SPO, CBS, s/26769, 8 May 1902.

12 N.L.I., Allan papers, ms. 29593, copy
of letter dated 29 September 1905.

13 Foster, *Yeats*, vol. 1, p. 331.

14 Joyce, *Ulysses*, p. 398.

15 McCracken, *Irish pro-Boers*, p. xix.

16 First proposed in the *United Irishman*,
15 March 1900.

17 Davy, *British pro-Boers*, pp 233–4.

18 *Irish Independent*, 28 October 1902;
and McCracken, *Irish pro-Boers*, p. 96.

19 Public Record Office, London, CO
904/70, RIC monthly reports, June
1902.

20 *Irish Daily Independent*, 9 June 1902;
*Northern Whig*, 21 October 1903; and
Monick, *Shamrock and springbok*, p. 69.

21 McGrath, 'The Boer Irish brigade',
*Irish Sword*, vol. v, no.18 (1961), p. 59.

22 Trinity College, Dublin, Library, Davitt
papers, Davitt to Dillon, 22 and 24
August 1902.

23 *Devoy's post bag*, vol. 2, pp 351–2.

24 See *Freeman's Journal*, 13, 20, 27
October 1906; 3, 10, 17 November
1906; 1, 29 December 1906; 5, 12

25 January 1907; 9 February 1907; 2 April 1907; and 29 July 1907.

25 Inglis, *Roger Casement*, p. 299.

26 *Freeman's Journal*, 20 August 1907; and *Irish Times*, 20 August 1907.

27 Staunton, 'Boer war memorials in Ireland', *SAIS*, vol. 3 (1996), pp 290–304.

28 *The Gael*, vol. 19 (Dec.1900); Lynch, *My life story*, pp 193–6 and 202–3; Ruda, 'Ireland and the *Boer fight for freedom*', p. 218.

29 *Devoy's post bag*, vol. 2, p. 442.

30 Walker, *Parliamentary election results in Ireland*, p. 350; and NAI, SPO, CBS, S/26362 and 27053.

31 Paul Hill to D.P. McCracken, 8 September 1997, Kingston-on-Thames Museum and Heritage Service; and *Surrey Comet*, 28 June 1902.

32 Revd V. Lynch, King's Bench Division, 21, 22, 23 January 1903, pp 444–60.

33 Lynch, *My life story*, p. 226; and *Natal Mercury*, 23 January 1903.

34 *Natal Mercury*, 26 January 1903; and Marjoribanks, *The life of Lord Carson*, vol. 1, chapter 21.

35 *Devoy's post bag*, vol. 2, p. 448; and Lynch, *My life story*, p. 192. See also N.L.I., pamphlets, NLI 1006, Arthur Lynch, *To Irishmen* and NLI, ms. 18138, Devoy papers.

36 See PRO, CO 904/208/258 (June 1903); and NAI, CBS, S/29989.

37 NLI, Allan papers, ms. 26756.

38 *Workers' Republic*, 18 November 1899.

39 PRO, War Office papers, WO/71/350 (MacBride); and Ryan, *The Rising*, p. 165.

40 Lowry, 'A fellowship of disaffection', *Etudes Irlandaises*, vol. 12 (1992), p. 107.

41 Churchill, *London to Ladysmith*, p. 181.

42 Healy, *Letters and leaders of my day*, vol. 2, p. 563.

43 *Freeman's Journal*, 29 December 1906.

44 NLI, Redmond papers, ms. 15235(4), Botha to Redmond, 29 April 1916, and ms. 15507(3), telegram dated 29 April 1918.

45 Pakenham, *Peace by ordeal*, pp 86–7.

46 McCracken, 'Fenians and Dutch carpetbaggers', *Eire-Ireland*, pp 120–3. William Cosgrave was sentenced to be executed on the same day as John MacBride in 1916. Cosgrave's sentence was commuted to penal servitude for life.

47 For a full account, see McCracken, 'The Irish Republican Association of South Africa, 1920–2', *SAIS*, vol. 3 (1996), pp 46–66.

48 T.K. Daniel, 'The scholar and the saboteurs', *SAIS*, vol. 1 (1991), pp 162–75.

49 *The Republic*, 22 April 1922.

50 Military Archives, Dublin, S 1984, Cassidy. This flag should not be confused with that in the possession of John MacBride at the time of his execution and which is in the museum too. There also appears to have been a third brigade flag which Maud Gonne donated to the National Museum of Ireland. This was given to her by Eamon Brugha, who in turn had received it from K.W. Wapenaar of Pretoria. What happened to the flag given to Father van Hecke is not known. The original Mitchelstown flag was buried in South Africa and lost. The fate of the standard of the second Irish corps remains a mystery.

51 *The Republic*, 22 April 1922.

52 See Herd, *1922: The revolt on the Rand*, pp 190–2; Martin, *The Durban Light Infantry*, vol. 1, p. 342; *Rand Daily Mail*, 13 March 1922; and *The Star*, 21 March 1922.

# Select bibliography

## A. MANUSCRIPT SOURCES

*Archives Diplomatiques du Ministère des Affaires Etrangères, Paris*
Correspondance politique et commerciale, 1897–1918: Grande Bretagne, t.4, Irlande, 1897–1914

*British Library*
Campbell-Bannerman papers
Viscount Gladstone papers

*Cory Library for Historical Research, Grahamstown*
Gold Fields papers

*Military Archives of Ireland, Dublin*
S1615 (1950) & S1984 (1952)

*National Archives of Ireland, Dublin*
State Paper Office: Crime Branch Special files

*National Archives of South Africa, Pretoria:*
Leyds archive
    191: Gesantskap, S.A.R., Nuusberigte en Koerantuitknipsels Ontvang van Ierse Geheime Korrespondent, 1899–1902
    320: Gezanischap, Z.R., 3/99
    615: Ierse Geheime Correspondentie
MGP, 205, c/19 (11 August 1900) confidential list of people travelling through or resident in Lourenço Marques since May 1900
PSY, 73, 'Affidavits in connection with alleged looting etc'
SO/POW, CT, vol. 4, file PR527

*National Archives, Washington DC, USA*
Army Service Record, personal file, file 4635 ACP 1889, J.Y.F. Blake
RG94, entry 297, file ALP2747, 1894, box 1238

*National Library of Ireland, Dublin*
Allan papers, mss.26755, 26756 & 29593
Celtic Literary Society minute books, mss 19934 (i) & (ii)
Devoy papers, ms.9827 & 18138
Dunne papers, ms.5181
Stopford Green papers, ms.15118
Irish Transvaal Committee minute book, ms.19933
Mahon papers, ms.19972
O'Leary papers, ms.8001
Redmond papers, ms.15235 & 15507
Walsh Boer war papers, mss 18287 & 21981

*Public Record Office, London*
Courts martial, WO 71/350
Irish Office papers, CO 906
Lists of Boer leaders, WO 108/401
Prisoner of war papers, WO 108/303 & 304
RIC monthly reports, CO 903 & 904
Secret South African Despatches, WO 108/380

*Public Record Office of Northern Ireland*
Craig papers, D1415
Crawford papers, D1454
Whyte papers, D2918

*Trinity College, Dublin, Library*
Michael Davitt papers
John Dillon papers

*University of Stellenbosch Library*
Lipp ms.

*University of the Witwatersrand Library*
Law ms.

*Privately held papers*
'Statement by Commandant Thomas F. Byrne' (signed & dated 30 July 1951), typescript
  [Mr & Mrs Art O Leary]
Papers of Gus Byrne [Mr Desmond Byrne]
Correspondence to D.P. McCracken, 1988–98


## B. PRINTED SOURCES

*1. Contemporary newspapers and periodicals*

| | |
|---|---|
| *Belfast News Letter* | *Ladysmith Bombshell* |
| *Birmingham Daily Post* | *The Leader* |
| *Chicago Chronicle* | *Le Petit Journal* |
| *Chicago Daily News* | *Natal Mercury* |
| *Contemporary Review* | *Natal Witness* |
| *Daily Express* (Dublin) | *The Nation* |
| *Evening Telegraph* (Dublin) | *Northern Whig* |
| *Fortnightly Review* | *Rand Daily Mail* |
| *Freeman's Journal* | *The Republic: The official organ of the Irish* |
| *The Gael* | *Republican Association of South Africa* |
| *The Graphic* | *Shan van Vocht* |
| *Hansard* | *The Star* |
| *Hibernia* | *Surrey Comet* |
| *Irish Daily Independent* | *Standard and Diggers' News* |
| *Irish Figaro* | *United Irishman* |
| *Irish News* | *Die Volksstem* |
| *Irish Times* | *Weekly Star* |
| *Johannesburg Times* | *Workers' Republic* |

2. *Books, pamphlets, articles and dissertations*

Akenson, D.H., *Occasional papers on the Irish in South Africa* (Grahamstown, 1991)
—— *The Irish Diaspora*, (Toronto, 1993)
Amery, L.S., *The Times history of the war in South Africa, 1899–1902*, 7 vols (London, 1900–09)
*Annual report of the Inspector-General of Recruiting for the year 1902*, cmd.1417 (London, 1903)
Aylward, Alfred, *The Transvaal of today* (Edinburgh, 1878 and 1881 editions)
Banks, Margaret A., *Edward Blake* (Toronto, 1957)
Batts, H.J., *Pretoria from within, during the war, 1899–1900* (London, 1900)
Beaslai, Piaras (ed.) *Songs, ballads and recitations by famous Irishmen: Arthur Griffith* (Dublin, n.d.): most of the songs refer to South Africa
Belfield, B., *The Boer war* (London, 1975)
Blake, Col. J.Y.F., *A West Pointer with the Boers* (Boston, 1903)
Blessing, Patrick J., *The Irish in America: a guide to the literature and the manuscript collections* (Washington DC, 1992)
Breytenbach, J.H., *Die geskiedenis van die Tweede Vryheidsoorlog in Suid-Afrika, 1899–1902*, 4 vols (Pretoria, 1969–1977)
Brink, J.N., *Recollections of a Boer prisoner-of-war at Ceylon* (Amsterdam and Cape Town, 1904)
Brown, Harold, *War with the Boers* (London, 1900)
Bulpin, T.V., *Storm over the Transvaal* (Cape Town, 1955)
Cammack, Diana, *The Rand at war, 1899–1902* (London, 1990)
*Cassell's history of the Boer war, 1899–1900* (London, 1903)
Childers, Erskine, *The framework of Home Rule* (London, 1911)
Churchill, W.S., *London to Ladysmith via Pretoria* (London, 1900)
Coetzer, Owen, *The road to infamy (1899–1902): Colenso, Spioenkop, Vaalkrantz, Pieters, Buller and Warren* (Rivonia, 1996)
Colles, Ramsey, *In castle and court house* (London, n.d.)
Collins, Mary E., 'Irish public opinion and the Boer war' (dissertation, University College, Dublin, 1963)
Colum, Padraic, *Arthur Griffith* (Dublin, 1959)
Conroy, D.J., 'The "loyal" Irish rebels', *Kommando* (December 1956), pp 22–3 and 74–5
—— 'Two incidents of the Boer war', *Irish Sword*, vol. V, no. 20. (1962), p. 194. Reply by D. O'Dowd, vol. V, no. 21 (1962), p. 266
Cook, A.J., 'Irish in the British army in South Africa, 1795–1910', *SAIS*, vol. 2 (1992), pp 91–105
Cullum, Maj-Gen. George W., *Biographical register of the officers and graduates of the US Military Academy* (3rd ed., Cambridge, Mass., 1891), vol. 3, p. 338; vol. 4, p. 335; and vol. 5, p. 311
Daniel, T.K., 'Erin's green veldt: The Irish Republican Association of South Africa, 1920–22', *Journal of the University of Durban-Westville*, n.s., vol. 3 (1986), pp 89–98
—— 'Faith and stepfatherland: Irish networks in the Cape and Natal, 1871–1914', *SAIS*, vol. 2 (1992), pp 73–90
—— 'The scholar and the saboteurs', *SAIS*, vol. 1 (1991), pp 162–75
Davey, Arthur, *The British pro-Boers, 1877–1902* (Cape Town, 1978)
Davidson, A.B., & Filatova, I.I., *The Russians and the Anglo-Boer war, 1899–1900* (Cape Town, 1998)
Davis, Richard Harding, *With both armies in South Africa* (New York, 1903)
Davis, Webster, *John Bull's crime* (New York, 1901)
Davitt, Michael, *The Boer fight for freedom* (New York, 3rd edn, 1902)
Denman, Terence, 'Irish politics and the British army list: The formation of the Irish Guards in 1900', *Irish Sword*, vol. XIX, no. 77 (summer, 1995), pp 171–86
—— 'The red livery of shame: The campaign against army recruitment in Ireland, 1899–1914', *Irish Historical Studies*, vol. 29, no. 114 (November 1994), pp 212–19
D'Esparbès, Georges, *Le briseur de fers* (Paris, *c.*1911)
*Dictionary of South African biography*, vols 1–5 (Tafelberg, Cape Town, 1968–87; published for the Human Sciences Research Council) contains the following entries:

—— 'John Blake' (A.L. Harington), vol. 3, p. 71

—— 'Michael Davitt' (B.J.T. Leverton), vol. 2, pp 161–2

—— 'Arthur Lynch' (S.J. du Preez), vol. 3, pp 549–50

—— 'John MacBride' (O.J. Ferreira), vol. 3, pp 552–3

Dillon, John, *Conduct of the war in South Africa. Debate on the King's speech. Speech by Mr Dillon, M.P., on Monday, February 25, and Tuesday, February 26* (London, 1901), pamphlet

*Disloyal Irish nationalists: The utterances of some of the Irish members on the Transvaal* (National Union of Constitutional Associations pamphlet, no. 93, November 1899)

Doyle, A. Conan, *The great Boer war. A two years' record, 1899–1901* (London, 1901)

Doyle, F.B., 'South Africa', in Patrick J. Corish (ed.), *A history of Irish catholicism* (Dublin, 1971)

Farwell, Byron, *The great Boer war* (London, 1977)

Fénélon, Revd J., 'Ireland and the Boers', *New Ireland Review*, vol. 12 (February 1900), pp 337–43

Ferguson, John H., *American diplomacy and the Boer war* (Philadelphia, 1939)

Flynn, J.F.M., 'Rife with possibilities: The Irish parliamentary party and the South African war, 1899–1902' (doctoral thesis, Columbia University, 1970)

Follis, Bryan A., 'Friend or foe? Ulster unionists and Afrikaner nationalists', *SAIS*, vol. 3 (1996), pp 171–89

Foster, Roy, *Modern Ireland, 1600–1972* (London, 1988)

—— *W.B. Yeats, a life. 1: The apprentice mage, 1865–1914* (OUP, 1997)

*The Great Transvaal Irish conspiracy* (anonymous pamphlet, *c*.1899)

Greenwall, Ryno, *Artists and illustrations of the Anglo-Boer war* (Vlaeberg, 1992)

Gregory, Lady, *Poets and dreamers* (Dublin, 1903; New York ed., 1974)

Griffith, Kenneth, *Thank God we kept the flag flying. The siege and relief of Ladysmith, 1899–1900* (New York, 1974)

Guelke, Adrian, *Interdependence and transition: the case of South Africa and Northern Ireland* (SAIIA pamphlet, Johannesburg, 1993)

Haldane, Capt. Aylmer, *How we escaped from Pretoria* (Edinburgh and London, 1900)

Hall, Darrell, *Long Tom* (Glenashley, 1994)

Hayes-McCoy, G.A., *A history of Irish flags* (Dublin, 1979)

Healy, T.M., *Letters and leaders of my day*, 2 vols (London, 1928)

Henderson, R.H., *An Ulsterman in Africa* (Cape Town, 1994)

Hennessy, Maurice, *The wild geese: the Irish soldier in exile* (London, 1973)

Henry, R.M., *The evolution of Sinn Fein* (Dublin, 1920)

Herd, N., *1922: The revolt on the Rand* (Johannesburg, 1966)

Hickey, D.J., & Doherty, J.E., *A dictionary of Irish history since 1800* (Dublin, 1980)

Hillegas, Howard C., *With the Boer forces* (London, 1900)

Holt, Edgar, *The Boer war* (London, 1958)

Inglis, Brian, *Roger Casement* (Belfast, 1993)

*The Irish in South Africa, 1920–22* (Cape Town, n.d., *c*.1922)

Jackson, Alvin, 'The failure of unionism in Dublin, 1900', *Irish Historical Studies*, vol. 26, no. 104 (November 1989), pp 377–95

Jordan, Anthony J., *Major John MacBride, 1865–1916* (Westport, 1991)

—— *Willie Yeats and the Gonne-MacBrides* (Dublin, 1997)

Joyce, James, *Ulysses* (London, 1937)

'The justice of the Transvaal: An Irish uitlander', *Dublin Review* (July 1900), pp 24–5

Kilfeather, T.P., *The Connaught Rangers* (Tralee, 1969)

(Kruger), 'A selection from a collection of tributes to President S.J.P. Kruger, compiled by Jacques Malan', *The Lantern*, vol. 33, no. 4 (October 1984), pp 54–60

Kruger, D.W., *Die Kruger miljoene*

Kruger, Rayne, *Good-bye Dolly Gray: the story of the Boer war* (London, 1974 ed.)

Lecky, W.E.H., *Moral aspects of the South African war* (London, 1900), pamphlet

Lee, Emanoel, *To the bitter end* (London, 1985)

Leeson, M.A., *Reminiscences of the Franco-Irish ambulance; or, our 'Corps' with the Mocquarts and on the Loire, 1870–1* (Dublin, 1873)

*Longland's Pretoria directory for 1899* (State Library reprint, Pretoria, 1979)

Lowry, D.W., 'A "fellowship of disaffection": Irish-South African relations from the Anglo-Boer war to Pretoriastroika, 1902–91', *Etudes Irlandaises*, vol. 12 (1992), pp105–22

—— 'Ireland shows the way: Irish-South African relations and the British empire/commonwealth, *c.*1902–61', *SAIS*, vol. 3 (1996), pp 89–135

Lucy, Henry W., *A diary of the Unionist parliament, 1895–1900*, (London, 1901)

Lupini, Mario, *Camillo Ricchiardi: Italian Boer war hero*, (Melville, 1988)

*Diary of Ernest William Luther of the 201st Regiment of New York Volunteers and of Blake's Irish Brigade, who was wounded in action near Weltevreden on Sunday 9th September and died in hospital, Machadodorp, 11th September 1900* (no place or date of publication given, but probably published by British Military Intelligence in London or Cape Town in early November 1900)

Lynch, Arthur, 'Lessons of the South African war', *New Ireland Review*, XV (1901)

—— *My life story* (London, 1924)

Lyons, F.S.L., *Ireland since the famine* (London, 1971)

—— *John Dillon: a biography* (London, 1968)

Lyons, George A., *Some recollections of Griffith and his times* (London, 1923)

MacBride, Major John, series of articles on the Irish brigade published in the *Freeman's Journal* on the following dates: 13,20 & 27 October; 3, 10 & 17 November; 1 & 29 December 1906; 5& 12 January; 9 February; 2 April; and 29 July 1907

—— 'The Transvaal Irish Brigade', *The United Irishman*, 22 December 1900

MacBride, Maud Gonne, *A servant of the queen. Reminiscences* (eds) A. Norman Jeffares and Anna MacBride White (Gerrards Cross, 1994 ed.)

McCracken, Donal P., 'Alfred Aylward, Fenian editor of the *Natal Witness*', *Journal of Natal and Zulu History*, IV (1981), pp 49–61

—— 'Insurgents and adventurers, 1806–99', *SAIS*, vol. 2 (1992), pp 39–53

—— '"Fenians and Dutch carpetbaggers": Irish and Afrikaner nationalisms, 1877–1930', *Eire-Ireland*, vol. 29, no. 3 (Fall, 1994), pp 109–26

—— 'The land the famine forgot', E.M. Crawford ed., *The hungry stream* (Belfast, 1997)

—— 'The impact of developments in South Africa on Irish politics in the period 1877 to 1902' (doctoral thesis, New University of Ulster, 1980)

—— 'Irish identity in twentieth-century South Africa', *SAIS*, vol. 3 (1996), pp 7–45

—— 'The Irish in South Africa: The police, a case study', *Familia: Journal of the Ulster Historical Guild*, vol. 2, no. 7 (119), pp 40–6

—— 'The Irish literary movement, Irish doggerel and the Boer war', *Etudes Irlandaises*, n.s., no. 22 (1995), pp 97–115

—— *The Irish pro-Boers, 1877–1902* (Johannesburg, 1989)

—— 'The Irish Republican Association of South Africa, 1920–22', *SAIS*, vol. 3 (1996), pp 46–66

—— 'Odd man out: the South African experience,' A Bielenberg ed., *The Irish diaspora* (Longman, forthcoming)

—— 'Irish settlement and identity in South Africa before 1910', *Irish Historical Studies*, vol. 28, no. 110 (November 1992), pp 134–49

—— 'The Irish Transvaal Brigade', *SAIS*, vol. 2 (1992), pp 54–72

McCracken, Eileen M., 'Alfred Aylward. A fenian in South Africa', *Irish Sword*, XII.49 (1976), pp 261–9

McCracken, J.L., 'The death of the informer James Carey', *SAIS*, vol. 3 (1996), pp 190–9

—— 'Irishmen in government in South Africa', *SAIS*, vol. 2 (1992), pp 25–38

—— 'Irishmen in South African colonial parliaments', *SAIS*, vol. 1 (1990), pp 73–82

—— 'Irish nationalists and South Africa, 1877–1902', *Christiaan de Wet Annale*, 5 (1978), pp 157–75. (Appendix on Irish brigades by A. Wessels, pp 176–84.)

—— *New light at the Cape of Good Hope: William Porter, the father of Cape liberalism* (Belfast, 1993)

McCracken, P.A., 'Arthur Griffith's South African sabbatical', *SAIS*, vol. 3 (1996), pp 227–62 & 282–9.

—— 'Shaping the times: Irish journalists', *SAIS*, vol. 2 (1992), pp 140–62

McGrath, Walter, 'The Boer Irish Brigade', *Irish Sword*, vol. 5, no. 18 (1961), pp 59–61

—— 'The Irish Brigade in the Boer war: Long forgotten fighters are to be honoured', *Evening Echo*, 30 May 1956

Macnab, Roy, *The French colonel, Villebois-Mareuil and the Boers, 1899–1900* (Johannesburg, 1975)

Marjoribanks, Edward, *The life of Lord Carson* (London, 1932)

Martin, A.C., *The Durban Light Infantry*, vol. 1 (Durban, 1969)

Martin, Christopher, *The Boer war* (New York, 1969)

Maurice, Maj-Gen. Sir Frederick, *History of the war in South Africa*, vol. 1 (London, 1906); vol. 2 (London, 1907)

May, Henry John, *Music of the guns* (London, 1970)

*Men of the times, Old colonists of the Cape Colony and Orange River Colony* (Johannesburg, Cape Town, London, 1906)

*Men of the times, Pioneers of the Transvaal and glimpses of South Africa* (Johannesburg, 1905)

Monick, S., *Shamrock and springbok. The Irish impact on South African military history, 1689–1914* (Johannesburg, 1989)

Murphy, Hillary, *The Kynoch era in Arklow, 1895–1918* (pamphlet, n.d.)

*The Natal who's who* (Durban, 1906)

Nicholls, B.M., 'Rebellions in retrospect: 1914/1916', *SAIS*, vol. 3 (1996), pp 67–88

O'Brien, William, and Ryan, Desmond (eds), *Devoy's post bag, 1871–1928*, 2 vols (Dublin, 1948 & 1953)

O'Bróin, Leon, *Revolutionary underground. The story of the Irish Republican Brotherhood, 1858–1924* (Bristol, 1976)

O'Casey, Sean, *Pictures in the hallway* (London, 1942)

O'Connor, Ulick, *Oliver St John Gogarty: a poet and his times* (Frogmore, 1964)

O'Donnell, F.H., *The history of the Irish Parliamentary Party, 1870–92* (New York, 1910)

*Official register of the officers and cadets of the US Military Academy*, 1877, 1878, 1879 & 1880

Ó Lúing, Séan, *Art Ó Gríofa* (Dublin, 1953)

Pakenham, Frank, *Peace by ordeal* (London, 1933)

Pakenham, Thomas, *The Boer war* (London, 1979; 1991 imprint)

Pearse, H.H.S., *Four months besieged: the story of Ladysmith* (London, 1900)

Pemberton, W. Baring, *Battles of the Boer war* (London, 1964)

Pottinger, Brian, *The foreign volunteers: they fought for the Boers (1899–1902)* (Johannesburg, 1986)

Preller, Gustav, *Kaptein Hindon* (Cape Town, 1921)

*Proceedings of the Irish Race Convention* (Dublin, 1896)

(Rankin, Reginald), *A subaltern's letters to his wife* (New York & Bombay, 1901)

Redmond, W.H.K, *Transvaal war: four speeches against it in House of Commons … together with two letters from Dr Leyds on the Catholic question* (Waterford, 1901), pamphlet

'Extracts from the report of Captain Carl Reichmann, 17th infantry, on the operations of the Boer army', *Reports on military operations in South Africa and China, July 1901* (War Department, Adjutant General's Office, no. 33, Washington, 1901)

Reitz, Deneys, *Commando: a Boer journal of the war* (London, 1932 ed.)

*Report of the director of census, 15 July 1896* (Johannesburg, 1896)

Rolleston, W.T., *Ireland, the empire and the war* (Dublin, 1900), pamphlet

Ronan, Barry, *Forty South African years* (London, 1919)

Rosslyn, earl of, *Twice captured: a record of adventure during the Boer war* (Edinburgh & London, 1900)

Ruda, Richard M., 'Ireland and the Boer fight for freedom: The Irish nationalist reaction to the South African war' (Yale University dissertation, 1973)

—— 'The Irish Transvaal Brigades', *Irish Sword*, vol. XI, no. 45 (1974), pp 201–11

Russell MP, T.W., *Ireland and the empire* (London, 1901)

Ryan, Desmond, *The Rising: the complete story of Easter week* (Dublin, 1949)

Ryan, Mark F., *Fenian memoirs*, T.F. O'Sullivan (ed.) (Dublin, 1945)

Schikkerling, R.W., *Commando courageous (a Boer diary)* (Johannesburg, 1964)

Scully, W.C., *Reminiscences of a South African pioneer* (London, 1913)

Seton, M.C., 'Irishmen in South Africa', *The Gael* (January 1900), pp 19–21

Sheehy-Skeffington, Francis, *Michael Davitt: revolutionary agitator and labour leader* (London, 1908)

Smith, Ken, *Alfred Aylward, the tireless agitator* (Johannesburg, 1983)

Smythe, Colin (ed.), *Seventy years, being the autobiography of Lady Gregory* (Gerrards Cross, 1974)

*South African who's who*, vols for 1908, 1921–2 and 1929–30

*Southern African-Irish Studies (SAIS)*:

—— vol. 1: 'Conference proceedings' (1991), 195pp

—— vol. 2: 'The Irish in southern Africa, 1795–1910' (1992), 290pp

—— vol. 3: 'Ireland and South Africa in modern times' (1996), 312pp

Southey, N.D., 'Dogged entrepreneurs: some prominent Irish retailers', *SAIS*, vol. 2, 1992, pp 163–78

Spaight, J.M., *War rights on land* (London, 1911)

Staunton, M., 'Boer war memorials in Ireland', *SAIS*, vol. 3 (1996), pp 290–304

Swift MacNeill, J.G., *What I have seen and heard* (London, 1925)

*Thirty-ninth annual reunion of the Association of the Graduates of the United States Military Academy at West Point, New York, June 12th, 1908* (Saginaw, Michigan, 1908)

Unger, F.W., *With 'Bobs' and Kruger: experiences and observations of an American war correspondent in the field with both armies* (Philadelphia, 1901; Cape Town, 1977 reprint)

Uys, Ian, *Heidelbergers of the Boer war* (Heidelberg, 1981)

Verney, Peter, *The Micks. The story of the Irish Guards* (London, 1970)

Villebois-Mareuil, Georges de, *War notes: the diary of Colonel de Villebois-Mareuil from November 24, 1899, to March 7, 1900* (London, 1901)

Viljoen, Ben J., *My reminiscences of the Anglo-Boer war*, (London, 1969)

Walker, B.M., *Parliamentary election results in Ireland, 1801–1922* (Dublin, 1978)

Ward, Alan J., *Ireland and Anglo-American relations, 1899–1921* (London, 1969)

Ward, Margaret, *Maud Gonne: a life* (London, 1993)

Wheatley, Comdt Pearse, 'The Irish who fought with the boers, 1899–1902', *An Cosantóir: the Defence Forces magazine* (December 1987), pp 26–7

White, Anna MacBride, & Jeffares, A. Norman (eds), *Always your friend: Gonne-Yeats letters, 1893–1938* (London, 1992)

—— (See also entry: Maud Gonne MacBride, *Servant of the queen*)

Wilson, H.W., *With the flag to Pretoria: a history of the Boer war of 1899–1900*, 2 vols (London, 1900 & 1901)

*Who's who in Natal*, 1933

Young, K.R., 'Chicago's wild geese: Irish-Americans in the Boer war', *Military Images*, vol. 7, no. 6 (1986), pp 14–15

Wessels, A. 'Irish Transvaal Brigades', *Christiaan de Wet Annale*, vol. 5 (1978), pp 176–84

Zimmerman, G.-D., *Irish political street ballads* (Geneva, 1966)

# Index